T0380675

JOURNEY WELL

Explore Your Deepest Needs & How to Meet Them

Laurie Krieg with Matt Krieg, LPC

WESTBOW
PRESS®
A DIVISION OF THOMAS NELSON
& ZONDERVAN

Copyright © 2019 Laurie Krieg with Matt Krieg, LPC.

All rights reserved. No part of this book may be used or reproduced by any means, graphic, electronic, or mechanical, including photocopying, recording, taping or by any information storage retrieval system without the written permission of the author except in the case of brief quotations embodied in critical articles and reviews.

This book is a work of non-fiction. Unless otherwise noted, the author and the publisher make no explicit guarantees as to the accuracy of the information contained in this book and in some cases, names of people and places have been altered to protect their privacy.

WestBow Press books may be ordered through booksellers or by contacting:

WestBow Press
A Division of Thomas Nelson & Zondervan
1663 Liberty Drive
Bloomington, IN 47403
www.westbowpress.com
1 (866) 928-1240

Because of the dynamic nature of the Internet, any web addresses or links contained in this book may have changed since publication and may no longer be valid. The views expressed in this work are solely those of the author and do not necessarily reflect the views of the publisher, and the publisher hereby disclaims any responsibility for them.

Any people depicted in stock imagery provided by Getty Images are models, and such images are being used for illustrative purposes only. Certain stock imagery © Getty Images.

Design: Calvin Chopp (cchoppdesign)
Editing: Hayley Mullins
Project Management: Lisa Kerr
Additional editing and proofing: Cassie Davito, Lisa Kerr, Michele Wells

Unless otherwise indicated, all Scripture quotations are taken from the Holy Bible, New Living Translation, copyright © 1996, 2004, 2015 by Tyndale House Foundation. Used by permission of Tyndale House Publishers, Inc., Carol Stream, Illinois 60188. All rights reserved.

Scripture quotations marked (NIV) are taken from the Holy Bible, New International Version®, NIV®. Copyright © 1973, 1978, 1984, 2011 by Biblica, Inc.™ Used by permission of Zondervan. All rights reserved worldwide. www.zondervan.com The "NIV" and "New International Version" are trademarks registered in the United States Patent and Trademark Office by Biblica, Inc.™

Scripture quotations marked (ESV) are from the ESV® Bible (The Holy Bible, English Standard Version®), copyright © 2001 by Crossway, a publishing ministry of Good News Publishers. Used by permission. All rights reserved.

ISBN: 978-1-9736-7992-9 (sc)
ISBN: 978-1-9736-7991-2 (e)

Library of Congress Control Number: 2019918668

Print information available on the last page.

WestBow Press rev. date: 12/04/2019

TABLE OF CONTENTS

INTRODUCTION: THE PHONE CALL

"No one can measure the depths of his understanding."
—Isaiah the Prophet[1]

"The way out of our loss and hurt is in and through. When Jesus said, 'For I have come to call not the righteous but sinners' (Matt. 9:13), he affirmed that only those who can face their wounded condition can be available for healing and enter a new way of living."
—Henri Nouwen[2]

I stared at my phone—a pink flip phone that I so had to have months before. Now it lay silently in my hand, mocking me with its bubbly pinkness.

"God?" I prayed, the tears immediately falling at the mention of the One I knew for nearly two decades. "If You really care about me, if You think I can make it, could You please have someone contact me who can encourage me? Please, make someone call and tell me, 'You'll make it through. You can do this, Laurie. You're not alone. Don't give up. There is hope for you.'" The tears fell. The begging of God continued. The phone did not ring.

Days later, I sat in the same position on the floor in my apartment, daydreaming about the knives in my kitchen and the tub in my bathroom. I craved death. The scratchiness of the cheap carpet cutting into my face reminded me I did not deserve comfort. I could remove this shame. I could come out—finally. *I could be who I am. I could find comfort and love in the arms of a woman for good. I wouldn't have to die.*

I was a recent college graduate, a full-time newspaper reporter, a Christian, and felt every minute of every day a monogamous, loving same-sex relationship was right for me. It made sense. It felt natural. I had experienced attractions throughout my life, been in a relationship with a woman, and had tried dating a guy for a while. (*What was that about anyway? I didn't know. An experiment?*) After graduating, I flirted around other relationships with women. Now was the time to decide my next steps: death or diving in.

Or . . . perhaps there was a third option. I had recently started seeing a new counselor, Carolyn, whose wrinkle-framed eyes and six-foot height bespoke an inner confidence and wisdom stemming from many years of walking with God. She also irritatingly (and intentionally) dodged my desire to focus on my same-sex attractions or for a pill to fix my depression and anxiety.

"Laurie, what are you really looking for?" she perceptively asked. "What do you really need?" I didn't say much because I didn't know the answer. *What do I really need? A woman! Right . . . ?* Instead of feeding my craving for my same gender with quick fixes such as trying to date more women or "just stop it," she taught me spiritual disciplines like listening prayer, lament, and forgiveness. I didn't know what she was doing, but she did.

Carolyn taught me to listen to my hole-riddled heart and translate its cravings to both validate their hunger and hear behind them. *Was a woman able to truly satisfy that desire I had to be held? To be nurtured? To be seen? For how long? Could God meet those needs?* She repeated odd things like, "He's closer than your very breath." And, "Laurie, let's bring it to Jesus."

I didn't understand what this meant or how it looked, but I wondered, *What if I could bring this to Jesus?* Not to take it away. I had asked God enough times to know that complete removal of the attractions was probably not an option for me. *But could He give me a way to work out my faith and my attractions? Was there a way to live a coherent life of integrity—struggles and all?*

I didn't want to come out as a Gay Christian (Gay in capital "G" identity sense, where I say, "I believe God allows monogamous, same-sex sexual relationships."[3]) I could not make such beliefs jive with the Spirit of God inside of me. My reading and interpretation of Scripture would not bring the two together. But even though my brain and spirit believed it was sin, the cravings of my body said otherwise.[4] What was I to do? I could not live in the hopeless tension much longer.

A guttural cry bubbled up from my chest—a cry that wanted to stay alive. It was a yell that wondered if it was possible to live with *joy and freedom* while still experiencing same-sex attractions. *Could I live in a hope-filled tension?* I didn't know another human who was doing such a thing. In 2008, I had not read one story of someone like me: a Christian who engaged in same-sex behavior as a Christian, repented of it, but still journeyed with the attractions. (*What kind of a weird Christian am I?*)

Carolyn's voice reverberated in my heart: *He's closer than your very breath.* "Fine!" *What do I have to lose?* I glared upward, instead of right or left, to this metaphorical third option of Jesus meeting my needs—whatever that meant. "Fine! If You are who You say you are," I spat. "If You are the real Need-Meeter of my soul, then You had better show up! If You can satisfy more than these women can, then show me how."

If I measured my faith in the idea that God could satisfy more than a tangible woman, I would guess it would measure 1/100th of a mustard seed.

But it was enough. God's math is not the same as ours. "He does not punish us for all our sins; he does not deal harshly with us, as we deserve" (Ps. 103:10). He is the prodigal's Father.[5] We take a half-hearted, ragged step toward Him, and He takes 492. We attempt another, and He runs 799. Meeting this Father is what made me change, not from gay to straight, not from pagan to saved, but from lost to loved—and to become one who *experiences love.*

I did not want to go on a journey to learn this. I would have preferred to have 10,000 angels descend, wipe away my tears, and tell me I'm the most perfect, humble, and ravishing human person ever. But God knew better. He knew I needed time alongside Him to fall in love with Him.

As you read, you may be sitting here wondering, "How do I do that?" The answer is what you hold in your hands. This is my phone call to you on your pink flip phone. (Perhaps you have upgraded by now?) This is my ongoing telephone conversation with you, where I try my best to share what was helpful in the past, what is currently useful today, and where I provide space to "listen" to you through reflective questions.

Ideally, you would read and answer these questions with a trusted counselor, a Journey Well Group[6], or a friend. But I get that even holding this book may be scary. That's okay. You don't have to share your story today.[7] I do hope that by the time you close the back cover, however, you will feel a confidence to open up even to one person, and especially to Jesus who so desperately loves you—even if you're secretly shaking your head saying, "No, He doesn't."

How you feel about God doesn't change how He feels about you.

This book has pieces of my journey, but it isn't about me.[8] In fact, I would feel like a total failure if you read my story and tried to cut-and-paste it to your life. I have made a lot of mistakes. But there are beautiful and breathtaking moments where the gospel (that is: the good news for everyone every day) came alive for me. Those Jesus-focused pieces are the ones I hope you siphon from this story.

The purpose of what we share here is not to "fix" anyone. (What a terrible word: "fix." Who is "fixed"? Who has perfect sexuality?) For those of you who experience same-sex attractions or identify as LGBT+, orientation change or reparative therapy is not on the table.[9] The only focus of this book is displaying how each of us can equally align our knees at the foot of the cross while our hearts equally receive living water. How God wants to transform us and use our weakness is up to Him.

Most books on sexuality do not consider my type of brokenness. They assume the reader simply struggles with too much lust for the opposite sex. My type of sexuality is reserved for a certain bookshelf and a certain web search.

But everyone struggles with sexuality, and the Church should be the safe space where we struggle with it together. For these reasons, I am taking my story off of the "special" shelf and moving it into general sexual brokenness. I am normal. Post-Fall-of-man, "normal" sexuality is broken sexuality. This includes my sexuality and yours—no matter how we struggle.

In these pages, I hope to serve as a helpful representative of the Church and of Jesus Christ by walking you through practical ways to connect your brokenness to Jesus, who was broken for you. We will start with the gospel; work through recognizing need, lament, forgiveness, celebration, gratitude, and oneness; and filter it all through the lens of my journey with my girlfriend, my boyfriend, my counselor, and Jesus, who became my joy, my hope, my Need-Meeter—the One who satisfies that aching hole in my heart.

This book seeks to answer the question "how?" *How do I live well with broken sexuality . . . in real life? How do I care well for my hole-riddled heart? How is the gospel good news for everybody every day—me included?*

I can't wait to show you.

Are you ready?

Ring ring. (I think that's your phone ringing.)

REFLECTION QUESTIONS:

1. Can you relate to any of what was written in this introduction? Which pieces and why?

    _____

    _____

2. What are you nervous about in reading this book? What are you excited about?

    _____

    _____

3. What is one goal you hope to meet by the end? (Ex. less shame, more hope, more understanding)

    _____

    _____

CHAPTER 1: I'LL NEVER HAVE A TESTIMONY

"I will say to the prisoners, 'Come out in freedom,' and to those in darkness, 'Come into the
light.' They will be my sheep, grazing in green pastures
and on hills that were previously bare."
—God[10]

"The gospel is not the ABC's of Christianity, it's A to Z . . .
The gospel is pretty much the solution to every problem."
—Tim Keller[11]

It's funny how often I share my testimony, considering how I never thought I would have one. When I was young, I remember watching the baptisms take place in church. Men and women came up, and with trembling hands, they read their soon-to-be baptismally drenched stories of before-and-after Christ—their "testimony." I smiled and clapped with the rest of the congregation while they were dunked and then brought up with a radiant glow on their faces. "I'll never have a testimony," I thought. "Or, it will be something like, 'I became a Christian at six years old, was a Christian, and I am still a Christian. I love God.'" I meant it. I glanced down the pew at my Christian parents and the entire row we filled with my eleven Christian siblings. (Yes, eleven. There are twelve of us kids born to the same mom and dad.) "There is no before-and-after for a kid who has always been a Christian."

Technically, I was not always a follower of Jesus. I "prayed the prayer of salvation" at six years old during a Bible club my mom led. Mom never missed an opportunity to tell people about the love of God, and I am a benefactor of her courage. In my elementary school gymnasium, I remember her holding up the Wordless Book. "Can anyone tell me what color this page is?" she asked, directing our eyes to the gold page. This book had different colored pages representing heaven (gold), sin (black), Jesus dying (red), Him making us white as snow (white), and us learning how to grow (green). The enchanting first page is what grabbed my attention.

"It's gold, and it stands for heaven!" a shaggy-haired kid shouted back.

"Good job!" Mom smiled. "It says in the Bible that the streets are paved with pure gold. I want to go there and be with Jesus forever. Do you, too?" She turned the page. "This color is . . ."

"Black!"

"Great! And what does that stand for?"

"It is for our sin!" someone else piped in.

"That's right." Mom flipped the page for all to see. "The Bible says, 'All have sinned and fall short of the glory of God.'[12] This means that if any of us have sinned even one time, we can't be with Jesus. Who knows what sin is?" I had heard this before from Dad reading the Bible every night after dinner, but that day I heard with fresh ears. I understood that I was a sinner and not allowed to go to heaven because I had been mean and lied. I knew I wanted to be washed clean like the white page showed. I wanted to be "white as snow."[13]

So when it was time to pray, I prayed sincerely with my six-year-old heart. "Jesus, I'm sorry for my sins. I want to be with you forever," I repeated, and I meant every word. "In Jesus's name, Amen!" I bubbled over with inner joy. Now I was going to go to heaven. I was especially elated because I knew my older siblings were going to be there someday, and I didn't want to be left out.

To increase my excitement, Mom said anyone who had "prayed the prayer" could go get a prize out of the treasure chest. That meant me. I carefully dug through the piles of rings, Bibles, and other trinkets until I found it: a glass red heart strung onto a keychain. It looked like a giant ruby. Yes, this is right, I thought.

I showed my mom, hoping she would be proud of my decision. She smiled at me amidst the chaos of the students looking for their after-group snack. "That can remind you of how Jesus is in your heart now," she said with a smile.

Grinning back at her, I nodded and then looked at my "ruby" with more delight than before. Jesus was in my heart.

OLD NATURE?

While wrestling with my sexuality in college, I would remember that red heart keychain and wonder what was wrong with me. "I must be the worst Christian." I read testimony after testimony online of people who had a before-and-after conversion experience that included their sexuality. Before: lost, making promiscuous sexual choices, and perhaps doing drugs. After: found, living a life of holiness, not doing drugs. I looked at them, and I looked at me. My only "before Jesus" time period was between ages zero to five. Was that my "old nature"?[14] Which parts of me now were old and which were new? I wasn't snorting crack while I had a girlfriend. I was a small group leader, getting a 3.9 GPA at my Christian university, and leading worship at a Bible-believing church while I had a girlfriend (whom I'll call Heather). I wasn't doing any of those "good" things out of obligation. I loved God as much as I knew how. And yet, here I was: in a same-sex relationship.

I was a Christian; she was a Christian. *There should be no issue here!* I often thought. *If only we could remove the physical aspect from our relationship, it would be perfect! Right?*

Well, there was the codependency. I had a hard time not sifting my thoughts through hers. *What would she think? What would she want?* I hated to be apart from her. The more I had her, the more I had to have of her. I felt the most peace (or at least a lack of anxiety) in her presence. *But, wait, that's bad . . . right? Idolatry and all that?* So we put limits on our in-person and phone conversations. We took breaks from each other. We even signed a contract with my pastor-father who cared enough about both of us to help us on our quest to make our friendship holy.

I never said, "Boy, you know what would be great? A same-sex relationship. My dad is a pastor, I go to a conservative Christian school, I lead worship, love Jesus . . . yup. Sounds great." To come out as a Gay Christian in the early 2000s would have been akin to declaring I had leprosy in Jesus' day. I did not want to be the leper, but I felt like one. And I felt like I couldn't not be one.

As much as I loved Jesus, I felt unable to stop pursuing my girlfriend. In my own strength, I could not release my death grip on the woman who made me feel good about myself. Desires inside of me took a good thing (friendship), paired it with sin nature (the attractions), and smashed them together and made her ultimate (an idol). I was addicted to her. "I want to do what is right, but I can't," Paul says, his words resembling mine.[15]

I did not understand why it wasn't working. Two Christians. Two friends, who both loved Jesus. Both of us were broken, but wasn't friendship supposed to be this great, God-glorifying thing that helped with brokenness? Wasn't this the Body of Christ? Why couldn't we do it? I read and reread Romans 6, 7, and 8 in that season of intense struggle, concluding each time that I was incapable of changing with my own willpower, conscious of the fact God did not condemn me, and aware that there was something to understanding the love of God that could help me. I did not know how it looked. A decade later, I am learning how it can look.

It began with examining what I was eating.

THE PASTURE LIFE

Let's pretend we are sheep in a pasture. *Bahh.* This pasture stands for our life. We like our lamb life, but we often find ourselves tempted to escape to eat the grass from the next pasture. It looks more lush and satisfying.

Next door's grass is our current favorite form of escapism: overeating, scrolling online endlessly, worrying, flirting with someone we shouldn't, looking at pornography, fantasizing and masturbating, or obsessing over another person and how *they* feel about *me* (or make me feel about me, i.e. I think I am loving them, but I really love me).

The traditional way to prevent us from eating the neighbor's grass is to put up bigger boundaries like porn blockers, locks on the fridge, or accountability partners who act like electrified fences or Taboo buzzers. (They beep at us when we break our commitments.) Those things are helpful for a time. But if you're anything like me, you are a sneaky little sheep. You are good at finding the holes in the fence to eat the neighbor's grass, or discovering the "off" button to the electrified fence/accountability partner. This can come in the form of being "too busy" to meet or even outright deceitful. I've done both.

But what if we ignored the fence for a while? What if we didn't focus on the boundaries but instead worked on tilling our own pastures? (Our own lives?) This would take studying the soil, the grass, and every inch of the terrain. It would look like taking note of what we are consuming. Are there big boulders from our past that we keep tripping over? Is the soil rich or sandy? Is fruit growing on the trees? Are we sharing the produce with others? Are there barren places where unconfessed sin reigns? Do we invite others into our fields to help us make it a better place to live? Where does Jesus live? Is He here? Where?

If we love our pasture, we are not going to care about what's on the other side of the fence or if the fence is even there. It will only serve as a boundary marker. If we are comfortable being our sheep selves while continually working on our pastures to make them smoother, more lush, and more peaceful, while simply enjoying God as He enjoys us, we will not want to escape. "The key to mortifying fleshly lusts," author and pastor Milton Vincent said, "is to eliminate the emptiness within me and replace it with fullness; and I accomplish this by feasting on the gospel."[16]

Good news: God's power through the gospel will help us cultivate our pastures so we can feast.[17] "I will say to the prisoners, 'Come out in freedom,' and to those in darkness, 'Come into the light.' They will be my sheep, grazing in green pastures and on hills that were previously bare."[18] This Shepherd in Isaiah cares about what we eat. We see it when he shows up in Psalm 23: "He [the Lord, our Shepherd] lets me rest in green meadows; he leads me beside peaceful streams."[19] In Israel, during the time of the writing of this psalm, green meadows came alive only a few months per year, and peaceful streams were the only way sheep could drink. Rushing water scared them too much, so shepherds had to either dig a dead-end channel to drink from or find quiet water source from which the sheep could satisfy their thirst.[20]

Jesus is the Good Shepherd. He loves His little sheep. He cares about what we eat and drink—about what grows in our pastures—because it is that vegetation that feeds us. "A wise person is hungry for knowledge, while a fool feeds on trash."[21] What we eat goes into our hearts and comes out of our mouths.

> A tree is identified by its fruit. Figs are never gathered from thornbushes, and grapes
> are not picked from bramble bushes. A good person produces good things from the
> treasury of a good heart, and an evil person produces evil things from the treasury
> of an evil heart. What you say flows from what is in your heart (Luke 6:44–45).

What we run *to* (pornography, food, friendships-turned-sexual) is not nearly as important as the reason we run. And to know that we must look at our pasture, examine what we are feasting on (is it self-hatred, people's approval, or our image?), and where we are sleeping (perhaps on a boulder of unforgiveness?). Looking at our pasture requires ripping our eyes away from our neighbor's yard of easy distractions and ways to numb out, and instead looking inward at our hearts and backward toward our past while following our Guide, the Good Shepherd, who has come to seek and save the lost sheep.[22]

BORN THAT WAY?

One place to begin tilling our pasture is to address the "born that way" question. If I was born with "the gay gene," for lack of a better term, isn't this whole book useless? Shouldn't I simply follow my heart, and resolve this dissonance by getting a wife?

Like I mentioned before, I said "yes" to Jesus at six. My attractions—my intrigue, more accurately— toward and preference for women over men began around that age. Girls were interesting. Boys were . . . like my five brothers. They seemed stinky and uninteresting. I picked fights with them and happily played Legos and G.I. Joes when they let me, but I wasn't interested in their gender as a whole.

Christian culture surrounding me in the 90s and 2000s dictated that I not only see same-sex behavior as a sin, but as the worst sin. No one in my church or family ever said this to me directly, but it was easily discoverable at a young age by a perceptive girl, simply by overhearing Christian radio and church conversations. "Those people!" "The gay agenda . . ." "An abomination . . ." "That is so gross . . ." Short phrases like these, said in a defensive tone with a grimace of hate and disgust, told me how I should feel. There were holy sins, and then there was . . . that one.

Whenever I felt a sexual draw toward my gender, whenever I secretly played computer games or toys in a way that I knew to be against God's design, I quickly suppressed it. Wrong. Bad. No—it was the worst. The worst, worst sin.

Was I born gay? Do I have the gay gene or at least the sexually fluid gene? I mean, I felt same-sex attraction from a young age. I liked to play with "boy toys" (and "girl toys"), and I enjoyed beating my brothers back when they hit me. (I probably instigated more than they did, honestly.) Was this who God created me to be? I am asking two important, but separate questions: 1) Was I born "that way" and 2) If so, is that God's good design? (For biblical arguments on God's design for marriage, please see the appendix written by Dr. Preston Sprinkle.)

The American Psychological Association says, "[N]o findings have emerged that permit scientists to conclude that sexual orientation is determined by any particular factor or factors. Many think that nature and nurture both play complex roles."[23] A recent study on sexual orientation by Johns Hopkins University comes to similar conclusions.[24] So, the answer to the first questions about whether or not I was "born that way" is . . . maybe.

But if they find a gay or sexually-fluid gene, doesn't that mean God made me that way? And if He made me that way, isn't it good? God doesn't make mistakes.

It is true that He doesn't. But He also does allow sin nature to interweave itself within us. We are inborn with a natural inclination toward self. I did not have to teach my often sweet, tender two-year-old how to throw a tantrum when she does not get her way. That was inborn—perhaps allowed by God to be crafted into her genes. Did God want her born with a sinful nature? I'm not sure He wanted it, but He allowed it. In Noah's day, "The LORD observed the extent of human wickedness on the earth . . . [and He] was sorry he had ever made them and put them on the earth. It broke his heart."[25] Even though He pushed "restart" on humanity with Noah's family, sin did not disappear. God allowed it, and He allows it. He will continue to allow it until the day the King vanquishes sin and the deceiver forever.[26]

Before that day of final defeat, I would not be surprised to learn that all sin tendencies have a genetic correlation. Scientists have found adultery genes, alcoholism genes, and murder genes.[27] If I have the murder gene, do I have to kill someone? "Sorry, honey, after breakfast, I gotta do it." Just because I have the adultery gene, do I have to cheat? Just because I have a natural inclination toward self, does Jesus' command to "give up your own way, take up your cross, and follow me" not apply (Matt. 16:24)? Living for myself is easier. It feels right. But I have made a commitment to put Jesus and His Word over me. I submit to them—and with the Lord helping me, I do not submit to my genes or desires.

The idea that sin's effects could be physically in our genes is biblical. "For we know that all creation has been groaning as in the pains of childbirth right up to the present time. And we believers also groan, even though we have the Holy Spirit within us as a foretaste of future glory, for we long for our bodies to be released from sin and suffering."[28] All creation has been groaning. All creation. Sin marred our mind, will, emotions, and bodies—including everyone's sexuality. Ask any heterosexual man if he ever struggles with lust. Ask any heterosexual woman if she has ever struggled with her sexual desires. Sexual brokenness is not limited to people who experience same-sex attractions. Every single human, besides Jesus (the God-Man), was born with a broken sexuality.

Additionally, we are never free from the war with sin. I was born into sin and then accepted Jesus, but I have not been instantaneously transformed from broken to whole. The sanctification process is lifelong. "The sinful nature wants to do evil, which is just the opposite of what the Spirit wants. And the Spirit gives us desires that are the opposite of what the sinful nature desires," Paul says. "These two forces are constantly fighting each other, so you are not free to carry out your good intentions."[29] This verse is assuring, because it reminds me that when I am struggling with any sinful desires as a Christian it is normal. The struggle may be inborn, it may be persistent, and it may be permanent until I go see Jesus. I am neither strange for struggling with any type of sin, nor am I free from the need to fight any type of sin, even if it is inborn. We all have a chronic sin illness, and our prescription is not more cowbell (sorry, Will Ferrell), but the daily medicine of the gospel.

The question, then, is not if we are born with an orientation toward sin, but how we are going to surrender our orientation toward sin.

WHAT IS THE GOSPEL?

Before we go on, let's clarify what we mean when we say "the gospel." I used to think it was simply "praying the prayer" of salvation. This proverbial prayer was summed up in Romans 10:9: "If you confess with your mouth that Jesus is Lord and believe in your heart that God raised him from the dead, you will be saved." Before praying: not a Christian. After praying: a Christian. Boom. Godspelled.

It's so much more than that. The gospel is creation, fall, redemption, and re-creation replayed every day in every way. "The gospel is not the ABC's of Christianity," said Tim Keller, referring to the "A–Accept, B–Believe, and C–Confess" gospel training some of us received. "It's A to Z. The gospel is pretty much the solution to every problem."[30] When I was engaging in same-sex sexual behavior with my girlfriend, I did not understand this. I was living post-"praying the prayer." I knew creation, fall, redemption. Bored. Next story. I was looking for something beyond the gospel; I did not know I needed to sink myself into it every day.

> **Creation:** I did not know the gospel meant starting each day knowing I am a beloved image-bearer.

> **Fall:** I did not know the gospel meant naming the sin that wounded me and confessing every time I choose sin, either because of wounds I'm carrying or just because sin is fun and easy.

Redemption: I did not know I could link my pain to Jesus' and learn how to forgive myself and others.

Re-Creation: I did not know God would be in the sanctification process with me while I still walked with a limp. I did not know that this sin struggle, too, was one with which I could walk into church and stay there. I thought my same-sex attractions had to be gone for me to go to church—or at least be honest in church.

Broken church people with us in the pews are not always great at exemplifying Emmanuel, God with us. They say, "Leave"; He says, "Come." And not only does He invite us, He says, "I will come to you." Not only does He come to us, He also died at the hands of legalists *for us.* Tim Keller articulates this well when he talks about Christmas:

What is Christmas? Christmas is saying something that no other religion in the world wants to say; no other religion dares to say: that the God of the universe has been [through it] . . . Hunger, loneliness, homelessness, grief, rejection, betrayal, torture, injustice—he's experienced it all. And what does that mean? Have you been betrayed? So has he. Are you broke? So was he. Are you lonely? So was he. Are you facing death? So did he. So you can go to him.[31]

Some Christians say you cannot come to church until you fix X, Y, and Z: *You are not gay. You don't have that addiction. There is no issue with your gender identity. You can come when your sins look holy like mine.* Jesus says, "Come now as you are." Receive *today* not only his acceptance of your image-bearing self, but real empathy, forgiveness, wholeness, and *power.* As Paul wrote, "I am not ashamed of the gospel, because it is the power of God."[32]

This is why I will not shut up about the gospel. I am addicted to it. Until the New Kingdom, I will always be in need, so I will always need the gospel. This is not because I struggle with gay sin, but because I struggle with *sin.*

REFLECTION QUESTIONS:

1. If you are a Christian, where do you mark the beginning of your walk with Christ? Was it with "praying a prayer" like I did?

_____

_____

_____

_____

2. When did you first learn about sex? How did you learn about it? (Parents, friends, the internet?) Was that first introduction helpful or unhelpful?

_____

_____

_____

_____

3. After reading the description of the gospel in this chapter, how does it relate to your first decision to follow Jesus? Has your journey been a deepening of that original understanding or something different?

_____

_____

_____

_____

4. How does your sexuality relate to your story of faith?

_____

_____

_____

_____

5. If you were to describe the "pasture" of your life, what does it look like? Lush? Full? Bare? Lonely? Are you focused on hopping the fence or tilling the soil?

_____

_____

_____

6. Was there a moment in the reading of this where you thought, "Yes! Me too!" Where and why?

_____

_____

_____

_____

7. Laurie's mentor often asks, "If the gospel is 'I am more loved than I can imagine and more sinful than I believe,' which side do you need to hear more often? The 'more loved' side or the 'more sinful'?" Why do you feel that way?

_____

_____

_____

_____

CHAPTER 2: THAT HOLE IN MY HEART

"[W]hat comes out of the mouth proceeds from the heart."
— Jesus[33]

"You have made us for yourself, O Lord, and our heart is restless until it rests in you."
— Saint Augustine[34]

Whether or not we cognitively recognize it, our hearts are restless, hungry, and looking for something. We crave true love. Ann Voskamp wrote, "No matter what they are saying, everyone's asking, 'Can you just love me?'"[35] Since the Garden of Eden, we all have been made for perfect relationship with God and with each other. Only in a give and take of love with the Church, reflecting the perfect give and take the triune God's love, do we feel complete—not permanently, but for heavenly foreshadowing moments. Like, perhaps for ten seconds during our favorite worship song—after we've warmed up with a couple others we especially like.

I experienced this unquenchable need for love, although I did not consciously know it until reflecting back years later. When I was in a relationship with another woman it felt so right . . . almost. I felt whole and complete, except for an annoying, small fraction of my heart that was left unloved, untouched, and incomplete. That void felt exponentially palpable when she had to go to work, when she didn't text or call when I needed her to, or when she couldn't show up physically when I wanted her there. Then I would grow surprisingly angry and hostile, because she wasn't meeting my needs. "We feel lonely . . . and thereby look—sometimes desperately—for someone who can take away the pain: a husband, wife, friend," Henri Nouwen said. "We are all too ready to conclude that someone or something can finally take away our neediness. In this way we come to expect too much from others. We become demanding, clingy, even violent."[36]

Those moments of demanding became the indicator light that I was looking to Heather for my completeness—not God. I was like a toddler demanding a favorite toy or a crack addict in need of the next hit. I thought I believed Psalm 16:2, but my actions proved otherwise. "I say to the LORD, 'You are my Lord;

apart from you I have no good thing.'"[37] Not so much. I wanted God and her, but we cannot hug both God and our idols. Try as I might, I couldn't reprioritize God as number one. Two women or two men together in a marriage-like way cannot represent a God who has both masculine and feminine characteristics. If men and women are both made in God's image (Gen. 1:26; 2:24; 5:1–2; Matt. 19:4–6), and if the Church is supposed to represent God's unity (John 17:22), and if marriage is supposed to represent the unity of the Church and Christ (Eph. 5:32), then marriage is supposed to look like God (from whom male and female were created). Therefore, marriage is supposed to be male and female in order for it to look like God. Because my relationship with Heather did not look like God, it didn't work well. This was not because He hates me, but because He loves me enough to show me a better way—not towards men, but toward Him.

I found myself in church every Sunday morning weeping, confessing, and telling God "I'm sorry," less for the same-sex behavior, and more for the idolatry of putting a person before Him. I confessed, I knew He forgave me, and I felt whole. For about three seconds.

That Fall of Man. It disrupted the perfect communion we once had with God. And so, when we feel the weight of a broken world (and grow anxious, lonely, or bored), our eyes shift away from the pasture we are planting, weeding, and resting in with the Father to a quicker fix. I knew this to be true, but the thing we don't talk about much in church is that sin works. Idols work. They can be quicker, more fun, and way more celebratory than the Isaiah 48:10 "furnace of suffering" God puts us through or the narrow road few find (Matt. 7:14).

However, sin only works for a time. That hole in our heart is a black hole. It sucks up more and more, demands more and more. We see this in the insatiable appetites we have for more money, grander houses, better iPhones, more Instagrammable food, and faster Wi-Fi. We see this in the consumerist way we look to significant others to make us feel better about ourselves. We see this in the way pornography viewers have created a demand for more intense images.[38] "You let yourselves be slaves to impurity and lawlessness, which led ever deeper into sin," Paul says in his letter to the Romans.[39]

Only when we refocus that black hole of our hearts on God does He turn its unquenchable sucking nature into a planet that rotates in perfect orbit around His Son.

But taking our need to God is difficult. I knew that truth, too, which is why I was so hesitant to go on the inward journey through counseling. (Who signs up for and pays for pain? It seemed like masochism.)

YOU CANNOT GO LOWER THAN ME

Before I decided to make a literal call for help, I stood silently in church during the singing portion of the service. I was in the first or second row. As much as I wanted to hide, I also wanted to be seen. I let my friend, Christen, notice my tears and hear my cravings for death. "Maybe you should get help for that?" she offered kindly. I didn't think I needed professional assistance until she pointed out my depression was growing out of control. I often talked about how much I hated myself and meditated on death.

I let the tears drip down my face while the surrounding worship of God washed over me. I did not feel strong enough to join in, but I could pray two words: *help me.* An image came to mind, interrupting my grief. I saw a dark, hollow, cavernous pit. I knew it was where sadness began, and I knew it was where I needed to go. *No, God. I don't want to go there. I don't like pain.*

"Come on, Laurie. You can do it." I looked deep into the cave, and in my mind's eye, I could see Jesus there. He was not shiny and haloed, but looked like a normal guy sitting in the dirt. He didn't seem to care that He was dirty or in a cave. He only seemed care about me. "Don't be afraid," I sensed Him saying to me, knowing I was. "You cannot go lower than Me."

Jesus was at the bottom. "I called on your name, LORD, from deep within the pit. You heard me when I cried, 'Listen to my pleading! Hear my cry for help!' Yes, you came when I called; you told me, 'Do not fear'" (Lam. 3:55–57). I had a sense that if I stepped into this pain, He would be with me. I also knew it was only there that I would find healing. Not "gay to straight" healing, but a healing that would take me from despair to joy, peace, and hope. "The cure for the pain is the pain," Rumi, an eleventh-century poet said.[40] I think Jesus might edit that quote to say, "The cure for the pain is going to the pain with an all-powerful, all-merciful Someone." Truly, He is "a man of sorrows, acquainted with deepest grief."[41] He gets it.

When I saw that image, everything in me wanted to cling to the edge of the cave, and say to Jesus, "No, thanks. Hard pass. I'll keep coping." But I couldn't. As Henri Nouwen in his book on grief reminds us, "The way out of our loss and hurt is in and through."[42] My toddler's *Going on a Bear Hunt* book agrees: "You can't go over it, you can't go under it, you've got to go through it."[43]

I called Carolyn the next day, and unknowingly I began the Hole in My Heart journey. I did not find despair at the bottom. I did not discover what I feared: "You guessed it! You're the worst." Yes, I became even more rightfully disgusted at my own sin, but the glory of the gospel is that you can simultaneously hate your sin while resting in the fact that you are a beloved human. Such a dual realization makes me lose my taste for sin and worship the Savior even more. When we are in a love relationship with God, John Calvin rightly said, such a soul "restrains itself from sinning, not out of dread of punishment alone; but because it loves and serves God as Father . . . even if there were no hell, it would still shudder at offending him."[44]

THAT HOLE IN OUR HEARTS

You may have been born like I was with a literal "hole in your heart" called a heart murmur. If so, I hope yours healed with time like mine did. Either way, without question, you were born with a metaphorical heart hole. All creation groans with examples of this cavernous need, even when we don't know what we long for. We even see it in popular songs.

We ask, we search, we party, and we wander, groping in the dark for something to satisfy. "His purpose was for the nations to seek after God and perhaps feel their way toward him and find him," Paul said to the Athenians, "though he is not far from any one of us."[45] However, instead of guiding the hands of the person seeking and feeling after God, we often run away, lobbing truth bombs such as "You need Jesus!" To stay, listen, and then point to how Jesus meets our needs is too hard. We often do not know how he can meet our own heart's cries, let alone another's.

With a palm to my face, I recall saying these exact words ("You need Jesus!") to a gay man who I worked with at a local Italian eatery a decade ago. (I was a server, and many of my co-workers identified with some letter of the LGBT+ alphabet.) One afternoon, this man went on and on about a guy he found attractive. Instead of listening beyond his words to places of pain and speaking hope there, with a contorted face I said, "You need Jesus." Nothing else. No care for him. Ann Voskamp wisely asked, "Why do we rush to defend God to a broken world, and not race to defend the image of God in the world's broken?"[46] I didn't want to defend the image of God in this man because apathy and truth bombs are easier to throw, and they made me feel more righteous. So I chucked a grenade, and then he walked away. Of course he did. I would have walked away if I was him.

Months after that explosion, I found myself engaging in same-sex behavior. The glimmers of attraction I had growing up all added up into one person who simultaneously felt like the best and worst thing to ever happen to me. She was the best because her attention answered the questions I had about whether I was special, if I could belong, and if someone would ever see me for me. But she was the worst because as good as the feelings were, they weren't enough. The joy she brought me didn't satiate my heart hunger. Yes, she told me that I was special, that I belonged, and that she saw me . . . but she never said it or showed it to me *enough.*

When I let myself lean in and put an ear to the space she did not fill, the Spirit of the Living God annoyingly seemed to whisper, "I have something better for you." I did not like those words, because it felt like the truth bomb I lobbed at my co-worker was now exploding in my face. "You need Jesus, Laurie." *I know! But I have Jesus, and He isn't cutting it.*

When I discovered the Core Needs and the Hole in My Heart (HIMH) Model, a light clicked on in my brain. "Oh, I need Jesus. I simply didn't know how I needed Him." I experienced life before this like going to a doctor who is a general practitioner. I had some general pain and could perhaps describe it as "a God-shaped hole in my heart," and I could simply take the prescribed pill of "You're a Christian. What more do you need?" But a good general practitioner knows when they need to refer to a specialist. Jesus is the specialist—a cardiologist. Working with Him and the Holy Spirit, we can diagnose more specifically what that hole in our heart needs.

THE HOLE IN MY HEART MODEL . . . EXPLAINED[47]

I need to fast-forward my story a bit. I'm married. To a dude. I will explain more of how this came to be later, but know I am not straight, Matt (this "dude") does not "fix" me (nor me, him), and we link arms as we run toward Jesus together. He is a licensed therapist, and although we don't have the same vocation, we both walk alongside people.

Matt likes to use an easy, not-intense example in his counseling practice to describe the HIMH Model. "What if I am walking around with my daughters, and a big dog starts running toward me? How am I going to react?" We, the listeners, do not know his likely response unless we know what has happened in the past with him and big dogs. Let's walk through the model to understand better.

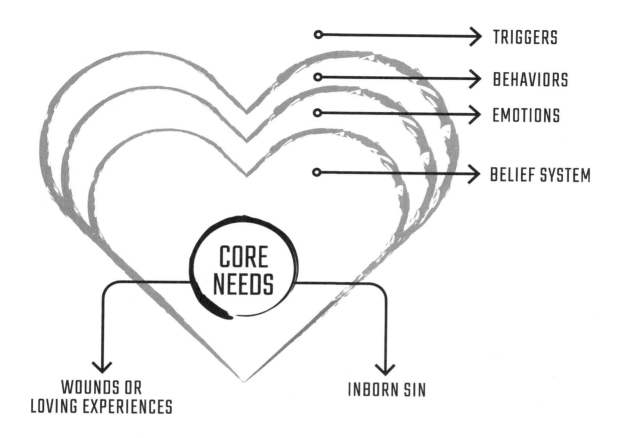

Triggers

At the top of the heart are triggers. Triggers are anything that set off a memory tape or flashback memory transporting the person back to the event of their original trauma.[48]

So, what about Matt and the big, tongue-lolling dog running toward him? The running dog is the trigger. Other triggers might be a smell, a certain word, a reaction from your child, the way a man looks at you, or a lack of "likes" on your social media posts.

Behavior

Our behavior is our physical response to a trigger based on our feelings about a past experience that the trigger resembles. For some people, having a slobbery dog run at them (trigger) invokes an immediate fight or flight response (behavior). For Matt, this is not the case. He grew up with giant dogs, and he can't help but want to let every one jump up on him and lick him, and encourage our daughters to allow the dogs to do the same to them (after he has assessed the dog's gentleness level). Matt responds to a running-dog trigger with a bending-down-and-letting-it-give-him-a-tongue-bath behavior. This behavioral reaction is because of something earlier in his life—and something deeper.

This is the only level we can control. Every other level is out of our control.

Emotions

According to Webster's Dictionary, emotions are "a conscious mental reaction (such as anger or fear) subjectively experienced as strong feeling usually directed toward a specific object and typically accompanied by physiological and behavioral changes in the body."[49] I see emotions as the light on the dashboard of your human car. They are the indicator of something going on "underneath the hood" or in the heart.

Emotions are tricky. They are often true indicators about how we feel about something, but they are not always true indicators about what is true. For example, Matt may see that dog and feel extremely happy about it. He may be daydreaming about this dog having a lovely licking fest with the whole family. However, the truth may be that the dog is rabid and wants to have a biting fest with my family. If Matt feels the dog is friendly and is happy about that (his truth), it does not mean the dog is friendly (the objective truth). Emotions are wonderful indicators, but they are not objective truth.

Some Thoughts about Emotions

Take a look at the feeling/emotion wheel[50] we've included. This tool and others like it have been extremely helpful for counseling because most of us who didn't grow up with Mr. Rogers like I did (thanks, Mom) didn't learn feeling words. Sad, mad, and happy were about it. "Mad" can be acceptable, "sad" is burdensome, but "happy" is ideal.

In this book, we are going to encourage you to feel all the feels. We can often think that emotions are "bad" or unholy—especially the negative feelings. (Unless we feel mad about sin; we can hate sin.) Research shows that one-third of us actively judge or shove away negative emotions such as sadness, anger, or grief.[51] But shoving them down will only strengthen them—like staring at a chocolate cake while saying, "I'm not going to eat that. I'm not going to eat that." Actively suppressing it only makes it grow in size. Psychologists call this "amplification."[52] Because of this and other biblical reasons, we are going to give you permission to feel—and even strongly encourage it. We believe sorrow and grief are critical pieces to healing and forgiveness. There is more on this in chapters 6 and 7, where we will explore lament and forgiveness.

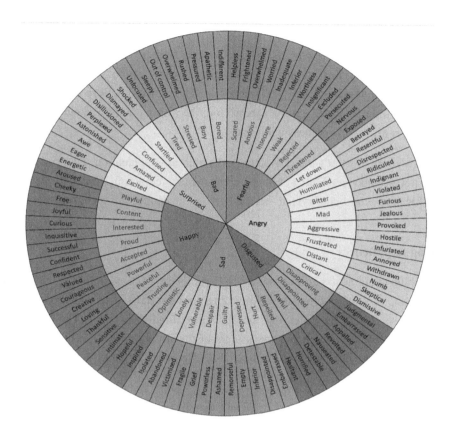

EXERCISE 1: HOW DO YOU FEEL RIGHT NOW?

This is possibly an easy one. Look at the Feeling Wheel words and ask, "How do I feel right now?" No need to judge the feelings, just observe. (And take note if you sense judgment or even resentment toward the question. Why do you feel frustration at the question?) Remember, emotions are an indicator light of what's going on underneath the surface. Write the word or words below if you choose.

Belief System

A belief system is what we believe to be true about God, the world, others, and ourselves. We can either operate out of false beliefs (lies) or truth. Our belief system is where the gospel is introduced. However, as we discussed earlier, we can know the ABC's of the gospel (I am fallen, I believe in Jesus, I am going to the new Kingdom), and still operate in false beliefs about God, the world, others, and ourselves (I am less-than, God hates me, I can get my own happiness without God).

We previously saw some of Matt's belief system in the emotion explanation: Dog runs at Matt (trigger). Matt bent down to pet it (behavior). Matt was happy about the dog (emotion). Matt believed the dog was kind (belief system). This particular belief system isn't about God or people, but it is about the world—dogs, in particular.

Wounds or Loving Experiences

Surrounding the hole in our hearts are wounds (or loving experiences) and inborn sin. Wounds are painful memories or the results of seasons of trauma. Wounding does not have to be something "big" like sexual assault or physical abuse. It could be something "small" like getting lightly bit by a Chihuahua once. Wounds have less to do with an objective observer's assessment of the situation ("You only got bit once by a little dog! No big deal!") and more about how the traumatized-one interprets the situation ("I was bit by a dog. Dogs are not safe. I am not safe in this world.")

Brandi Lea, author and advocate for single moms in Uganda, described well how we can perceive wounds in a podcast interview. "A lot of times we are looking at our degrees of trauma to decide whether or not we are traumatized," she said. "None of us have perhaps faced what [the moms in Uganda] have faced (the LRA [Lord's Resistance Army] rebel forces have not come through our town to rape and murder), but that doesn't mean we are not traumatized in some way."[53] From devastation in Uganda to the soccer mom's embarrassment at forgetting the soccer snack in Grand Rapids, Michigan, pain is pain.

One of the more difficult but less-emphasized forms of trauma is what my counselor, Carolyn, used to call "leaky faucet wounds." These wounds include drip-drip-drip pain such as daily cutting remarks, frequent withholding of love, or constant passive-aggressive comments. This can be more painful and take more time to process because we don't see them as a major wound to heal. We tend to brush the wound and the wounder off with an, "I'm fine. Oh, that's just the way that person was." But it's not "just the way that person was"; it is sin. And that sin must be grieved and forgiven for us to truly move on with our lives.

The effects of one-time trauma or faucet trauma can be the same. Consider the difference between getting in a major car accident where your back immediately shifts (one-time trauma), and waking up every morning and being shoved by someone (faucet wounds). In the second example, the first time you may straighten up and think, "That was weird." But after a decade of being shoved every morning, your back becomes permanently misaligned. It resembles that of the car accident victim. But instead of going in for help, you learn to walk with a crooked spine. It is not until you run into a door that everyone else walks through fine that you wake up and say, "Huh, maybe I should deal with the spine thing," and go to counseling.

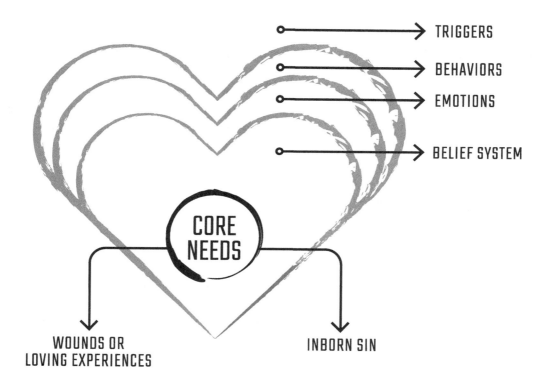

In contrast to trauma, loving experiences are memories laced with patience, kindness, gentleness, self-control, a rejoicing in the truth, honor of others, safety, trust, hope, and/or perseverance.[54] Matt's experience with big dogs in his past would be categorized as a "loving experience." To Matt, dogs embody safety, hope, and kindness.

But what about that sin nature? Isn't it in here, too? Our sinful nature wants to sin. It wants to do evil, and we are not free from it until we see Jesus.[55] So, perhaps Matt was born with a genetic predisposition toward rage. (Scientists have found a genetic correlation with uncontrollable anger.)[56] Let's say that a dog runs toward him (trigger), and he starts to tense up (behavior). He feels mad (emotion), he believes this dog is going to hurt his kids (belief system), he remembers a time when a dog hurt his brother badly (wound), and his sin nature is turning the volume up on everything (sin nature: quick to get angry). So he wants to kick the dog and the owner. But does he have to? Through the power of the Holy Spirit, there is no sinful behavior we have to engage—no matter our genetic predisposition.

We are not done yet. One more level to go, and this is the level that changed everything for me.

Core Needs[57]

At the bottom of our hearts is not a pit of sin, but a black hole of need—what we call Core Needs. Core Needs are God-given desires that make us whole. God placed them inside of us to be met by him, with his people as the supporting cast. The Body exemplifies Christ. "[T]he church is [Christ's] body; it is made full and complete by Christ, who fills all things everywhere with himself."[58] This verse talks about "fullness,"—or *pleroma* in the Greek, which means "complete."[59] People can help to make the cross of following Christ easier to bear by dulling how loudly Core Needs speak inside of us through tangible, human love.

The following is a list of some of those needs we have gathered from resources and developed from working with people we have had the privilege to walk alongside.

EXERCISE 2: YOUR CORE NEEDS

As you read the Core Needs, listen to the beating of your heart. Does it race when you read certain words? Perhaps that is your spirit connecting to the Holy Spirit, telling you, "This is what you need. Let me guide you to how we can meet this in a way that glorifies me." Underline, circle, or mentally note two that stand out to you the most.[60]

I need to be . . .

Affirmed: Overwhelmingly approved of

> "The Lord is for me, so I will have no fear." —Psalm 118:6

> "It is God who enables us, along with you, to stand firm for Christ. He has commissioned us, and he has identified us as his own by placing the Holy Spirit in our hearts as the first installment that guarantees everything he has promised us." —2 Corinthians 1:21–22

Desired: Specially chosen as myself—no pretense necessary

> "I have called you back from the ends of the earth, saying, 'You are my servant.' For I have chosen you and will not throw you away." —Isaiah 41:9

> "You didn't choose me. I chose you." —John 15:16

Included: Wanted in this group, team, or partnership; I belong

> "I have called you by name; you are mine." —Isaiah 43:1

> "[Y]ou Gentiles are no longer strangers and foreigners. You are citizens along with all of God's holy people. You are members of God's family." —Ephesians 2:19

Loved: Unconditionally accepted

> "I have loved you, my people, with an everlasting love. With unfailing love, I have drawn you to myself." —Jeremiah 31:3

> "No power in the sky above or in the earth below—indeed, nothing in all creation will ever be able to separate us from the love of God that is revealed in Christ Jesus our Lord." —Romans 8:39

Nurtured: Cared for; held

> "No one can measure the depths of his understanding." —Isaiah 40:28

> "How often I have wanted to gather your children together as a hen protects her chicks beneath her wings." —Matthew 23:37

Purposed: Filled with a sense of profoundly mattering

> "I cry out to God Most High, to God who will fulfill his purpose for me." —Psalm 57:2

> "And we know that God causes everything to work together for the good of those who love God and are called according to his purpose for them." —Romans 8:28

Rested: Re-centered and reset in mind, body, spirit; includes having fun

> "You have six days each week for your ordinary work, but on the seventh day you must stop working . . . to be refreshed." —Exodus 23:12

"It is useless for you to work so hard from early morning until late at night, anxiously working for food to eat; for God gives rest to his loved ones." —Psalm 127:2

Delighted In: Seen as unique and special

"Thank you for making me so wonderfully complex! Your workmanship is marvelous."
—Psalm 139:14

"All of you together are Christ's body, and each of you is a part of it."
—1 Corinthians 12:25

Protected: Unafraid; trusting everything is under control

"The name of the Lord is a strong fortress; the godly run to him and are safe."
—Proverbs 18:10

"Don't be afraid of those who want to kill your body; they cannot touch your soul. Fear only God, who can destroy both soul and body in hell." —Matthew 10:28

Noticed: Seen inside and out

"Hagar used another name to refer to the Lord, who had spoken to her. She said, 'You are the God who sees me.'" —Genesis 16:13

"I can never escape from your Spirit! I can never get away from your presence! If I go up to heaven, you are there; if I go down to the grave, you are there . . . I could ask the darkness to hide me, and the light around me to become night—but even in darkness I cannot hide from you. To you the night shines as bright as day. Darknes and light are the same to you." —Psalm 139:8, 11, 12

EXERCISE 3: CORE NEEDS INVENTORY

Can't figure out what's missing? The following questions may help direct you toward recognizing the unmet needs that may be driving your decisions right now.

While answering, listen to your inner voice sense of, "Ugh. This hasn't been met in a while; there is a void here." Or simply a guttural movement of the Holy Spirit where you think, "There is something to this question." Hold up that feeling of a missing Core Need as transparency paper against your day-to-day interactions.

When you feel mad/sad/fearfully triggered, ask, "If I felt _____ (Core Need) in this moment, how would I respond differently?" If you envision a more confident, uplifting posture to the situation, it is an indicator of need. Let yourself feel it. We will work on learning to fill the need later, but for now, simply feel it. Get comfortable with discomfort. That's where God tends to move.

1. When was the last time you *felt* God loved you? What happened?

2. When was the last time you were doing something vocationally or for a volunteer project and felt like you were flying and never wanted to come down? What elements stand out to you as important to creating that feeling?

3. When was the last time your soul rested—when you both stopped and recharged?

4. When was the last time you belly laughed? How did you feel? Who were you with?

5. When was the last time you felt like someone saw you—the real you? Who was it? Why did you feel seen?

6. Who was the last person to affirm you? Why did you feel affirmed?

7. How have you experienced someone taking care of you physically and/or emotionally? When was this?

8. When was the last time you felt desirable? By whom?

9. If you stopped doing everything you're doing today (work, extra-curricular activities, friendships), would your worth be the same in your eyes? In others' eyes? In God's eyes? How do you know how God feels about you?

10. What or who, if they were taken away, would make you feel like the rug was taken out from underneath you and your world was crumbling?

11. When was the last time you thought, "These are my people and I am theirs?"

12. When have you felt special—like royalty special? What was it about that time that made you feel this? What elements were in place?

"Answers" (Core Need most closely associated with the question): 1. Loved, 2. Purposed, 3. Rested, 4. Rested, 5. Noticed, 6. Affirmed, 7. Nurtured, 8. Desired, 9. Loved, 10. Protected, 11. Included, 12. Delighted In

Learning about Core Needs altered my whole worldview. Like I said earlier, I knew I needed Jesus, but I didn't know how I needed Jesus. When I was taught to slow down my thinking and identify my needs while looking at a woman, I was undone. Instead of, "I see her, I want her, this is who I am," my thinking shifted to, "I see her, I desire to be close to her. What do I really want to have happen with her?" Sexual language did not come out of my mouth; instead, I uttered heart words. I spoke of Core Needs. "I want to be noticed inside and out (seen). I want someone to see that the real me is delightfully special (unique). I want to be taken care of physically and emotionally (nurtured)." So, was a woman actually going to satisfy that? Could a monogamous, loving same-sex relationship meet those needs my heart cried out for? I had tried it and knew the answer: No. But I had also tried Jesus, and wasn't He worse? He wasn't tangible. So if Jesus is the real answer, *how in the world could He meet these needs of my heart?*

We will get there. I promise. But first, let's finish up with Matt and that ever-running dog. We need to fully understand this model to be able to talk about it in the rest of this book. How do Matt and his relationship to that running dog relate to the Core Needs? Inside of Matt is a need to be desired. He wants to be "specially chosen as myself—no pretense necessary." Dogs, a creation of God, reflect God in how they (often) love people unconditionally. They seemingly desire to be with you without any requirements or pretense.

So, to review, Matt has this desire to be specially chosen (Core Need: to be desired), he had great memories with dogs growing up (loving experience), he believed they were kind (belief system), he was happy seeing one (emotion), he bent down to pet it (behavior), and it all began with a dog running toward him (trigger).

Who knew petting a dog could be so deep?

REFLECTION QUESTIONS:

1. How do you see the world searching to fill the "hole in their hearts"?

2. Have you ever felt the hole in your heart? What does that need look like? When was it the most palpable?

3. Did you grow up with permission to feel negative emotions? How do you feel about feelings now?

4. What sorts of trauma have you endured? The continual "faucet" wounds or a one-time trauma?

5. Which Core Needs spoke to you? Can you think of a time in your childhood when one of those needs was not met? When was this, and what happened (trigger)? What did you do with that pain (behavior)? How did you feel (emotion)? What did you believe about yourself, the world, or God (belief system)? How did sin nature play into this?

6. When have you been triggered this week? What happened? Follow the Hole in My Heart Model to trace that experience as far down into the hole in your heart as you can. Can you see what Core Need the trigger hit?

_____
_____
_____
_____

CHAPTER 3: THE MOST IMPORTANT THING

"Even if my father and mother abandon me, the LORD will hold me close."
—King David[61]

"What comes into our minds when we think about God is the most important thing about us."
—A.W. Tozer[62]

I was recently asked, "If a fifteen-year-old boy came out to you, telling you he was wrestling with his sexuality, what is the first thing you would do?"

I would listen, thank him, ask questions to understand more, and try to find points of agreement. Such a response is our regular practice in Matt's counseling, my mentoring, and on the streets. "Thank you so much for trusting me with your story," we say. "You are welcome to ignore or say 'pass' to any of our questions, but we'd love to know how it has been for you? How did you get to this place or to this wrestling point?" We listen, thank, and ask to understand more.

If our initial conversation grows into a mentorship or counseling relationship (only ever offering this, never demanding it), our primary focus with this person would be to discover what he believes about God and what he thinks God believes about him. Does he believe God hates him? Wants to squish him? Is indifferent toward him? Likes him when he's perfect? Loves him unconditionally? "What comes into our minds when we think about God is the most important thing about us," A.W. Tozer said.[63] That is not just a nice quote; that is truth.

Undoubtedly this young man is going to experience rejection. His local church could be the kindest and most amazing, affirming, exhorting, grace-filled, and truth-speaking church on the planet, but one Sunday morning, someone may say something that unintentionally communicates rejection.

Let's pretend our young gay man's name is Sean, and some morning, there is an elder named Roger making coffee at the church. Sean was dropped off by a friend, and he is terrified walking in. He's been gone for a few weeks, but now he wants to get involved. *Will I be able to get into a small group? What if they find out I'm gay? Will I still be able to talk about what's going on with me? Will they kick me out?* Sean walks up to Roger, who is making coffee, and says, "Hey! Can I help?" Remembering the rules he just posted about who is allowed in the kitchen, Roger says, "Oh, I'm so sorry, but the coffee team is the only one allowed in here." Sean's face falls. "Okay . . . thanks," and he walks away, hurt.

What happened? Because it is my made-up story, I'll fill in behind the words. When Roger said "no," he was thinking, *I'd love some help. I've met Sean before, and he is a great guy. But, rules are rules.* Sean is thinking: *Rejected again. He probably knows I'm gay and thinks it's a catchable disease. Church people hate me. God must hate me.*

People with broken sexuality—especially LGBT+ people—have often been rejected many times by their families, churches, friends, and themselves. Repeated wounding in the same place only needs a light bump from someone like Roger to set off a pain dating back to childhood. For Sean, if he has endured many rejections from others, *any* human rejection is going to hurt exponentially more. If he finds out that the church (and Roger) actually will not love him as a fellow co-beloved sinner as he is, where he is (while still holding to a traditional biblical sexual ethic—it's possible!), at best he might say, "Goodbye, church," but he may also say, "Peace out, God."[64] He may even join the too many LGBT+ teens who have said, "Farewell, world." Indeed, LGBT+ teens are two to four times more likely to attempt suicide than their straight, cisgender peers, and they are eight times more likely if they come from highly rejecting families.[65] That is a devastating reality that should not be. But what can we do about it? We must create safe spaces in the Church and inside every one of us.

A REAL FRIEND'S REJECTION

I once met a young man who shared his story of rejection. To preserve his identity, we will call him "Frank." Frank had no safe space inside himself or inside the Church. "I felt that since I was four years old," he admitted quietly about his same-sex attractions. I shook my head. "I can't imagine what it was like to feel that as a young black man." From what I had heard, admitting you experience same-sex attractions in some areas of the black community can be brutal. Many LGBT+ people never say anything.

"Oh, yeah," he shook his head slowly back and forth. "In my world, people don't just make fun of you. They bully you to death—to death." He continued: "Since I was six, I considered killing myself. I used to write notes and hide them under my bed . . ." My heart dropped. He mentioned how he coped by stealing and using drugs. "It got so bad, I ended up in prison." Instead of going deeper into coping strategies, Frank turned to God in his cell. "I said, 'God, if you are who you say you are . . . if you are the One I am looking for, then show up.'"

My jaw dropped. That is almost verbatim what I yelled at God when I had my own come-to-Jesus moment nearly a decade ago—not in prison, but in my apartment. Lostness is lostness. "In that cell . . . I don't know how to explain it other than the whole room filled with God's love." He shook his head back and forth slowly again. "I heard God's voice. He didn't call me fa*, He didn't call me sissy . . . He called me 'son.' And I called Him 'Lord.'"

The story didn't end at that point, even though I felt we had just done church. "I felt like I was supposed to share my testimony in the prison." He had become the leader in the chaplaincy program, and it was his turn to share. But to open up about same-sex attractions or behavior as a young black man in prison is asking for (at best) rejection, and at worst, a beating. "I did not want to do it. I argued with God and fasted and prayed for three or four months." I held my breath, waiting to hear what he decided. "I realized that I had surrendered my heart to God but not my will."

"What did you do?" I asked, knowing I was standing on sacred ground with him.

"I finally concluded this was not my story," he said. "This was God's, and I had to share it with others." He did, and he was rejected—not by all, but by some. He said he felt sad and withdrew for a season, until he brought even this pain and rejection to God. "And He poured out more love on me than I could imagine."

SAFE SPACES ARE NECESSARY INSIDE, TOO

Creating safe spaces in churches, homes, and schools is unquestionably critical for people like Frank and Sean. But physical safe spaces mean nothing if there is not a safe place with Jesus inside their own hearts. Telling rejected people, "You are loved," 20,000 times in 20,000 different ways won't help forever—especially if we hold to this historical, Christian sexual ethic. Any truth statements can sound condemning if a person never experiences love from the Lover of his soul in his places of deepest shame and pain.

This is easier said than done. We cannot duct tape nice verses to our brain and hope for transformation. Experience trumps truth. "[T]he heart's distrust is greater than the mind's blindness," John Calvin said. "It is harder for the heart to be furnished with assurance [of God's love] than for the mind to be endowed with thought."[66]

Remember the Hole in my Heart Model? Beliefs are higher up on the model (closer to the surface of where we live most frequently) than wounding (a wound in this case being someone at church rejecting this young man). Now, the wound of someone offhandedly rejecting this man while making a batch of coffee at church is not a giant issue. But the issue is not the issue. The person who bumps him emotionally while making coffee is simply hitting the surface of an infected wound that has perhaps been stabbed repeatedly since childhood.

So, shouldn't Sean just toughen up? Recognize we didn't mean to hurt him? Why should we have to be so sensitive?

There are two right answers to such questions, and one answer focuses on the young man and the other focuses on the Church.[67] Yes, he needs to "toughen up"—if toughening means that he is strengthened by the love of Jesus Christ in his core.[68] But at the same time we, the Church, need to be a part of that strengthening—not the re-injuring. "[W]arn those who are lazy. Encourage those who are timid. Take tender care of those who are weak. Be patient with everyone," Paul said.[69]

I am in no way saying every LGBT+ person is weak, but I do believe most (if not all) have been rejected in small to outrageous ways. We have talked with kids whose parents have told them they wished they had cancer, would die, or had never been born rather than for them to wrestle with sexual or gender issues. The parents sometimes mean it well: "We love them so much we wish they didn't have to struggle!" Intentional or not, such words make for gigantic wounds. The child hears, "I shouldn't be alive. I am worthless. I don't belong." If left unhealed and unprocessed, that wound's only option is to grow infected.

We, as the Church, need to be sensitive to those who have been hurt frequently and deeply—both LGBT+ people and others. One of our friends rightly called himself "a rejection junkie." "I am waiting for people to reject me," he said, and often times he did not have to wait long. Our friend, Sean, and Frank all needed to experience love in the Church and in their places of deepest need in order to gain strength and resilience. But that takes time. And that takes love—from the Father and from the Church.

This book is not focused on fixing the Church. (I'm grateful for fellow laborers in the same field seeking to do that.) It is instead focused on creating safe spaces inside of our hearts. To do that, we need to get at the infection and wounding.

EXERCISE 4: IT'S TIME TO READ

As you walk through this book, I want to encourage you to walk with the Bible, too. This is not because it is good to do so; it is because you *have to if you want to grow at all*. God speaks through people and through prayer, but mostly through His Word. The Word of God is the lens through which we view *everything*. It's how we discern what we hear in prayer or from people.

I know the Bible can trigger people. When I was despairing, there were times that I would open it up, read a "safe book" like Luke, and all I would hear was Jesus yelling at me. I threw my Bible across the room more than once, asking, "Why do You hate me?"

I don't know what to say other than to hang out in super safe passages for a while. For me, they are the

Psalms. Isaiah 40–60. Romans 8. Ephesians. Colossians. Galatians. John 14–17. Read safe passages (or even a single chapter or verse) over and over. It will change your heart. If there is one verse that speaks to you, read it until it becomes a part of your DNA.

In addition to simply reading daily, when you feel the question mark bubble over your head asking, "Is this true?" check it out. Do the work. Test it. "Test everything that is said. Hold onto what is good."[70] Write down your questions, and see if you can find them to either be proved or disproved in the Bible. For example, as I began my journey with Carolyn, I imagined God crossing His arms, waiting to punish me. I thought such an image was an accurate one of the true God, but I began to question it. Is it true? Does He hate me? *God, do You hate me?* Instead of simply going with my feelings, I dug into the Bible. And in my searching, my feelings were proved wrong: I discovered a lover-God. A God with both masculine and feminine attributes. "O Jerusalem, Jerusalem, the city that kills the prophets and stones God's messengers! How often I have wanted to gather your children together as a hen protects her chicks beneath her wings, but you wouldn't let me" (Matt. 23:37). I heard God's mercy, His nurture, and His motherly characteristics in this. (Which makes sense since both men and women were made in God's image.) Verse after verse challenged my beliefs until when I thought of God, I saw Him as next to me—with me—more often than I thought of Him as distant and uncaring. I could (and can) still see Him as unloving, but when I do, I know I can say, "No. Not true. I refuse to believe it," and say a verse of truth instead.

If I found verses that seemed to "prove" His hatred, I took them to people smarter than I am. This means I read articles, read good theology books, sought out wisdom from people farther along the road than me, and asked Carolyn. "There is safety in having many advisers" (Prov. 11:14).[71]

THE CAREGIVER/GOD TRIANGLE

So, how do we get below the surface to our wounding? We have to start by looking at our primary care-givers: our parents or those who took care of us growing up.

Before you slam this book closed, declaring it to be reparative therapy or something else, please give me a minute to explain. I understand referring to parents *at all* in this conversation can make LGBT+ people or those who experience same-sex attractions bristle, saying, "Don't say my parents are to blame! I had great parents." Parents of LGBT+ kids can say the same thing. "Don't blame me! I was great! They were born this way." Or, "I didn't do it. They chose this."

I hear you. I see you. I am not about to point fingers. All I am going to say is every parent since Adam and Eve has done an imperfect job of emulating God to their kids. If you identify with my same-sex attractions or wrestle with more mainstream, "acceptable" sins like pride, fear, or greed, we have to take it back to the parents. We all have to grieve that our parents were imperfect. I had to do it; our kids will have to do it. "At some point in your life," author and worship leader Christa Black Gifford wrote, "whether your family had a white picket fence or your parents were drug addicts, there were times when you didn't receive what you needed to thrive as a human being. And those experiences were always painful for a heart that was created for love."[72] We children are not born with the knowledge that God is our Father and Completer. Parents act as a surrogate for God, while siblings, cousins, neighbors, and the Church support the child's God seeking process. Once we make the decision to follow Jesus, people continue to push us to more knowledge, wholeness, and holiness while we do the same for them.

My parents were and are amazing. So were Matt's. But they had days where they were tired and cranky like everyone else's parents. (And my parents had eleven other children to deal with, for crying out loud!) There was no way they could see the especially-loud Core Need of my heart to be seen, for example, and meet it as much as I needed. No parent can—no matter the size of his or her family. My unmet need paired with sin began to tiptoe toward whatever would satiate that void in my chest. This came in the form of same-sex fantasy, perfectionism, and control.

Matt is literally a counselor, and we both know and believe everything we say here, but we have already emotionally wounded our kids—not just the toddler, but also the baby! Parents, we have wounded our kids. Kids, we have been wounded and then have turned around and hurt others. Our job is not to blame, but to name the pain in order to take it to God, to help us confess, forgive, and heal. "We can reclaim only what we name. If we refuse to look at our past with honesty, sensitivity, and wisdom, the harm of the past will continue to war against the present," psychologist Dan Allender wrote.[73]

Carolyn Schroeder, my counselor who taught me much of what I write here, said we not only need to name past wounding, but to name it as *sin*. "When we don't see what happened to us as sin," she said, "we will more easily excuse sin in us."[74] To put it another way, when we look at others' sin against us as, "Oh, that's the way they are," we will do the same to our own reflections. When we sin, if we say, "That's the way I am," then we will never change. We never grow. And we lose out on intimacy with God. "When you lift up your hands in prayer, I will not look," God said to His people, Judah, whom He loved and wanted to be close to. "Though you offer many prayers, I will not listen, for your hands are covered with the blood of innocent victims. Wash yourselves and be clean!" (Isa. 1:15–16). Jesus's brother James agreed by connecting the nearness to God to cleanliness—a metaphorical washing off of sin: "Come close to God, and God will come close to you. Wash *your* hands, *you* sinners; purify *your* hearts, for *your* loyalty is divided between God and the world" (James 4:8, italics mine).

When we don't name sin as sin, we repeat it, lose out on intimacy, and then pass the whole mess to our kids or to those we mentor.

So, how do we start looking at sin against us by our primary caregivers? We're going to do a little exercise. Ready? I'm guessing not. This is never fun. I get it. I don't like it either. But I promise you it is worth it, and it may actually promote better relationships with your parents and God.

EXERCISE 5: THE CAREGIVER/GOD TRIANGLE[75]

God is God. Parents are not. Start talking to anyone about his or her issues with God, however, and we start to hear parent problems. Nine times out of ten, the "god" they hate is not actually God. It's mom-god, dad-god, sister-god, or pastor-god. Doing this practice helps to highlight the differences between God and the caricatures of God we developed in our formative years.

Fill out the following diagram about your primary caregivers. (If pastor-god, and not a primary caregiver, is the one you are mad at, keep reading. We will focus on that later.) While filling this out, answer this question: *Growing up, how did _____ treat* [the other caregiver and/or you]? While writing, also consider: *How did your caregivers reflect God well? Were they kind to each other? What did love look like? How did they show affection toward you and each other? Where were there voids in their way of relating to one another or you?*

Your answers do not have to be absolutely, inarguably true. If your caregivers were in the room with you while you filled this out, they might disagree. That doesn't matter in this moment. Simply write your perception. Right or wrong, it is what you observed, and it undoubtedly affected how you view God and live your life.

CARE GIVER 1:

How did Caregiver 2 treat
Caregiver 1?

_____
_____
_____
_____
_____

CARE GIVER 2:

How did Caregiver 1 treat
Caregiver 2?

_____
_____
_____
_____
_____

YOUR NAME:

_____

How did Caregiver 1 treat you?

_____
_____
_____
_____
_____
_____

How did Caregiver 2 treat you?

_____
_____
_____
_____
_____
_____

WHY IN THE WORLD ARE WE DOING THIS AGAIN?

Good question. Why are we doing this? Why are we going deep into the depths of our history and wounding? This does not seem fun. It seems as if the world we have set up could come crumbling down. The house I've built around me is working. I am living in the Matrix, and I want to live in it. I've literally said to a counselor, "Can't I take the blue pill from The Matrix to forget all I learned?" In case you were born after 2000 or somehow missed seeing this movie, let me get you up to speed. There is an important scene where the main character, Neo, has a choice to make: should he bravely take a red pill to learn more about the depths of his reality, or should he take the blue pill and forget it all—and go back to a life of comfortable denial? "But it's inside you, Laurie," my counselor responded. "You've been living with the depths of your reality whether or not you forget it again. The truth of your history is in you, and you will live out of that reality even if your brain forgets."

So, it's not a matter of living without wounding again, it's a matter of waking up to what's inside of us and doing something about it. Dan Allender said this about this desire to avoid the pain of looking inside:

> The majority of people I see for therapy come because their relational realm is broken. Something has penetrated the bubble, and though it has been resealed, the ache can't be denied. Most want the fractured relationship restored without having to give up their insulation. It is simply not possible. But seldom are the roots of the core issue addressed; to do so means to reenter memories of betrayal that are full of pain and bitterness. It is better to wall off the memory, insulate themselves, and carry on. That works until the bubble gets pierced and the ache demands attention that harshness or denial will not resolve.[76]

Jeepers, who is excited now?

When I recently had another wound triggered by a life experience, I went back to my now-mentor-not-counselor, Carolyn. "Carolyn! I thought I was *done* with the big stuff. I thought I was through doing this past-digging stuff."

She paused, wisely choosing her words, a half-smile lining her eyes. "Laurie, I am in my seventies now, and God is still showing me areas of growth for me." My jaw dropped. She's not done yet? She's not all healed up? She still sins? "But I am so glad when I see where I can grow, because it shows more room for God to be present in me."

I had no words. This woman was grateful—*truly grateful*—for growing pains. She was glad to find areas of weakness in herself. I didn't know it was possible to feel that way. I mean, Paul says it: "I am glad to boast about my weaknesses, so that the power of Christ can work through me."[77] But that is *Paul*. He wrote a substantial chunk of the New Testament and saw Jesus with his eyes. There are real humans today who are really glad to find weakness? They are grateful to go deep into their areas of lack so the power of Christ can fill them?

I know it is true because I have felt it in me. I have taken big wounds to the Healer and watched Him transform ashes into a garden of life. Please know I'm not talking my same-sex attractions. That's not a wound to heal. That's a mix of inborn desires and temptations that I believe will not leave me until I see Jesus someday. No, I'm talking about actual trauma. He uses it for my good and the good of others. Is God the author of this trauma? No. Can He take it and use it for good? Yes. "He comforts us in all our troubles so that we can comfort others. When they are troubled, we will be able to give them the same comfort God has given us. For the more we suffer for Christ, the more God will shower us with his comfort through Christ."[78]

So, why are we doing this painful, digging, retrospective processes? We are doing this so we can experience more of Christ and then give His comfort to others.

But we have to dig. We have to do the work. And sometimes God brings his own jackhammer to our hearts. The pain is brutal, but the gifts are plenty. Don't give up. I'll come with you as much as I can, but more importantly, God's comforting Spirit will never leave you nor forsake you.[79]

Reflection Questions:

1. What comes to mind when you think about God? Do you think this reflects the real "capital-G" God or a "little-g" caricature of God? How can you know?

_____

_____

_____

_____

2. Consider your Caregiver/God Triangle. What surprises you from what you wrote? What did not surprise you? What stands out?

_____

_____

_____

_____

3. Consider your Core Needs. How did your caregivers meet these well? How did they not?

_____

_____

_____

_____

4. Considering your Core Needs again, where do you feel they are not being met by both others and God? Are there similarities in today's feeling of emptiness to a lack in your childhood?

_____

_____

_____

_____

5. Picture a specific moment when one of these Core Needs was not met by a caregiver. What happened? How did you feel? Take this memory with you as we walk into wounds in the next chapter.

_____

_____

_____

_____

6. So that you do not have to walk around this week carrying a ripped-open wound, find two verses that speak to that specific, unmet Core Need. (You can cheat by looking at page 28.) Although we do not want to slap a Band-Aid on a festering wound, the Word of God is alive and active. It can be a balm for our painful places, and an alive-and-powerful truth-infuser into your belief system (Heb. 4:12). Write down two verses that speak to the aching Core Need and put them in a place you will see them often (the refrigerator, your phone's lockscreen, a mirror). Memorize them if you can. Do these verses differ from any caricatures of God you have had in your mind?

_____

_____

_____

_____

EXERCISE 6: BE KIND TO YOURSELF

This book is intense, and judging yourself while reading it isn't going to help you connect your heart to Jesus' heart. Self-judgment is not going to produce lasting change; it's going to burn you out. There have been times I have shifted from digging deep into wounds with ferocity to complete numbness. I am all or nothing. As you walk through these pages, I want to caution against all-or-nothingness. Take it a step at a time, a day at a time, and speak kindly to yourself as you do it—and speak in the third person. I'm not kidding. A recent study done by Michigan State University and the University of Michigan shows that saying encouraging things to yourself in the third person ("Laurie, that was really awesome what you did," as opposed to, "I am a great person") dramatically improves your ability to process stressful situations.[80]

If, like me, you are hard on yourself and tend toward extremism, ask God, "What is one kind sentence I can put on repeat in my mind this week?" (Put it in the third person.) It might be an adaptation of a verse or simply something true.

CHAPTER 4: WHERE THERE ARE WOUNDS THERE'S A WAY

"Where are your accusers? Didn't even one of them condemn you? . . . Neither do I."
—*Jesus*[81]

"[W]hen we learn to move through suffering, rather than avoid it, then we greet it differently. We become willing to let it teach us. We even begin to see how God can use it for some larger end. . . . Ultimately mourning means facing what wounds us in the presence of One who can heal."
—*Henri Nouwen*[82]

It was the first English class of my college career. I already knew I loved the teacher, Professor Cynthia Beach. Her well-chosen words and kind eyes said, "I am smart and compassionate." Two years later, I tested what I thought to be true by telling her my secret: "I am in a same-sex relationship, and I don't know what to do." She responded gracefully and compassionately like I hoped. She listened, asked questions, and listened some more.

"I stink," I said, the tears hitting her desk.

"Is that your name?" she asked. "'I Stink?'"

I could not verbally respond because of the shame. *Yes. That's who I am*, I thought. *I stink. I am a failure.* Her tenderness, kindness, and gentle prodding to meet with her counselor-husband (and my second-favorite professor) would propel me toward life: *Keep moving. Don't give up. Even your breath is a prayer for life. You are valuable. There are good men out there; they just don't wear signs.*

But in class that late summer day, she asked all of us a series questions which prompted similar introspection: "I want you to think of a time when you were especially happy or sad. How did you feel? Why did you feel that way? You have ten minutes to write whatever comes to mind."

I froze, and then I broke. The suppressed memory surfaced to my brain like a geyser. A man, a stranger, touching me . . . I was eleven. *Was this real?* I could hardly ask the question, knowing it to be true.

Minutes before the memory flood, I was Super Christian Girl who had no problems. I had curled my long, blonde hair, chosen my outfit specifically for this moment, and I had monologues ready to answer "Who are you?" and "Why did you choose this university?" and "What are you going to do with your life?" I was *that girl. Christian leader girl.*

Now I was *that girl with a story.*

I always wondered why I flinched when men would come up next to me. Now I knew. Men triggered me.

The memory gushed over the ridges of my brain as I sat, stunned, trying to hide wetness on my cheeks. *Shut it back down!* I couldn't find the cork.

I was eleven; he was forty-something. I was looking at toys while my siblings wandered the rest of the store in search of Christmas presents. The man saw a kid alone, and he went after me. I had no words. But finally, I found the strength to lightly push him away and whisper "stop." He slinked away into the crowd.

In a daze, I found my older sister. Feeling shame covering me like a wet blanket, I shakily relayed what happened. I couldn't look at her. *What did happen?* She found my mom and told her, my dad called the police later, and then . . . just me. Standing alone in my room. "Is this going to affect me the rest of my life?" I wondered. "No way."

Kids always interpret things incorrectly. I was no exception. I stuffed it, deciding it didn't matter. Before I locked it away, I attached God's wrath to that man. I recalled demanding that my mom take me to the store where it happened. My mom didn't want to. I was defiant. *God sent that man to hurt me as punishment. It was my fault.*

I took the lie and swallowed it.

It was not the first time I was hurt this way. I had a family friend play a "game" with me—that wasn't a game—at eight, and at nine, a female ballet teacher engaged me in a way that was not appropriate.

At one point in that eight/nine-year-old season, I stood in our house, considering all of my siblings scurrying around the home. They all seemed to have an identity. Alicia was the funny, creative one. John, the artist. David was smart. Suzie, a kind servant. Angela, she had a big heart that liked to give. Me? I looked down inside of myself, and saw . . . nothing. I was invisible. I could picture myself with an outline of my head, my shoulders, but nothing else. A non-person. Worthless.

The hole in my heart was taking over the whole of me. Did anyone see me? *Did anyone care about number 9 kid out of 12?* That perpetrating family friend said I mattered—because of what I could give him. The ballet teacher said the same thing: "You matter because I can take from you." The man in the store agreed.

They saw me and said I mattered, but it wasn't the real me they saw and valued. It was my outline. My body. Because I didn't consent, it wasn't the *real me* they were stealing from nor even saying that mattered. What they could steal from me had value, but because they stole it, it only served to confuse me: I matter, but I *don't* really.

I looked at friends and family with the same wary eyes. *Do you really love me? Or do you love me because you have to because we share the same blood? Do you love me because I can perform well? (Because I get good grades, smile right, and say the right Christian things?)* Instead of processing this internal mess, I leaned into it. I took the outline that they said mattered, and I made it shinier.

I sought to become the popular girl who got good grades. This approach got a thumbs-up from my parents and teachers, and I felt the eyes of the most respected people in my school on me. Our family relocated homes and school districts every three years, and each move gave me the opportunity to deepen my chameleon transformation. I become more of *that girl* who was cool, mean, and smart. Slowly, I lost the real me who enjoyed wandering the fields in her backyard and finding stray animals to cuddle. I became someone who desperately wanted to be loved and would claw her way to the top to get that desire met.

The Core Need in my heart to be seen nodded. *Yes, that's a good idea. Get the right people to like you. Even the boys. Do whatever it takes.* The best defense, I decided, was to have a great offense. I would get boys to like me, to notice me, but I would not let them touch me. *That's gross and scary.* I flirted and won them over. When their eyes were on me, I knew I was in control. I flirted with the girls, too, *but that was all in jest, right?*

There were times I felt convicted, such as in youth group worship time when the songs especially penetrated my heart. I thought I could hear the true love of God speaking to my spirit, saying, *I have something better than flirting and being mean, Laurie. I want to meet that need in your heart.*

I would cry and confess, but then . . . well, sin is fun and easy. And I still loved God, and He loved me, so, I was good with Jesus, right? Plus, I was only hurting me. And it didn't even hurt. It helped.

That idea was shattered in college, when I ran into a girl I socially tortured in junior high. "Oh, hey! It's great to see you again!" I was so changed by that time that her look of terror in response shocked me. I realized, whenever she tells her testimony, I am a part of it. Not as the hero, but as the villain.

We cannot quarantine brokenness. We cannot quarantine sin. The stranger in the store bled on me, and I reacted sinfully—bleeding on others. This bloodbath does not end until we take our wounds to the Healer.

So what wounds do we need to take to the Healer? For one, sexual assault and abuse.

I am not alone in this. LGBT+/SSA people have experienced sexual assault at an outrageous percentage. Nearly half of lesbians (46%) and three-quarters of bisexual women (75%) reported sexual violence other than rape in their lifetimes. Four in ten gay men (40%) and nearly half of bisexual men (47%) report sexual violence other than rape in their lifetimes.[83] 50–66% of people who identify as transgender have experienced sexual abuse or assault.[84]

The sexual stealing from my body did not cause my same-sex attractions. I had intrigue toward women my whole life—before the assaults. Yes, the violence did not help my relationship to men, but they did not cause my attraction to women.

I highlight these percentages only because non-Christian, seemingly unbiased research shows that LGBT+ people are at a higher risk for sexual assault than other groups.[85] Also, as much as I want to focus on all brokenness in all people, I need to press on the LGBT+ wounding for a while. I think there is a sad reality in some people's subconscious that because LGBT+ people are "open sinners" we don't have to love them and care for their wounding as much. Guess what? We are all open sinners. We all thumb our noses at God defiantly every day. All fall short. All are loved.

So, let's talk more LGBT+ pain.

- 74% of LGBT+ youth are bullied compared to 20% of the general youth population.[86]
- Only 37% of LGBT+ youth report being happy, while 67% of non-LGBT+ youth say they are happy. However, over 80% of LGBT+ youth believe they will be happy eventually, with nearly half believing that they will need to move away from their current town to find happiness.[87]
- With each instance of verbal or physical harassment, the risk of self-harm among LGBT+ youth is 2 ½ times more likely. [88]
- LGBT+ youth in highly rejecting families are 8 times more likely to attempt suicide.[89]
- Gay, lesbian, and bisexual youth are 4 times more likely to attempt suicide than their heterosexual counterparts.[90]
- Those who expressed a transgender identity or gender non-conformity while in grades K–12 reported alarming rates of harassment (78%), physical assault (35%), and sexual violence (12%); harassment was so severe that it led almost one-sixth (15%) to leave a school in K–12 settings or in higher education.[91]
- 41% of people who identify as transgender have attempted suicide compared to 1.7% of the general population.[92]
- An unknown number of LGBT+ people are murdered globally each year.[93]
- 40% of homeless youth identify as LGBT+ verses 7% of the general population.[94]

- LGBT+ teens are 3–7 times more likely to engage in survival sexual acts to meet basic needs.[95]
- 46% of LGBT homeless youth ran away because of family rejection.[96]

Don't we care? How can we say we do, but not do anything about it? Matt and I attended the one-year memorial services of the deadliest shooting in the United States at the Pulse gay nightclub in Orlando. There, someone who seemingly had a specific hatred for LGBT+ people murdered 49 people.

Standing amidst the waving rainbow flags, the people gripping each other while weeping, and the smiles and encouragement to "keep dancing" and pursuing love, my heart ached. "Where are the Christians?" I wondered. I was with a group of like-minded people who want to show the gospel of grace, truth, and love to LGBT+ people. I'm sure there were more Christians there—some perhaps doing the gripping of their same-gendered partner, weeping. But what about the churches? What about the small groups of people who believe theologically like we do, but choose to minister to LGBT+ people? Where are the people who want to care for people as they are, where they are? Where are the Christians?

"What good is it, dear brothers and sisters, if you say you have faith but don't show it by your actions? Can that kind of faith save anyone?" (James 2:14) We need to show our love—not only speak it from a distance—and certainly not with phrases like, "I love you, but I hate your sin." If we really loved people, then we would demonstrate it by caring for tangible needs no matter who the person was or what they did.

WOUNDING FOR SEXUAL MAJORITIES (NON-LGBT+ IDENTIFIED PEOPLE)

But, non-LGBT+ identified people have their own risk for sexual assault, bullying, homelessness, and suicidal ideation. You may be a part of the one in four women or one in six men who have been victims of childhood sexual abuse.[97] You may be one of two million teens who face homelessness each year.[98] You may be one of 30–60% of Millennials wrestling with high anxiety.[99] You may be one of 1.4 million teens or 1.2 million adults in the U.S. who have attempted suicide.

These are painful wounds and emotions that need to be brought into the loving, wise hands of the Healer—no matter how one identifies. Pain is pain, and wounds are wounds. Jesus is an equal opportunity doctor.

DON'T I DESERVE IT?

Who deserves life? No one. "All fall short of God's glorious standard" (Rom. 3:23). But who paid the price we can all live forever? Jesus Christ. His blood does not cover me more than it does an "acceptable sinner." His blood equally covers each of us.

Without a question, the biggest problem people bring into Matt's counseling practice is not sexual sin—it is shame. Beloved people wear it like a wet blanket. I believe nothing invites the enemy of our souls to wreak havoc on our inner person like self-hatred via shame—and Satan is a shame expert. He takes a good thing like conviction of sin and links his slimy shame-laden claws into it.

But the Lord never shames; He convicts.[100] Conviction points to our sin: "Dear one, bring your heart to Me. Give Me your need. Apologize for that one thing right there." Satan always shames. Shame says our whole person is worthless because of our sin: "You did what?! You are worthless! You are a failure. You deserve death. You deserve the bullying, the pain, the homelessness." These are all lies.

But our Christian silence agrees by default. Silence defers to the loudest voice, and the enemy's voice is loud when we are isolated. Most Christians swimming through the conviction/shame cesspool are isolated and silent.

The world tries its best to fix the shame problem: "No! You don't have to feel that way! Get rid of it. Remove both the conviction and shame, and come out as a proud, affirming LGBT+ person!" Or, "Be promiscuous and date around!" Or, "Look at all the porn you want!" Or, "Just cheat on your spouse. You will be free. Join us, and you will not feel inner turmoil." True . . . for a time . . . until the Spirit of the Living God within you pricks a place of conviction again, perhaps more loudly this time.

HOW DOES JESUS FEEL ABOUT THE SEXUALLY BROKEN?

Simultaneously removing shame and conviction is not the answer. Before we dive into separating the two, we must first bathe the whole shamed/convicted mess in God's love. To do that, we must see how He feels about the sexually broken.

In John 8, some Pharisees and teachers of religious law bring to Jesus a woman caught in adultery. A sexual sinner. They are ready to stone her. They ask Him what to do. And what does He do?

1. **He saves her life.**
   He steps in the middle, and instead of grabbing a stone, He stoops. He boldly and peacefully writes in the sand. He calms the wave of the legalists' rage.

2. **He points the finger back at the Pharisees.**
   "Let the one who has never sinned throw the first stone!" He writes in the sand and says this. What does He write? We don't know. But no matter what, we do know that what He wrote and how He responded convicted the accusers' hearts of their hypocrisy.

3. **He does not condemn her.**

"Didn't even one of them condemn you? . . . Neither do I."

4. **He talks about sin.**

"Go and sin no more," Jesus says finally. Jesus saved her life, convicted the accusers, removed condemnation, and then talked about sin . . . at the end. He made sure she was *alive* first so she could experience His redeeming-from-death love. Such love should make us want to obey the command to flee from sin. But we need to first experience that love.

Jesus loved those perceived by the legalists as "the worst" so much that His interactions made them think He was not from God. "If this man were a prophet, he would know what kind of woman is touching him. She's a sinner!" (Luke 7:39)

I love this so much because in reality, the opposite was true: His love of "the worst" sinners *proved* He was Emmanuel. God with us. God with the lowest of the low. God who became the lowest of the low and died as the lowest of the low so that *everyone can have life.* Me too. You too.

AM I REALLY WOUNDED?

If you're reading this book, you may know you are bloodied up. When I began counseling with Carolyn, I said, "If you cut me open right now to look inside me, you would see chopped meat. Nothing inside feels whole. It feels ripped to shreds by pain—caused by others and myself."

But maybe you cannot relate to what I am saying at all. Maybe you have read line after line of what's written here and felt no chopped meat, nothing. Numb. "Numb is an emotion," Terry Wardle, a psychologist and author said.[101] Even though your emotion is a lack of an emotion, that lack is information about what is going on underneath. Whenever I feel something greater or lesser than a situation calls for, I know I am getting triggered. And where there are triggers, there are wounds. For example, before a certain moment when I sensed God's releasing to do this ministry, when anyone talked about things related to LGBT+ people, I became nearly catatonic. I felt nothing. I could say nothing. I was so overwhelmed with emotion that I felt emotionless. Numb is an emotion. Somewhere inside of me, I wanted to get the feelings out, but I simply didn't know how. I had not developed the brain-heart-mouth connections to be able to recognize pain, feel pain, and then say, "Wow, I feel pain." I was fragmented *into* brain, heart, and body due to assault. Assault teaches you to detach your brain from your body in order to survive a horrific event. My get-stuff-done personality type only adds fuel to the detachment fire. In intense situations, *I can operate* at a high level of professionalism even if inside my heart is racing. I don't feel nervous; I feel nothing *except focus*.

We have seen such focused, numbed-out looks from many of those with whom we have worked. They talk about outrageous assault done to them without batting an eye. They speak as if their brain is on the ceiling, their body is on the chair in front of me, and their heart was left at the place of assault. The disconnect is nearly visible.

FOR REAL, I DON'T HAVE REAL WOUNDS

There are also people I meet who may have a general sense of "My life wasn't perfect, but I didn't have any major trauma . . . so I think I'm good." But when we look at the fruit of their life in their pasture, we see the opposite of love, joy, peace, patience, or kindness growing. We may see bitterness, rage, jealousy, fear, or selfishness growing. If the individual in front of me is saying, "I'm fine," but the fruit is bad, I can 100% guarantee there are ungrieved, unprocessed "small" wounds that must be taken to the Lord for healing. (Along with confession, forgiveness, etc.—but we aren't there yet.)

The way I see it, most of us live in our sheep pastures (our lives) blindly. We cannot see the giant rock we stumbled over, we cannot feel the edge of the fence, we do not know if there is a gate or what type of tree we just slammed our heads against. These things are remnants of the past: An unkind word, a passive rejection, or a word misunderstood. We didn't ask for these items to be included in our present-day pasture lives, but here they are. We cannot magic them out. (Much to my dismay, magic is not real.) We also cannot avoid them forever. We keep blindly slamming into them, and cursing in reaction. Instead, we must stop running blindly and take the time to touch, feel, grieve, and identify (name) what they are. Then we will see more clearly. Then we will not continue running into the same barriers. Then we are no longer haphazardly living and stumbling around, we are consciously, intentionally living.

But we have to name the wounds. We have to see them—no matter how "small."

To help us focus on these "smaller" wounds, here is a list to help you consider passive wounds in your life:

Passive wounds: never being told "I love you"; never being hugged or touched; being ignored; not having your needs taken care of—physically or emotionally (neglect, abandonment); being told or made to believe you were not good enough; experiencing your parents' constant conflict and feeling responsible; having parents that didn't love each other (and feeling responsible); having work-addicted parents (and being ignored); or being depended on by your parents for their emotional wholeness (emotional incest).

Characteristics of this passive wounding might be: super-sensitivity, perfectionism, low self-esteem, a sense of unworthiness, mis-perceptions of God, fear of failure/success, depression (not biochemical), fear of commitment, fear of rejection, lack of trust in self or others, and unforgiveness, bitterness, and resentment.[102]

WHAT DO I DO WITH MY PAIN?

So what do we do with this wound-finding or general sense of, "Okay, maybe I do have some wounding"? Where can we take it? ("Please don't say, 'Take it to Jesus!'" you may be repeating.) We are going to take it to Jesus—but hopefully in a way you never have before. Like I say to every client I ever meet: "I am not smart enough to help you. No one is." There are some specific things we can look at together, but it is the Counseling, Healing, and Sovereign God who has power to find our pain, take it into His hands, and mold a masterpiece from it.

Reflection Questions:

1. What wounds, memories, or traumas (or seasons of trauma) have come to the surface for you while you read the last few chapters? Even if you feel you "have forgiven or forgotten," if you feel an emotion about the situation greater or lesser than the situation calls for, perhaps that is the Holy Spirit nudging because there is more work to do.

---

2. How do you feel right now? Can you name it? (Look at the feeling wheel again and find a word or words to describe your emotion.)

EXERCISE 7: MEDITATE

Again, I don't like to leave people ripped open as they leave this book. To re-center, find a comfortable, quiet place. Turn off your phone (unless you're reading this on your phone—then just turn off all your apps). If music helps you focus, turn on a quiet song. But if it's taking too long and it is too distracting to find a song, just stop.

A. Close your eyes and breathe: in for two seconds, hold for four seconds, then out for another two seconds. Picture every inch of your lungs filling. This is not some Eastern religious practice; this is utilizing the bodies God made to calm us down.[103] Breathe deeply several times. If something comes to mind you have to do, let it go like a leaf in the wind. God will bring it back to you when you need to think of it again.

B. Pick one of the following verses under "D." below and meditate on it. To "meditate" means to murmur, sigh, and muse.[104] In Joshua and the Psalms, God calls us to meditate on the Word "day and night" (Josh. 1:8, Ps. 1:2). Martin Luther said of meditation, "To meditate means to think persistently, deeply and diligently. Properly speaking, it means to chew over (ruminare) something in the heart. So to meditate means to engage as it were in the middle (medio), or to be moved in the very middle (medio) and centre."[105] Meditation is more like digesting food than processing a thought. Whatever imagery helps you envision it, the point is to take those places of rawness or numbness in the heart to God and let Him apply balm through the Word via meditation on truth.

C. Begin with a prayer of honesty and humility (and even confession if your heart is pinpricked with conviction—not shame).

D. Read these verses repeatedly until a word, phrase, or idea speaks to you.

"For he stands beside the needy, ready to save them from those who condemn them." —Psalm 109:31

"Some wandered in the wilderness, lost and homeless. Hungry and thirsty, they nearly died. 'Lord, help!' they cried in their trouble, and he rescued them from their distress . . . For he satisfies the thirsty and fills the hungry with good things . . . Some sat in darkness and deepest gloom . . . He led them from the darkness and deepest gloom . . . Some were fools; they rebelled and suffered for their sins . . . He sent out his word and healed them . . . Those who are wise will take all this to heart; they will see in our history the faithful love of the Lord." —Psalm 107:4–6, 9, 10, 14, 17, 20, 43

"Instead of shame and dishonor, you will enjoy a double share of honor. You will possess a double portion of prosperity in your land, and everlasting joy will be yours . . . I will faithfully reward my people for their suffering." —Isaiah 61:7–8

"I will deal severely with all who have oppressed you. I will save the weak and helpless ones; I will bring together those who were chased away. I will give glory and fame to my former exiles, wherever they have been mocked and shamed." —Zephaniah 3:19

"Since he himself has gone through suffering and testing, he is able to help us when we are being tested." —Hebrews 2:18

"I myself will tend my sheep and give them a place to lie down in peace, says the Sovereign Lord. I will search for my lost ones who strayed away, and I will bring them safely home again. I will bandage the injured and strengthen the weak." —Ezekiel 34:15–16

"He will not shout or raise his voice in public. He will not crush the weakest reed or put out a flickering candle. He will bring justice to all who have been wronged." —Isaiah 42:2–3

E. How do you feel now? How do you feel about God? How do you think God feels about you? Do these verses match any long-held perceptions of God? Were those long-held perceptions real God or little "g" god?

CHAPTER 5: LISTENING PRAYER

"What God wants is simply our presence, even if it feels like a waste of potentially productive time. That is what friends do together—they waste time with each other Simply being together is enough without expecting to 'get something' from the interaction. It should be no different with God."
—David Benner[106]

"My soul, wait in silence for God alone, for my expectation is from him."
—King David[107]

I knew I needed Jesus, but I didn't know how I needed Jesus. Listening prayer taught me how, and so Matt and I teach it to about 90 percent of our clients. What is listening prayer?[108] Listening prayer is talking with God in prayer while utilizing our imagination. It involves setting a scene in our mind where we feel at rest, inviting Jesus into it, and talking with Him there. It takes prayer that sometimes feels like talking to the ceiling and makes it three-dimensional. Listening prayer includes four main pieces: 1. Safe Place or "being with" God in a restful, quiet state; 2. Lament or grieving pain to God; 3. Forgiveness, which also includes confession; and 4. Thanksgiving and celebration.

Listening prayer is not sitting in a cross-legged position, waiting for divine revelation to fall, but it is rather primarily listening, rather than talking, in prayer—hence the name. "A man prayed, and at first he thought prayer was talking. But he became more and more quiet until in the end he realized that prayer is listening," Søren Kierkegaard said.[109] It is me, Bible in my lap, reading, hanging out with God, getting my heart out before Him, and listening to what He might say through the Word, other people, or the still, small voice in my spirit—which is also filtered through the lens of the Bible in my heart/brain. That is critical. As Keller says, "Without prayer that answers the God of the Bible, we will only be talking to ourselves."[110] I don't want to talk to myself. I want to talk with and listen to Jesus.

We intentionally call the overarching heading of what we do *listening* prayer because we humans are very chatty. The name forces us to remember that true prayer has both speaking and listening. Until I met with Carolyn, 98 percent of the praying I did was me babbling on and on about *my* needs and *my* desires for *me* (and sometimes for my family and friends). I talked. Listening prayer taught me to quiet my heart like David told his soul to do. "Let all that I am wait quietly before God, for my hope is in him."[111] I currently engage this specific type of praying 10 percent of my prayer life, but it may increase to more like 40 percent of my time when I feel there is a memory or pain inside that I am having a hard time articulating or when I feel very distant from God.

The gifts of this process are many, but the primary one I saw initially was the way it helped me visualize the truth of the Bible. Instead of flatly reading God saying, "Give all your worries and cares" to Me (1 Peter 5:7), I could envision Him saying it with tenderness, compassion, and with a look into my eyes. He stretched out His arms to me, asking to take the fourteen backpacks of burdens I carried. He saw me. He told me I had worth. (Core Need alert!) I fell in love.

This is where, once again, you may toss this book aside. "This girl is *one of those*." I'm not sure what "one of those" is, but I assure you, if your image is of someone who throws their brain and Bible out the window while they wait for God to speak, I'm not. I am simply someone who believes in the Jesus of the Bible who said, "But in fact, it is best for you that I go away, because if I don't, the Advocate won't come. If I do go away, then I will send him to you" (John 16:7). *It is better for us to have the Holy Spirit than Jesus in physical form? What?!* I believe the Holy Spirit is real. I believe he speaks today—affirming and confirming what is written in the Bible. If you do not believe the Holy Spirit still speaks today, then you might not like the next few chapters.

Matt and I did not grow up in charismatic churches. We primarily attended Baptist and non-denominational churches. When Carolyn first introduced all of this to me I thought, *What is this? Is this okay?* But she was my fifth counselor, and I was either going to kill myself or leave the faith completely, so what did I have to lose? In retrospect, had I not learned this and other practices (which are spiritual disciplines such as meditation, lament, and forgiveness in the context of Listening Prayer) I am 99.9 percent certain I would be dead or an atheist. I knew all the right answers before seeing Carolyn. I *believed* a historical Christian sexual ethic was God's way. I tried obedience. I tried confession. I tried literal signed contracts. I tried just gutting it out. I concluded this sexual ethic only offered a life of death and loneliness.

Not true.

This process showed me what I was missing: not doing more Christian stuff, but doing less, and sinking deep into the soil of Christ's marvelous love more (Eph. 3:17).

SOME BIBLICAL SUPPORT FOR LISTENING PRAYER

Since first journeying with Carolyn, I have been compiling research to confirm listening prayer's biblical soundness. I am going to give you our best arguments so that as we step forward you are not held back by my same question of, "Is this biblical?"

One of the first stops of listening prayer is Safe Place. Safe Place is an imagined location where you feel safe to talk to Jesus. It is setting the stage for the other pieces of this process: lament, forgiveness, confession, and thanksgiving. Your Safe Place could be sitting at the top of a mountain, having your feet buried in sand at the beach, or walking in the cool shade of a forest. It doesn't matter if you have physically been to the location or if you can only imagine it; the point is to ask the Lord to bring to mind a place where you feel you can sigh deeply.

So . . . am I a heretic for introducing Safe Place to you?

Let's look at it: When you pray now, do you close your eyes? What are you seeing when you do this? The back of your eyelids? Is it more holy to look at the back of our eyelids than to picture a scene where we can envision our loving Father meeting us? And as we envision Him, using the Word of God as a filter to see His expressions, countenance and responses to us? What is more holy?

R.A. Torrey said, "We should never utter one syllable of prayer either in public or in private, until we are definitely conscious that we have come into the presence of God, and are actually praying to Him."[112] Torrey goes as far as to say to pray without recognizing that we are speaking to the one "who lives in eternity" (Isa. 57:15) and whose thoughts "are nothing like your thoughts" (Isa. 55:8) is to take God's name in vain.

Some say the imagination is "the devil's playground." To this, I would say any part of our bodies created by God (minds, hands, mouths, eyes) could be used for good or for evil. Jesus agrees: "Your eye is like a lamp that provides light for your body. When your eye is healthy, your whole body is filled with light. But when it is unhealthy, your body is filled with darkness" (Luke 11:34). Our eyes are not intrinsically evil. They can be used to do evil like lust or covet, but Jesus used his to look deeply into the hearts of others.[113] Our imaginations are not intrinsically evil. They can be used for evil like lusting or coveting, but they can also be used to remember, be grateful, plan, hope, write worship music, envision the parables of Jesus, and help us pray. Richard Foster believes God uses imagination to speak to us because He is Emmanuel, God with us.

To believe that God can sanctify and utilize the imagination is simply to take seriously the Christian idea of incarnation. God so accommodates, so enfleshes himself into our world that he uses the images we know and understand to teach us about the unseen world of which we know so little and which we find so difficult to understand.[114]

We already try to take massive theological truths and make them more understandable—like Jesus with the parables. We see this in Narnia, *Pilgrim's Progress*, The Lord of the Rings, and songs like "Oceans," "10,000 Reasons," and old hymns such as "When I Survey the Wondrous Cross." We are taking theology and making it visual.

So I'll ask you: Where is your favorite place to pray? Where are you physically when you feel most connected to God? For me, it's either next to water, on the top of a hill, or in my room, sitting on the window seat, looking over the forest behind our house. Without question, my two critical pieces for focused prayer are solitude and some sort of connection to nature (especially water).

Jesus was the same way. He "often withdrew to lonely places and prayed."[115] He told us to pray alone.[116] The Greek word for "lonely" or "solitary" is *eremos*. Just outside of Capernaum, there's a place called Eremos Hill. People believe this to be the place where Jesus withdrew. It has a variety of flowers and birds, and a gorgeous view of a lake. It is the mountain where Jesus spoke some of my favorite words in Scripture—the Beatitudes.[117] Jesus was like me while He was on earth in that he liked nature and views of a lake. Rather, I am like Him in that I like what He likes. It makes sense that such locations would re-center and position Him for focused prayer. It's possible that it reminded Him of when He, the Father, and Spirit designed Creation, and exhorted Him to continue on the hard path of redemption of everything—including this very view.

One of the problems of living in our current culture is we cannot often get away to lonely places to pray. We may live in a city apartment, have children to watch, or have jobs that keep us tethered to technology. But one of the gifts of prayer is that no matter where we are, God is there. God made us with the gift of our imaginations to travel with Him to Mount Eremos, or in the case of my Safe Place, to the shores of a backyard pond. When we begin our praying by imagining a place where we can sigh deeply inside of ourselves and invite Jesus there, it can open up our hearts and minds to better commune with the Creator of our imaginations.

After learning this practice, I have taken it with me everywhere. When my second daughter was born, I was wrecked with heightened emotion from the entire birthing process. I knew I needed time to myself in a place to reflect, but often times, I physically couldn't do it. So in the dead of night, after waking up more times than I could count to comfort this dear baby, I often rocked her back and forth while I mentally hung out with Jesus next to a still pond in my Safe Place. I didn't do much there except perhaps weep, sit, and simply "be" with Jesus. Even five minutes "away" to pray in this three-dimensional way met the Core Need of feeling seen by my Creator enough for me to go on through the night.

NEUROLOGICAL SUPPORT FOR LISTENING PRAYER

Different locations in our brains have different functions. When we go through a traumatic experience (wounding), the trauma is stored in the sub-cortical regions of the brain—the raw emotion, image area. Our fight-or-flight instincts kick in, and the ability to logically process the event in a linear, linguistic way turns off.[118]

Through a complex process that neurologists are just beginning to understand, trauma can be stored in sub-conscious places in the brain.[119] However, it is not completely hidden (or always hidden). Trauma can be seen in flashbacks and in the way our physical body responds to triggers. For example, before I consciously remembered the assault from the man in the store, I stood in a sandwich shop, waiting for a meal with my mom. A man sidled up next to me much like the man did in the store six years earlier—not to hurt me, but to order. My heart began to race, my back tensed, and I had an insatiable urge to run. I looked around me and didn't understand why. There was nothing to fear according to my eyes. My body said otherwise. "Mom, what is wrong with me?" I asked. I could not and did not remember for another two years.

This is because when we encounter trauma, the memory of it—implicit (seemingly "forgotten") or explicit (remembered)—is stored in the emotional parts of our brains and in our body. Our body "remembers" even if we do not. My heart raced when the sandwich-shop man triggered the memory of the man in the store.

What this neurological response to trauma has to do with listening prayer is the usual talk-therapy modes of sharing trauma can actually re-traumatize a client.[120] Have you ever shared something traumatic with a friend and felt your heart racing as if it was happening? Your brain "thinks" something traumatic is happening. The part that is reacting actually doesn't "think"— it reacts in the deeper, sub-cortical or primitive part of our brain, which is in charge of breathing, digestion, sexual attraction, and safety (fight of flight again), rather than in the later-developing cortex—the intelligent human brain that is in charge of logical, rational thinking.[121] The primitive brain immediately responds more quickly than the cortex—which has the ability to process what we are seeing. Simply talking about the trauma can either send us into a place of fight or flight or numbing out even if we force ourselves to think, "I'm safe. I'm okay."

Matt and I have seen it happen in our practices. When clients begin to talk about events without going through the listening prayer (specifically the Safe Place "scene setting") process, we watch them either shut down from fight or flight or shift completely to a numb place and simply state the trauma without emotion.

If we begin and end in a place of visual, peaceful calm with Jesus, the slow pacing, the visual nature of it, and the power of the Holy Counselor (John 14:16–17) opens up the cortex (thinking part) of the brain to help it interact with the memory stored in the sub-cortical part. Simple talk therapy can help (and has helped me), but I have found the counseling process to be exponentially more profound as we engage Listening Prayer with a living, holy, sovereign, all-knowing, and wise Counselor.

This is all a bit heady, so I am going to walk you through how the Safe Place part of listening prayer looked for me.

SAFE PLACE WITH CAROLYN AND LAURIE SCRIPTED

The following is not verbatim of a conversation I had with Carolyn, but it is an honest example. You can follow it on your own or with a caregiver if and when you both sense you are ready.

Wait! But first:

Interruption #1: Self-Assessment Questions to Know If You Are Ready

1. What comes to mind when you think about God?

If more of your thoughts are "God hates me" than "He loves me," I would not recommend going through this process on your own. It is critical to have a safe person alongside you.[122] This person will help discern what is true based on the Bible. Additionally, you need to be chewing on/meditating on the Word of God as your breakfast, lunch, and dinner. This way, if you "hear" or "see" anything that does not jive with the God of the Bible (who answers prayer), you can quickly reject it.

2. Are you willing?

You don't have to do this. Like I said, I was *so desperate for something real*, I was willing to try it even before I studied all of its biblical soundness. I trusted Carolyn, and I was willing to give it a whirl. I was afraid—mostly that God wouldn't talk to me. *What if I don't hear from Him? Does that mean He's not real?* He will. And He is real—no matter how you feel or see him. You may not "hear" Him in an audible voice (I never have), but you may receive from Him through the prompting of a verse in your heart you learned as a kid or read that morning, or in an image only you understand. God has used jet contrails in the sky as a symbol of "I see you, Laurie" more times than I can say.

If you are willing, then we say to you what we say to clients all the time: "Only engage as much as you feel comfortable and one half-step more."

Let's step into Safe Place with Carolyn and Laurie like a script:

Carolyn: Laurie, get into a position where you feel comfortable.

Laurie: [I adjust my posture so I am not distracted. If I had to use the restroom, for example, I left. I wanted to be focused.]

Carolyn: Before we begin, I want you to read this verse from Isaiah 43:1 aloud. [She hands me her giant, worn Bible with the verse highlighted.] When you read it, fill in your name for "Israel."

Laurie: Ok. "But now, O Laurie, listen to the LORD who created you. O Laurie, the one who formed you says: 'Do not be afraid, for I have ransomed you. I have called you by name; you are mine.'"

Carolyn: Good! Now, close your eyes, and simply focus on your breath. Breathe in deeply for two seconds, hold it for four, and out for two. [She breathes deeply like this with Laurie for a couple minutes.] Breathe in, hold it, breathe out. Picture your lungs filling from the top to the bottom.

Interruption #2: Breathing

We talked about this before, but I'll talk about it again. There can be anxiety surrounding things like breathing deeply because it nods toward Eastern religions. I will offer a few thoughts to those of you who feel a bit itchy about it: 1) You don't have to do this. 2) God made our breath. Just like our eyes, our hands, our imaginations, we can use our very breathing for evil (like centering it on something like idol worship), or we can use it for good (like breathing and focusing on God's love which drives out fears[123]). 3) God made us holistic beings. Utilizing the science of our bodies' ability to calm down with deep breathing can bring us to a place of peace. This is not because of Eastern religion, it's because a holy God made us holistic and breathing calms us.[124] 4) God's name, YHWH, is the sound of a breath.[125] A baby's first "word" is breathing the name of God. Our last word before dying is a breath—God. Our breathing can be a prayer if we focus it on the Creator of Life.

I choose to do it because I am quite an anxious person. It helps to calm me down so I can focus on being with my Savior-King, the Lover of my Soul.

Laurie: [Breathes deeply]

Carolyn: Good. [Praying] Now, Lord, I bring Laurie before you. I ask that nothing evil would be allowed in this space, around Laurie, or able to afflict her at all. If there is something coming against her, we tell it in the strong and mighty name of Jesus Christ to go to the foot of the

62

cross and not return. I pray with the same power that raised Jesus from the dead and is living in me that nothing evil is allowed in this place.[126]

Interruption #3: Praying Against the Enemy

Okay. This may be a bit "out there" for you, too. Did she pray for the enemy to be gone? Is that okay? I can tell you with absolute certainty that there is an enemy prowling around like a roaring lion who wants to devour you. There is an enemy who wants to steal, kill, and destroy you, but this is darkness over which you have authority.[127]

When I walk with people through this listening prayer process, I do not always tell the darkness to be gone, but I often do. There are times I can tell that there is something major blocking potential growth. The "block" isn't always the enemy, but it's important to clear it out of the way just in case. The enemy is not pro-freedom in our lives. He hates you. He likes death and destruction, so any time I'm leaning into places where he has wreaked havoc, I want to pray.

I take the authority given to me by Jesus Christ to tell it to be gone in "the strong and mighty name of Jesus Christ."[128] I am not afraid when I do this—okay, I might feel a bit shaky, but I refuse to cower. I refuse because my brain is bathing in the truth that I have the power of Jesus Christ living in me. "The Spirit who lives in you is greater than the spirit who lives in the world."[129] Is that true or not? As my sister, Suzie, says, "Compared to the great lion, Jesus, Satan is a paper lion. You could flick him away with your finger because of the power inside of us." Or as Oswald Chambers puts it, "The prayer of the feeblest saint who lives in the Spirit and keeps right with God is a terror to Satan. The very powers of darkness are paralyzed by prayer; no spiritualistic séance can succeed in the presence of a humble praying saint. No wonder Satan tries to keep our minds fussy in active work till we cannot think in prayer."[130]

One more thing to remember is that it is important to clear the spiritual air aloud because Satan and his minions are not omniscient (able to read your mind) nor omnipresent (able to be everywhere at the same time). The enemy can speak things like headphones in our ears, but he cannot hear our thoughts. He knows if a whispered lie lands by watching our actions.

To review, 1) We have a real enemy. 2) We have real power because of Jesus to take authority over any territory he may want to claim for his own.

Carolyn: [Praying] God, I ask that you would sanctify Laurie's imagination. Would you use it now for your glory? [Talking to Laurie] Now, Laurie? I want you to ask the Lord to bring to mind a place where you feel safe. In this place, you can pray this aloud or in your heart.

Laurie: [A couple minutes goes by, and I silently pray to myself.]

Carolyn: When an image comes to mind, nod to me so I know you see something. And Laurie? If distractions come to mind, let them go like a butterfly flitting off of your hand.

Laurie: [I smile then nod, recalling a childhood home where we lived from my second to fourth grade years. It was an abandoned nursing home before we renovated it into a family home for the dozen of us kids. There was an Olympic-sized swimming pool inside, but my favorite part of that behemoth home was the backyard. It was there I felt I was my true self: wandering the fields, looking for stray kittens, daydreaming as I watched the clouds stroll across the sky. My favorite spot was the pond where we younger kids liked to fish. I enjoyed going there all alone to think. It has been my consistent mental Safe Place for a decade.]

Carolyn: What are you seeing?

Laurie: It's the spot I always go to.

Carolyn: The pond in the backyard of your old house?

Laurie: Yes. I see the fields, the pond, and the wind rustling through the tall grasses.

Carolyn: [She walks through each of the five senses, pausing to listen to what I say, and perhaps commenting.] What does it look like today? If you look left? Right? Above you? Below? What type of weather is it? What is the temperature? Can you feel the wind? What do you hear? Any birds or water rippling? What do you smell? Perhaps grasses, the pond, or trees? A good earthy smell? Is anyone with you? How are you positioned in this scene? How do you feel about being here in this scene?

Laurie: [I answer each question, the picture becoming more and more solidified as I take notice of details.] I feel peaceful externally, but also like there is a big boulder inside of me that wants to get out.

Carolyn: Okay, that's good to notice. [Even if I said something like, "I feel He hates me!" She never reacted badly. She just noticed—perhaps writing it down.] We will take note of things like that and offer it to the Lord to help us sort through it. [Praying] God, I ask that you would increase that feeling of peace, and we offer you this boulder inside. [Talking to me] Laurie, whenever you are ready (if you want to), ask Jesus to be with you here in this Safe Place.

Laurie: [I don't want Him here but I do. (Do you know that push-pull of wanting to be near Jesus but terrified of Him at the same time? Will He see you and confirm everything you hate about yourself or show you love? I have the memory of a goldfish when it comes to knowing His love for me.)] Jesus? Will You please be with me here?

Carolyn: He might show up in bodily form, He might show up as a lion or a lamb, or you might recognize the Spirit's presence by feeling aware of Him there. Nod to me when you sense His presence.

Laurie: [I nod.]

Carolyn: Where is He today? [If you do nothing else, I would encourage this. Noting where you "see" Jesus helps you understand how you really feel about Jesus' presence in your life. Is He far? Close? Do you want Him to be closer? Farther?]

Laurie: I see Him across the pond, far away.

Carolyn: Are you okay with that?

Laurie: Yeah, I don't want Him near me.

Carolyn: [No judgment, just hearing. I get the sense that anything I say is simply information for her to know . . . not information to judge.] That's good to note. How are you positioned in the scene?

Laurie: With my arms crossed and my knees bunched up close to my face.

Carolyn: Can Jesus hear you if you talk to Him?

Laurie: Well, yeah. He's God. He can do anything. [I was a bit sassy. Plus, I was mad at Him.]

Carolyn: Will you talk to Him?

Interruption #4: Talking with God

Do you know what Carolyn and I just did? Instead of saying, "Dear Jesus . . . blah . . ." we visualized our "Dear Jesus." I used to pray by only shifting from looking at my real world to closing my eyes, talking *at* God. Both can work, but I find no matter how I speak, I need to know with whom I am speaking.

We can become tongue-tied when we speak with people who are famous or powerful, but with God, we become casual. No matter our style of praying, we must give honor and gratitude to the Alpha and Omega—who in spite of His bigness takes notice of man.[131]

Laurie: [I immediately start to cry, feeling the lack of judgment from Carolyn, sensing Jesus' kindness far away, and remembering the words I have been reading in Scripture about God's tenderness, His kindness, and His motherliness. He is far away not because He *is* far away, but because I *feel* He is far away. Listening Prayer shows me how I feel about God. I speak and let the tears fall . . .] Jesus! I am in so much pain!

Carolyn: [My eyes are mostly closed, but I sometimes catch a glimpse of her leaning in, her hand outstretched. I hear her praying under her breath off and on. This woman knows God, loves Him, and has done her own inner work. She knows the gospel is good news for everyone every day—herself included. There is no way she could lead me where she hasn't and doesn't go.] Laurie, can you ask him if He hears you? Can you ask Him if he cares about your pain?

Laurie: [Pauses. *What if he doesn't say anything?*] Jesus, do you hear me? Do you care about my pain?

[Instantly, He is next to me in my mind's eye. I both want him there and know He wants to be there. There are no words. There is only His sitting next to me, His arm around my back as I feel His with-ness. I cry, and let Him hold me. After letting me hang out with Jesus for some time, Carolyn says with tear-filled eyes . . .]

Carolyn: Jesus, thank you for hearing Laurie, and for letting her be with You. Thank You for showing her how You are Emmanuel. We seal this in Jesus's name. Amen.

We did not engage trauma (i.e. lamenting), but we set the stage to gently engage it with God holding my hand and a wise caregiver walking with me . . . in the future.

I will leave Carolyn and me there for now. In the next chapter, we will demonstrate how holy lamenting like Jesus and the psalmists did can be infused into this place of listening prayer.

Reflection Questions:

1. Where is your favorite physical location to pray? What elements are required for you to feel closeness to God? (Solitude, nature, or a large worshipful building? Music?)

_____

_____

_____

_____

2. What do you think about this idea of listening prayer? Have you ever done something like it before? What hesitations do you have?

_____

_____

_____

_____

3. If you were to estimate what percentage of your prayer life is devoted to listening/resting/meditating/ hanging out with God versus talking to God, what would those percentages be?

Listening/Resting/Meditating/Hanging out with God: _____ %

Talking to God: _____%

4. When you imagine Jesus getting away to the lonely places to pray, how much of His time do you think was spent talking and how much was spent listening? (There is no right answer; there is only imagination.)

_____

_____

_____

_____

EXERCISE 8: SAFE PLACE SCRIPTED FOR YOU

Either on your own or with a caregiver, go through the Safe Place Script on your own. If you are on your own, pretend like Carolyn is your caregiver, and if you have a caregiver, ask them to ask the questions she asks, inserting my name with yours.

Where did you go?

How did you feel doing it?

CHAPTER 6: LAMENT IS THE WORST BEST

"[Jesus] can always be found in the thickest part of the battle. When the wind blows cold He always takes the bleak side of the hill. The heaviest end of the cross lies ever on His shoulders. If He bids us carry a burden, He carries it also. If there is anything that is gracious, generous, kind, and tender yea lavish and superabundant in love, you always find it in Him."
—Charles Spurgeon[132]

"Have mercy on me, LORD, for I am in distress. Tears blur my eyes. My body and soul are withering away. I am dying from grief; my years are shortened by sadness."
—King David[133]

Carolyn and I walked through the nuances of Safe Place, cementing it in my mind for a while before we moved on to what we'll cover in this chapter. By "a while," I mean until I was able to get to the pond location in my mind fairly quickly, and I was not bogged down by misinterpretations of who God is. How this looked is when I "arrived" in my Safe Place I may have still seen God far away, but there were hardly any moments in that counseling room, with Carolyn praying over me, that I "heard" something from God that wasn't God.[134] I may have yelled at Him, but He slowly shifted in my thoughts from a raging Sky Judger to the slow-to-anger, rich-in-love God.

The beauty of this training was that it was bleeding into the rest of my life. I wanted to "hear" what was true from God in this space, and so I read and read and read the Word with eyes searching for the antithesis to the caricature in my mind. When I felt God's deep rage toward me and my same-sex lusts, I tore into the Bible, searching to know whether or not that rage I felt was true. It wasn't true. I found tenderness, kindness, graciousness, and a special reaching out to the sexual sinner.[135] Granted, I may have had to confess some things to Him, but I did not confess toward a raging God, but a right-with-me-at-the-pond God. I wanted to confess to Him. He was kind. I saw it—in the Word and in prayer.

At that point, I was ready to learn the next part of listening prayer: lament. But first, I needed permission to feel.

Feeling All the Feels

"Laurie, I want you to write down how you felt about the assault." I stared at Carolyn, feeling nothing about the assault with the man in the store. "You need to get the emotion up and out of you before you can forgive your perpetrator." I cocked my head like a puppy learning a new command. I did not understand the concept. I had been able to cry out some pieces of my journey, but not all. Definitely not the assault from the man in the store about whom I felt . . . zero. Now she wanted me to feel it before forgiving? *I've tried, lady. I just can't. Also, I have forgiven him, if "forgiveness" means throwing a white sheet over a dead body and pretending I don't smell the decaying flesh. Next topic, please.*

By the time I began meeting with Carolyn, I had so completely stuffed my emotions that I felt nothing most days. Or I felt like dying. Or I felt everything. There was no middle of the road, seemingly healthy tears for appropriate things. I dammed up all the emotions or felt all of them simultaneously. Now she wanted me to selectively grieve one thing? I did not know how to do that, nor did I necessarily believe that feeling the depth of what this man did to me was biblical. Forgive and forget. (Or, just forget. Where *is* that Matrix pill?)

Since that decade ago in Carolyn's office, I have also been building a mental file of "biblical reasons we can feel negative emotions." The thickest part of the file includes the seemingly negative emotions of Jesus.

Jesus Was Spitting Mad

Many of us grew up with a dash of pride at quickly knowing the answer to, "What's the shortest verse in the Bible?" "Jesus wept!" we said, referencing John 11:35. Good job. Go get a sticker.

I did not know the significance of the passage until I heard the post-9/11 sermon Tim Keller gave in New York City immediately following the attack. There, he referenced the verses preceding Jesus's weeping. "Every translation ancient and modern are afraid of what the text says," Keller said of John 11:33: "When Jesus saw her weeping, and the Jews who had come along with her also weeping, he was deeply moved in spirit and troubled."[136] But "deeply moved" doesn't translate the written Greek accurately. It doesn't describe the true emotion that led to weeping. "In extra-biblical Greek, it can refer to the snorting of horses; as applied to human beings, it invariably suggests anger, outrage or emotional indignation," theologian D.A. Carson wrote. "It is lexically inexcusable to reduce this emotional upset to the effects of empathy, grief, pain or the like."[137] To help us, Tim Keller retranslated the "deeply moved" verse: "The best translation would be, 'bellowing with anger, he came to the tomb,'" he said. "At the very least it would mean his nostrils flared with fury, and it might mean he was yelling in anger."[138]

I'm sorry, what? Jesus? Wasn't Jesus a pacifist hipster? Who is this yelling, spitting, bellowing-like-a-bull Jesus I never knew? I knew He flipped some tables, but I didn't know about the tomb rage. Why was He so angry?

It is the answer to the "why" that makes me fall in love with Emmanuel again. Commentators do not all agree on the answer.[139] Some say it is because he was frustrated at the hypocrisy of the mourners grieving alongside Mary (her grief was sincere and theirs was false). Some say it was because Jesus knew the miracle He was about to do would usher in his death. Some say He was simply grieving loudly. I agree with other commentators who said Jesus was spitting mad because He visibly saw the effects of sin: death.[140] I envision a spitting-mad Jesus recalling Eden and internally roaring, "This is not the way it was supposed to be! They were not supposed to die!" We were not designed to perish, so in the days before His own death (to save us from death), Jesus refuses to restrain his righteous rage. "No! This is not what We designed! Sin has marred My beloved!"

Yes, and thank you, Jesus. You give us permission to say the same thing. How many times in our lives do we reach a jaw-dropping, spitting-mad moment where we say, "What. Is. This. Life?! There is no way this is the way it is supposed to be!" Perhaps it happens at the gravesite of a friend, or under the harsh lights of a doctor's office, or when God chooses not to remove a certain thorn from our flesh. Instead of raging upward at God, because of Jesus we can rage next to Him, who also says, "This is not the way it was supposed to be."

After college, my friend Libby met with me when I was wrestling over my decision of what to do with my discovered sexuality. "Laurie? Do you know what you are doing?" No. I didn't know. Please tell me. "I believe everyone gets to a point in their life where they need to scream, and you are screaming, *'Life is not fair.'*" Because it isn't. It doesn't even operate in the way God intended when he created Eden. Jesus knew this, and so He bellowed. We can, too.

EXERCISE 9: YOUR SCREAM

When have you "screamed"? When have you hit that wall of, "Life is not fair"? What did your bellowing look like?

_____

_____

_____

Jesus Agonized in the Garden

Another reason we can feel negative emotions and lament them is because Jesus did not go skipping glee-fully to the cross. If He did, we would think He was mentally unhinged. He was not skipping, but He did go willingly—joyfully even, according to Hebrews 12:2. (His joy in suffering demonstrates how we can be present and joyful—but perhaps not happy—in the midst of excruciating pain.) How could He do this? How could He go willingly without detaching from His emotions? What sane, innocent person would endure beatings, walk up a hill, carry a cross and then be fully present while suffocating and getting rejected by the Father, and *in the midst of that* extend additional grace to someone dying on a cross next to Him?[141] Certainly His deity factored into His ability to forgive, but He was also human.[142]

Jesus could forgive because He felt the weight and measured the cost of forgiveness earlier in the garden. "My soul is crushed with grief to the point of death," He said to His friends in Gethsemane (Matt. 26:38). Every gospel narrative speaks of His agony. Luke goes so far as to say, "He was in such ago-ny of spirit that his sweat fell to the ground like great drops of blood" (Luke 22:44). This sounds like a description of an emotion deeper than I've ever felt.

I have wondered if fear of death—or this type of death was the reason for Jesus' crushed soul. But that doesn't make sense. He fearlessly walked on stormy water and courageously faced Satan himself (Matt. 14:22–23; 4:1–11). He also commanded others not to fear or be anxious (Matt. 6:25, 14:27, 17:7, 28:10; Mark 6:50; Luke 5:10). Jesus is not a hypocrite. He confronted hypocrites (Matt. 7:5). He is and was the most au-thentic human to ever live. He would not say one thing ("don't fear") and do another (live in fear). So, then, why was He so distressed? Was it dread? I believe He grieved so deeply because He felt the emotional weight of the sin before He physically died for it. He did not detach from the weight of it on the cross. He felt it—all of it, starting with the sin of Adam and Eve in the Garden. He counted the cost, grieved it, and then paid the price. This process is known as forgiveness.

Perhaps Jesus's Gethsemane-to-the-cross grief is not only permission to feel pain, but the holiest example of how to forgive someone. Stereotypical forgiveness looks a lot like how I jokingly referred to it at the beginning of this chapter: We see the injurer like a dead body decaying in that sheep field of our life. We don't say, "Oh my word, there is a dead body here!" and then ask God and helpers to help us remove it from our pasture. Instead we put a Febreezed sheet over it and work really hard at craning our necks away from looking at the rotting flesh. When people come to our territory and ask us about the smell, we say, "What smell?! What do you mean?!!! [Smile smile] It's FINE. I FORGAVE THEM."

Ahem. I have no personal experience with such a thing. I'm only hypothesizing.

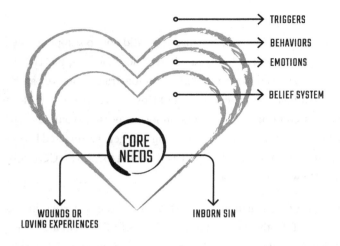

TRIGGERS

BEHAVIORS

EMOTIONS

BELIEF SYSTEM

CORE NEEDS

WOUNDS OR LOVING EXPERIENCES

INBORN SIN

To put it into our Hole in My Heart model, the wound is legitimate. There is true, real pain coming from an unmet Core Need or a Core Need stabbed by some sort of injury. Instead of acknowledging the wound and grieving its presence, we allow it to become infected. The wound also brought friends with it called false beliefs (filed under "belief system"). "You deserve this. You are worthless." As much as we pretend we don't believe it, as much as we avoid the growing infection or the deep wound, *it's still in there*. We see the results of the infected wound in our emotions. We react in the "What smell?!" sort of overreaction, or in a total lack of emotion. Hysterics imply history.

We cope (behave) in whatever form of coping we like that day: cleaning obsessively, eating mindlessly, or surfing social media endlessly. The triggering of an infected wound could be anything. It could be a slight bump from our friend who doesn't "like" our posts quickly enough, or it could something large like a husband cheating—but the pain quadruples because there is an internal infection that's been festering for decades.

Grieving or lamenting like Jesus did at Gethsemane is the only way to remove the infection so we can truly forgive. Lament rips off the Febreezed sheet, stares at the decaying body, and says, "What is this dead body?! This is terrible!" We feel the weight of death. We count the cost of what avoidance has done for us. We look to see how this death has spread into other areas of our life. Once we name it and feel it, we forgive by an act of the will, saying, "I choose, with God's help, to remove this dead body from my pasture." We may remember it, we may feel some of the effects forever, but because we have grieved the pain, and with God's help, eliminated it, there is a chance for the soil once covered by decay to grow a healthy garden of life.

We will look more closely at forgiveness, but we must first to do the grief part: lament.

What Does Lament Look Like?

The writers of the Psalms showed us how to lament or "express sorrow, mourning, or regret," as Webster defines it.[143] Did you know about 25–44% of the Psalms are songs of lament (mourning and grief) and imprecation (calling for God's justice)?[144]

I must have missed this growing up. I think I focused more on the "praise you, God" psalms and the ones that petitioned for help and protection. Are there really examples of prayers that look like grief?

Yup. Check out Psalm 77 and 88, or David's words in Psalm 13:

> O LORD, how long will you forget me? Forever?
> How long will you look the other way?
> How long must I struggle with anguish in my soul,
> with sorrow in my heart every day?
> How long will my enemy have the upper hand?

I think I can read the Psalms and hear a professional audiobook reader with a British accent in my head. But there is no way expressive, dancing, poetic David wrote in such a formal way. If his heart was like God's, and Jesus was God, and Jesus got rip roaring mad and wept sometimes, I can envision that this God-hearted guy named David wrote with agony in his chest and tears on his chin.

That's the emotion with which we can lament. Getting out the raw, gritty, mad, sad, raging, [insert angry Feeling Wheel words here] is what will release the infection, allow God to enter into the wound to heal it, and prepare us to forgive the offender. But to skip the grieving part of forgiveness is to say, "Jesus, you had to agonize over sin (this sin) and even die for it, but I don't have to." To grieve sin done to us is a small way to thank Jesus for paying the price through His tears, blood, and life. It says, "Jesus, I acknowledge this cost You something. It hurt me, but it killed You. Oh Jesus, thank You for feeling with me as I feel with You."

But we have to lament to the right person. While we met with a client together, Matt used this example to describe the appropriate way to lament (or to get out any emotion) and why we need to. "Let's say your body is a skillet, and your emotions are the fiery heat of a stove. If you leave the skillet (your body) on the stove (your emotions) with nothing inside the pan, what is going to happen?" The client answered, "The pan is going to burn up." Right. "You alone + all your emotions = you burning up. But if you put something inside of the pan, it will cook it. You need a place to put the emotions. You need to put the emotions somewhere productive."

So where is productive? That's a good question. Have you ever taken your feelings (good or bad) from friend to friend to friend and left from each one feeling disappointed? No one quite feels what you feel? I recently stumbled upon a proverb that addresses this. "Each heart knows its own bitterness, and no one else can fully share its joy."[145] It's annoyingly true. No one—not even a very skilled, empathetic counselor—can ever feel what you feel enough. As I said in counseling with Carolyn, "No one can handle all my crazy or all my happy." They can't. So who can? Look at Jesus and the psalmists.

Where did Jesus direct his pain at the tomb of Lazarus? Was he mad at Mary? No. He was raging heavenward. What about in Gethsemane? Yes, He was frustrated at the disciples who couldn't seem to stay awake, but He wasn't telling them to "take this cup from Me." That agonizing phrase was directed at God. And the psalmists? They wrote about their pain and the people who wounded them, but they took it all to God. God is the only one who can receive all our pain with gentleness and do anything about it. He is the Comforter (2 Cor. 1:3–5), the Healer (Mark 2:17), the Provider (Gen. 22:14), the One Who Sees You (Gen. 16:13), and the Mighty One (Gen. 49:24). In other words, God is everything we need. So lament takes this pain and directs it at the Healer—the only one who can heal anything. "Lament is not meaningless rage, but a rage that finds meaning in His outrageous love. Lament is an outrage . . . that still trusts in God's good outcome."[146]

But how, Laurie, how? How do we do this?

I'm so glad you asked.

What Lamenting Looks Like[147]

Actually, I'm not. I feel really bad for you. I am lamenting about you having to learn lament. Every time I have assigned it to a group or an individual, I grimace and say, "I'm so sorry. This is the worst best. It's going to be painful but worth it." They stare at me like I just handed out a surprise midterm exam. "Really, just do it. It's terrible but worth it." When Matt and I meet with Carolyn and her husband for "checkup" counseling, and she assigns a lament to us, we still groan. I promise you it is terrible, but I also promise you it is twice as worth it.

I am going to continue the scripted conversation with Carolyn and me from the previous chapter, but with this included context: The previous week, let's say Carolyn and I were talking, and the trauma about the stranger in the store surfaced. I had processed it with other counselors, but she saw what we have learned to see in clients: increased emotion around the event such as intense anger or fear, or decreased emotion around the event like, "Oh, well. Forgive and forget." Both are indicators of work to be done with Jesus. True processing looks like grief, an honest assessment of pain, and eyes that read, "Jesus paid for it. I have scars, but I am not carrying it. Jesus is."

Ask the Lord every time if He wants you to go to this place of pain. If you sense a "yes," and safe people around you are saying, "Go there, dear friend," just do it—ideally in the context of safety with a licensed professional.

EXERCISE 10: WRITE THE LAMENT

To write your lament, carve out about 45 minutes of time by yourself 2–3 days before you are to bring this to your caregiver or Journey Well Group. We say to wait until 2–3 days before so if writing it puts you in a dark place, you are not there for very long. You are close enough to feel it when you meet with a caregiver or Journey Well Group, but you are not in a sad state for long. To write:

1. **Get quiet**: Get quiet before God with your Bible, a notebook/journal, and a favorite pen. Read a comforting, favorite passage of Scripture. Ephesians 3 and Isaiah 40–43 are always go-tos for me. For inspiration on writing laments, read Psalm 66, 69, or 77.

2. **Ask:** Ask the Lord, "God? What would you like me to lament? What in my life has not been grieved?" A memory may surface that has been catching on your brain for years. You may think, "Why am I thinking of that?" It may be a place to start. Or, your caregiver may have assigned you one to write about. Ask God if you should begin there.

3. **Wait for a trigger:** If nothing comes to the surface after at least 10–20 minutes, put your writing aside and trust God is going to reveal it in His time. Wait instead for when you feel triggered, and write then. This would look like you going about your day and something happens where you are responding greater or lesser than a situation calls for. The trigger may be bumping against a deeper wound. When you can (that night or the next morning), begin writing about the trigger and see where it leads. If we use our pasture metaphor, we can envision you walking through your pasture and finding the top of a weed. As you pull it up, you recognize it as a vine, and you pull and pull, seeing it has a root system connected to something planted long ago. We want to get to the root system, but we have to start with the top of the plant (the trigger).

4. **While writing:** Puke it out. (Another metaphor. Yippee.) Get the grief out. Get the feelings out. Get the infection out—any way you can. The Psalms are beautiful, but yours doesn't have to be. Actually, we discourage lovely writing unless you are naturally a great writer. Whatever comes out of you, get it on paper. The point is to be raw and honest. Swearing is acceptable.

5. **To whom?** Write it to God. He is the receiver of your words. He can handle anything you throw at Him. He's already heard it silently in your heart/head, so why not get it out? It will feel better when you do.

6. **What do you write?** Specifically, write what happened in the trauma/wound/series of wounds. Tell the story. Start with the what/why, and then move to the how it made you feel. Write what the event made you believe about yourself, about God, and about people. Tell God what you lost as a result of this happening to you (what it cost you, such as time, friendships, depth of a spiritual walk, etc.).

7. **Don't worry:** If you don't feel anything while writing, it's okay. There have been times Matt has walked in while I was writing a lament and asked me, "What are you doing?" I smiled and said, "Writing a lament." It used to be a bit disturbing, but since learning more of how the brain works, I don't worry anymore. The "feeling" part of my brain is shut down while I'm writing about the pain, but I know through listening prayer I will most likely re-access it.

8. **Take it to your caregiver or Journey Well Group:** There is power in bringing these laments to God in listening prayer with someone who loves Jesus and/or in a group who is seeking God with you. I can write laments and feel nothing, but as soon as I get in the presence of safe people, while I picture Jesus' face hearing my heart, in a place we have hung out so many times, I lose it—in a good way.

Lament with Carolyn and Laurie Scripted

Ready? Let's look behind the scenes.

[Imagine we have already set up the Safe Place process. I am "there" in my mind's eye. I see Jesus across the pond. I am holding the lament I wrote two days ago about the man in the store. I felt nothing while writing it, even though I wrote a lot of feeling words about what I think I felt.]

Carolyn: Okay, Laurie, I want you to ask God if He wants you to read this.

Laurie: [I see myself with my knees to my chest. I feel Jesus next to me, but I am growing frustrated even thinking about the stupid lament I wrote. *Please say no, please say no.*] Do you want me to read this, Jesus?

Laurie: [I wait, then sense His encouraging but empathic smile. An affirmation.] Yeah. I am supposed to read it.

Carolyn: Are you supposed to read it in your Safe Place or somewhere else?

Laurie: [I ask, knowing quickly what to do.] I'm supposed to go back to the dollar store where it happened.

Carolyn: Okay. [Praying] Lord, Laurie feels she is supposed to go back to the dollar store where she was hurt all those years ago. Will you please go with her? [Pauses] Can you ask Him if he will come with you?

Laurie: [Everything in me is resisting this entire process. If it wasn't for Carolyn's patient, authoritative, God-loving presence and the nod from Jesus, I would bolt.] Jesus, will you

76

come with me? [A tear falls. Crying is rare for me except here—in this room with Carolyn and in this Safe Place with dear Jesus. Will He come? Yes. He reaches His hand out to me as we go back to where I was when I was eleven. My body feels cold, but Jesus is here.]

Carolyn: Okay, whenever you are ready, read your lament . . . [I hear her start to pray quietly under her breath. She doesn't know I hear her, but I do. It is comforting to know how much she trusts God, even when I don't.]

Laurie: I was in the store, looking at toys. I was just a kid. I was confused about who I was—a kid or a teenager? [I continue to read it, going through the what/why, how I felt, and what it cost.] Jesus! Where were You? Why didn't You stop this? I was just a kid. Why didn't you care? I believed You sent that man to hurt me. Did You?

Carolyn: [She is listening throughout, and perhaps prompting with, "Tell Him. Tell Jesus how it made you feel." She is trying to get at my heart so all the infection gets out. She wants me to pull the entire weed from the pasture—roots and all. She wants me to look at the dead body and grieve its presence in my life for years and years. If she doesn't sense me going deep enough into it, she may come back another day with me, or she may push where she senses emotion The skills necessary for her to do what she does are an attentive ear to emotion, the Holy Spirit, and the ability to wait as someone feels pain.] Laurie, I want you to go back and tell Jesus what this event cost you.

Laurie: What it cost me? [I am wiping dripping tears by now, the lament to the side. I stopped reading it at some point, going off the page to follow my emotions. This is totally acceptable.] It cost me so much. It cost me my childhood. It cost me believing I am safe. It cost me friendships with men. It cost me believing I am worth something.

Carolyn: [Carolyn hears the wound, but she is looking at all the levels a wound hits . . . including my belief system. She goes there next, hearing me say something about "worth."] Laurie, ask the Lord what you believed about yourself in that moment. [She has a pen and paper ready. She is going to write down all the lies I say so we can reject them later. They have been clinging to my heart for years, and they aren't allowed inside anymore.]

Laurie: What did I believe, Jesus? [I wait.] I believed I was just a piece of meat. I believed I was worthless. I believed I have to take care of myself. I believed I am the only one who is in charge of my safety.

Carolyn: What did you believe about people?

Laurie:	Men are not safe. Men are terrifying sex monsters who hurt kids. They want to steal from women. They will steal from women—and little girls—if they can.
Carolyn:	And about God?
Laurie:	I believed He was unkind. He sent mean people to hurt me. He was happy when this happened.
Carolyn:	[She knows the Word. She knows I just said something(s) counter-biblical. She does not jump on me about it, but she trusts the Spirit inside of me to speak about this. If He doesn't, she will have me read something in the Bible to counteract what I said.] Ask Him, Laurie. Ask the Lord if that is true. Was He happy when this happened? Did He send those people to hurt you? Ask Him, "Where were You, Lord?"
Laurie:	Where were You, Lord? [I wait . . . and suddenly, the picture changes. I knew God was with me as I felt like an 11-year-old again, getting hurt by that man as I stared at toys, but I didn't see where. I felt like He was above me like an evil genie. Now, the image is clearer. God wasn't in the sky, sending the man. No, He was Jesus. He was with me. He was the One I have been learning to see. The One I had been getting to know better in the Bible.

As the man approaches my right, Jesus is just behind me. His hand is on my back, His muscles rippling in pain. He wants to stop it, but He isn't. He's allowing it, suffering as He does so. I see myself hurt, but I feel Jesus' presence. He is helping me, strengthening me. He is always ready to help in times of trouble.[148] He didn't remove the trouble, but He was with me.

He didn't send that man. He actually felt it more than I did and He felt it when I stopped feeling. [Suddenly I felt sad for Jesus who had to feel that pain, too.] Oh, Jesus. You were there. |
Carolyn:	Yes! Yes. He was. Okay, Laurie, can you still see Jesus with you?
Laurie:	Yes.
Carolyn:	Does he want you to stay there or go back to Safe Place?
Laurie:	Go back. [I am exhausted. I sense His permission to leave this place of pain—even if I don't see it as terribly anymore.]
Carolyn:	Okay, go back. Do you see your Safe Place now?
Laurie:	Yes. I'm hanging out with Jesus again. We are resting by the pond. I'm wiped out.

Carolyn: Okay, you said a lot of things that you believed about yourself, the world, and God. I want to get them off of you so you can walk in freedom from here. [I nod, and she takes me through each one.] Laurie, repeat after me, "In the strong and mighty name of Jesus Christ, I reject the lie that I am worthless. I take back the ground that I intentionally or unintentionally gave to the enemy, and I give it back to You, Lord. I instead believe the truth . . ."[149] [Then she would wait for me to hear what is true from the Holy Spirit. Often it was verses or truth from the Bible.]

Laurie: [I repeat it all, and we go through each one. If you have a hard time of "taking back the ground," just note, I too used to balk at its forthrightness. Now I'm like, "Who cares? The enemy isn't allowed to have me. I'm going to tell him to his face."]

Carolyn: [After some time, she says . . .] Thank you, Jesus, for all you did in and through Laurie today. I pray You would seal this good work in Jesus's name. Amen!

Post-Lament Care

Every time I walk through this process with a client or myself, it is always a little bit different. As a caregiver now, I *have* to make sure that I am on top of my seeking-Jesus game in order to have an ear of discernment. I want to be able to hear lies, hear where the client needs to feel more *or* hear if the client is completely overwhelmed and we need to stop.[150]

For homework with a client after doing this process, I offer a few things:

1. *When* the enemy brings back lies you rejected to mind, say (aloud), "No. I reject the lie that I am worthless (for example), and I believe the truth that _____." Satan doesn't want you free, and he doesn't want you alive. *Say truth even if you don't believe truth.* "Hold up the shield of faith to stop the fiery arrows of the devil" (Eph. 6:16).

2. Find verses to support the truth you found today. The Word is a sword of truth that can fight the lies of the enemy. "For the word of God is alive and powerful. It is sharper than the sharpest two-edged sword, cutting between soul and spirit, between joint and marrow. It exposes our innermost thoughts and desires" (Heb. 4:12).

3. If I sense most (or all as best as we can figure) of the pain has gotten out, I assign forgiveness work. Try not to hate me too much. Here it comes . . . next chapter.

Reflection Questions:

1. Lament, huh? How are you doing? On a scale of 1 to 10, with 10 being you really want to do it and 1 being you never want to do it, how much do you want to engage this process?

   _____

   _____

2. Same type of question: On a scale of 1 to 10, how much do you think it would be helpful to do this lament process?

   _____

   _____

3. Have you ever studied Jesus' righteous anger? What did you think about His spitting-mad self at the tomb of Lazarus? Did it encourage you to feel negative emotions or not?

   _____

   _____

4. What stood out to you from the lament script between Carolyn and Laurie?

   _____

   _____

5. If you feel you could benefit from a lament process, with whom could you do it?

   _____

   _____

CHAPTER 7: TRUE FORGIVENESS

"Forgiveness is an act of the will, and the will can function regardless of the temperature of the heart."
—Corrie ten Boom[151]

"If you refuse to forgive others, your Father will not forgive your sins."
—Jesus[152]

There is nothing that has taught me the gospel like forgiveness.

Forgiving the stranger in the store who molested me was difficult, but it was merely uprooting a large weed compared to relocating a boulder of pain in Matt's and my marriage.

We had been married six years. When the calendar flipped to the start of our seventh year, I remember thinking, "Wow! Maybe we will be one of those couples who don't go through the seven-year fighting thing. No 'seven-year itch' for us." Wrong.

Two months into that seventh year of marriage, I was growing increasingly frustrated with Matt. We were living as missionaries in California reaching out to at-risk youth. He ran gang-prevention therapy groups in schools, and I worked at a local teen center for the same crew. But Matt's heart didn't seem into our vocation or our marriage. He was disengaged, angry, and apathetic toward God. Meanwhile, I was diving into a small group with women who weren't just walking with God, they were sprinting toward him. They taught me things like spiritual warfare, how to discern the Holy Spirit in a group, and how to read the Word like you are feasting on the richest meal. But . . . our marriage. I didn't know what to do with the increasing anger I felt about it and about Matt. "This must be how marriage is," I silently concluded. "This must be what men + women in marriage look like." I had heard enough marriage podcasts at that point to know men can detach while women dive into the Spirit. This was my marital cross to bear. I was following Jesus by marrying this man, *so deal, Laurie.*

I didn't want to deal. Marriage podcasts also taught me "you can't change your husband, but you can pray for your husband." What did I have to lose? So every time I wanted to growl at Matt, I prayed, "God, make him like Jesus." Short. Sweet. I thought it might be nice to be married to Jesus.

About a month after I began praying, the light of God began to rid our house of darkness. "Everything exposed by the light becomes visible—and everything that is illuminated becomes a light" (Eph. 5:13 NIV). Matt was going to become a light.

On Thursday evening, I returned home from small group and went straight to bed. I woke up at about 1 a.m. with a sense that there was something dark in our home. I had only begun waking up to the fact that we are in a spiritual war, and it can mess with you. "For we are not fighting against flesh-and-blood enemies, but against evil rulers and authorities of the unseen world, against mighty powers in this dark world, and against evil spirits in the heavenly places" (Eph. 6:12). What we see with our eyes is not all that there is. I felt it.

I went into our living room and prayed over the place. I was only slightly afraid, but I was not going to allow the enemy who is a paper lion know my fear. I prayed boldly, but could tell I needed backup. *Wake Matt up*, I sensed. Really, God? I knew I needed to. "Matt! Get up!" I whispered loudly—but not too loudly to wake up our seven-month-old daughter. "There is something dark in our house, and you need to do your manly duty and get it out of here."

Matt got up groggily but quickly. I could tell he was a little nervous. He loved God the best he knew how—he just didn't know how much God loved him. He walked through the house, praying with me. "God," he concluded, "let there be nothing in this house that is not of You." I felt the darkness mostly leave, and I was okay to go back to sleep. Finally.

We crawled back into bed, and I immediately fell back asleep while Matt stayed up.

Tell her. Matt thought he heard God say in the quiet of his heart. The final words Matt prayed over our home convicted him. "Let there be nothing in this house that is not of You." Matt knew he had to confess to the one he had wronged.

The six years of hiding and lying about pornography use came to his mind. *No, God, no! Anyone but Laurie!* He was terrified to tell me. As much as I am in training now to see all sin as equal, I was not an equal-opportunity lover of sinners back then. I held onto some remaining beliefs about heterosexual men from when I was wrestling the most with my sexuality: straight men are often addicted to pornography and therefore are dogs. I did not have the same standard for LGBT+ people or for women. Only heterosexual men.

I thought Matt was different. We had talked about his wrestle with pornography in junior high and high school, but by the time we dated it was past tense. It was back then . . . in college, when he had a group of guys holding him accountable. When we were married, he lost those friends and lost the battle of his will. Matt and I grew distant with busy jobs and lives, but porn wasn't too busy for Matt. It began to meet the hole in his heart of needing to feel significant—for a few minutes each day. But then the shame descended, making the insignificance he felt all the more palpable.

But he had recently met with my small group leader for spiritual direction. She walked him through something like listening prayer. There, Matt saw himself carrying a backpack full of anxiety and pain. While praying, he seemed to encounter Jesus, and he saw himself hand his backpack of cares to Him. As he did, Matt did not sense Jesus sighing in impatient relief that Matt had finally cast his cares onto Him. He sensed Jesus looking into Matt's eyes, saying that he needed to know His love. "I have loved you even as the Father has loved me. Remain in my love" (John 15:9). Know that God loves you. It will change everything.

Back in bed, he begged this loving Jesus not to make him confess to me. "She struggles with hating men because of this, God! This is the area of weakness she judges." I was not a safe person for Matt. *You must tell the one you have wronged*, God seemed to be saying.

"Fine!" Matt said. "I'll tell her if she wakes up."

There was no way I was waking up. Unless the baby was crying, I was dead to the world. I didn't wake up in the next few minutes, and Matt sighed in relief. Sleep time. But as if his hand was controlled by a string from heaven, it reached out and flapped me on the back. "What?" I said, waking immediately.

Matt gulped, flipped on the light, and began, "Laurie, I have to tell you something, and it may not be easy for you to hear."

The next few days felt like torture.

Matt did not cheat on me with a physical person, but in some ways it would have been easier than dealing with six years of lies and cover-ups because of porn. Had he cheated with a woman, I could have understood the relational and emotional development that comes from being with another real person. But porn? In my broken, angry, hurt perspective it was the non-emotional seedy underbelly of sex that degraded women and promoted sex trafficking. Those were cardinal sins in my book.

*Now is your chanc*e, a voice—not God's—whispered to me. I knew it was not God's because it did not align with the Word I still read. *Now is your chance to leave this man. Go . . . be who you are. He's just like every other man.* Women who heard what happened came out of the woodwork, inviting me to join them in their man-hater club.

It would have been easy. It would have solved a lot of problems—and caused even more. I toyed with it, let it dance around my brain for a few minutes, and then with hardly any energy behind the word I said, "No." The more I put myself on lockdown with the Bible, solid worship music, and people in my life who were *pro-our-marriage*, the stronger my "No" became. "No! I don't know why, other than the word 'covenant,' but no. We are together. We don't know *how*, we just know what is true. So, shut it down, lying voices!"

On day three of me asking questions of Matt, Matt repenting with tears, me responding with weeping, and us looking at God with a loud "How?!", I began to see the light. Matt and I sat on the floor of our apartment while our daughter slept, unaware of the relational earthquake. I looked out on the deck, and a prayer idea came to my heart. "Jesus?" I silently prayed. "What are Your emotions about this situation? I'm tired of feeling mad. How do You feel?" I was immediately overwhelmed with hope. I was nearly bowled over with the impression that Jesus was bouncing with anticipatory joy. *You have no idea how I am going to use this.* In response to Jesus's smile, I glared at Matt. "I don't know how we are going to do this, but as I sit here I sense Jesus's joy," I spat. "He is going to use this for greater things than we can imagine. Our brokenness is His gain." Matt's jaw dropped.

Jesus had one more thing to impress on my heart as I sat there, resisting feeling His hope for us. His finger of conviction pointed at my heart—where I struggle with same-sex lust. *There, Laurie. Right there. What about that? You struggle with lust toward women.*

So does Matt.

Oh, dear Jesus, I am undone. Is my sin more holy than Matt's? Is my lust better than his? *Which sin nailed Me to the cross more?* But the lying! Immediately, the Lord reminded me of the dozens of times I lied to my parents and friends while sneaking around to engage in sexual sin.

There is nothing so humbling as the cross of Jesus Christ.

And what motivated you toward relationships with women, Laurie? Sexual desire, sure, but what else? My heart. The hole in my heart. I was lonely, craving someone to see me. Was that same truth true of this *man* in front of me? I thought men were emotionless. I thought husbands detached and didn't feel. I asked Matt. "Why?" His answer then and his answers over the next year helped me to understand my husband—and men—more. Yes, hormones and sexual desire played into it, but the original and frequent motivations toward porn were heart words. "I wanted to know I was desirable," Matt said. "I wanted to know I was worth something, and that I am seen."

We were the same.

Understanding our hearts more, I stared at my wedding ring. "This still feels cheap. According to Jesus, you cheated on me so many times." So have you, the Spirit whispered in my heart. Gah. That conviction. It doesn't miss anything. How many times had I looked "at a woman with lust"?[153] Perhaps not with porn, but with my real eyes in a real world.

"What can we do?" I asked Matt. "How can we symbolically restart our marriage here?"

We got inked. (Sorry, Mom). That evening, Matt and I got matching tattoos with the word "victorious" written in Greek. Mine surrounded by swords and his by a shield—two parts necessary to fight a battle.

But four months later, we were fighting the same battle but on opposing teams. We decided to move back home to Michigan and launch Hole in My Heart Ministries while our marriage learned how to walk on shaky baby deer legs. I continued to ask many questions. "Why? What about this time?" and "What was going on in your heart?" Hearing his Core Needs helped me to understand. *Perhaps men are not complete sex monsters. Perhaps they are more like me than I thought.*

As much as my brain grew in understanding to Matt, as much as I said I forgave him, there were indicators I did not. Every time I remembered a fond family memory and asked him the "behind the scenes" questions, every muscle inside of me tensed with rage at his answer. A velociraptor stormed out of my mouth ready to "justifiably" destroy him. *Maybe I haven't forgiven him . . . But he deserves to be punished!*

I could feel the bitterness growing around the wound in my heart. *How long can we survive this way?* I knew it would not be long. So, I had two choices: fortify the bitterness with a wall of hatred and then cover it with a whitewash of civility, or forgive him from my heart (Matt. 18:35).

Because I love Jesus, because I want a heart free of infection, because I want Jesus's forgiveness of me (Matt. 6:15), and because I was committed to oneness with Matt for life, I chose to forgive. I did not feel like it. I chose it.

You can, too.

The following is what I walked through with Matt. You are welcome to join us.

EXERCISE 11: THE FORGIVENESS PROCESS

Before we begin, let's see if we are ready to forgive.

1. **Assess, "Do I need to forgive this person?"** What's our rule? Whenever our reaction is greater or lesser than a situation calls for, I need to do some internal work. My reaction was still unequal to the situation. For example, when I would think about Matt looking at porn on our vacation years before, I wanted to find him in this moment to bite his head off. He had already apologized, I had already said the words "I forgive you," but the storm in my chest said, "No you don't."

2. **Do the lament.** Lament is the critical step before forgiveness. I had grieved—LOTS—with Jesus, with Matt, with friends. I needed the Lord to suture the wound through forgiveness.

3. **Set the stage.** Find paper and a pen, write the person's name on top that you are going to forgive, and then divide the page top to bottom. At the top of the left column write, "What did they do?" On the top of the right write, "How did I feel?" Writing the answers is painful. You—like me—may want to blitz through this quickly. Don't. That's only going to prolong the lack of forgiveness, and you're going to be in a painful state for more years. You can choose that, but I'm offering another way.

NAME OF THE PERSON: _____

WHAT DID THEY DO?	HOW DID I FEEL?

4. **Make a list.** List everything they did on the left side. This is important: We cannot quickly say, "They lied, they cheated, and I feel sad." We must look at each way they sinned against us because we feel

each way they sinned against us. If a stained glass window is a relationship, wounding (especially major wounding like this) takes the window and throws it on the ground. Windows don't break in one nice piece—they shatter. Each piece must be picked up and examined. For example, on the left column I wrote, "You missed out on being more present with Gwyn when she was very young," "You lied to me when I openly asked if you were struggling," and then I wrote specific times when I felt hurt because of his actual location. On the right-hand column, I wrote how I felt regarding each sin against me, such as "hurt" or "ripped to shreds" or "abandoned" or "lonely."

5. **Avoid using only angry words.** Something to remember while doing this is that you may be tempted to write all the angry Feeling Wheel words down. It's okay to use some of them, but anger is a mask emotion. It often covers up a "weaker" emotion like fear or sadness.[154] Try not to default to anger to cover up what may be going on underneath. Let your eyes roam to the other feeling words that may be truer inside. This takes practice. In tough conversations now, I often swallow the first five sentences I want to say because I know they are not how I really feel. Getting the deeper emotion out will help heal the infection around the wound.

6. **Take it to the Lord with a caregiver or in a Journey Well Group.** I actually brought it to Matt. Oh, boy. I did not want to do it. Matt is not a caregiver or a member of a Journey Well Group. He is a care-about-er (about me and I am the same for him). Some people do not recommend processing laments or forgiveness with spouses or close friends, but we did it and do it. We find the spiritual intimacy it grows between us is worthwhile. We would only recommend processing your lament and forgiveness with someone who has been trained as a caregiver.

Processing the forgiveness of Matt's lying with Matt was the first time we did anything like it together. I didn't know it would work. Spoiler: it did. Here's how it went down.

Forgiveness Scripted with Matt and Laurie

Laurie: [I am secretly glaring at God.] Matt, I'm supposed to read what I wrote about you with you.

Matt: [Seeing I don't want to do this . . .] Uhh . . . okay.

Laurie: [I sit down with him, take in a big breath, and try to keep my velociraptor claws to myself.] Okay, let's go.

Matt: [He leads me in Safe Place, and I get to a place where I can begin to talk to Jesus.]

Laurie: [I see myself lying on the ground, angry journal page in hand (the what he did/how I feel list), my face is buried in it, and I am weeping. I can see Jesus too, sitting next to me with His hand gently on my back as He has done so many times. I am next to the pond—being here is comforting.]

Laurie: This hurts, Jesus.

[Jesus nods, a sad smile on His face. There's no judgment for how long it has taken me to get here. Just a sad smile. I look at the ground, and see the shards of glass of our broken marriage mixed in with the sandy dirt. I pick one up, giving it to Jesus. As I do, I name a sin I wrote on the left side of the page.]

Laurie: Jesus, Matt did _____

[I see myself giving him a piece of glass as I say each one. I am aware of Matt's presence, and a part of me is trying not to slam each piece in Jesus's hand to somehow hurt Matt even more for what he did. I am trying to surrender my heart and not make Matt pay—even now. But fighting my will is hard. *Help me, Jesus.*

When I look down at Jesus's hands, I see blood dripping from a cut the glass made. He continues to smile at me, inviting me to give Him all the sin—all of the broken pieces. The more I gave Him, the more He bled. *Why is Jesus bleeding for the sin Matt did?*

> [H]e was pierced for our rebellion, crushed for our sins. He was beaten so we could be whole. He was whipped so we could be healed. All of us, like sheep, have strayed away. We have left God's paths to follow our own. Yet the LORD laid on him the sins of us all (Isa. 53:5–6).

Oh.

I hand Him all the sin, but I still feel gross. *The feelings, Laurie. Give Me how it makes you feel.*

Our bodies were not made for sin or for pain. Our bodies were created for Eden. This is why it hurts so much when someone sins against us. Our spirit is doing as Jesus did at Lazarus' tomb, crying out, "This is not right!" and Jesus agrees. "No, it's not. This isn't what I created you for." But the way to heal it is not to keep screaming, it's to give it to Jesus. He is the only one with arms strong enough to carry both the sin and the pain.

I see the pain inside of me like black ink. I begin to pull it out and hand it to Jesus. He helps to siphon it from my veins, and He takes it onto Himself. A steady flow of tears washes my face as the poison of bitterness leaves. I didn't know it could happen this quickly. I didn't know I could ever feel this free again.

Jesus is very bloody. I see Him now with His arms outstretched on the cross, dying. This is critical—we must see Him there. We must envision Him dying for the sin done to us in the place He really died. There, we can see how He wore our current pain even then. The cross is real, and its results are real. The death may be past tense, but the covering of His blood is current. He knew how Matt would hurt me even then, and He died for it.

I see him in agony. The sin Matt did to me hurt God worse than it hurt me. He feels it more than I do. He is my Father and Creator. I am His beloved daughter. He not only sees and feels the effects of sin, He also feels the spiritual battle behind it. How much more must He agonize over sin?

But then . . . one more critical piece of this forgiveness process: My sin. I need to give Jesus my sin, too. Have I been perfect—totally sinless in my response to Matt? No. *Search me, O God, and know my heart,* I pray (Ps. 139:23). I still see Jesus hanging on the cross above me, but now I have a new scattering of glass, which I broke, at my feet. I put my sinful responses to Matt in Jesus' hands. I see each one cutting Him and digging into His flesh. My sin kills Him, too.]

Laurie: I'm so sorry, Jesus. I'm sorry for how I was bitter. How I yelled in unrighteous anger. How I bit back at Matt. How I withheld love from him. I let myself boil in bitterness. [Nothing is so sobering as seeing my sin equally kill Jesus, too.]

Even though Matt sinned against me and *the world* would justify sinful responses to him, God doesn't. The cost of sin—any sin—is death. Not to name my responses as "sin" is to say to Jesus, "You had to die for Matt, but not me. I am a better judge than You. Judge him. Not me. I am right. Matt is wrong. You are wrong." The problem is, I am neither Alpha nor Omega—the beginning nor the end (let alone both!).[155] If I am the judge, I will either be too harsh or too lenient. The sovereign King is the only equally loving judge of us both. Can I trust that? Can I name both of us as sinners and surrender the right to disperse consequences to God? To do so is to say, "Oh, Jesus, *thank You.* You paid the punishment for us both. We deserve Your place on the cross. I accept You as judge."

I am exhausted but not done. I must envision Jesus rising again from the dead. I am back in my Safe Place with Jesus. I see Him in all white. I see Him with nail scars in his hands. *I see the scars from my sin and Matt's sin on His flesh.* My eyes are still full of tears, but they are no longer bitter tears. They are grateful. I let Jesus hug me. I reach over for Matt's hand to hold.]

Laurie: Oh, Jesus, thank You.

Do you know what I did right there with Matt? Forgiveness. When I walk clients through this process, I often do not say, "We are going to forgive." I simply go through the process, and they experience forgiveness. It shocks them when I say what we did. This is because forgiveness is often offered as a holy lobotomy, not an experience of the gospel of Jesus Christ. From death comes life. We are all broken equally. We are all loved equally.

Why Forgive in the First Place?

I can find a lot of articles on why you need to forgive. I understand the reason for the massive word count on the subject. It feels like you are giving up the right to pay someone back.

That's exactly what we are doing.

"It's taking someone off of your hook and putting them on God's," Carolyn said.[156] It is saying, "I am refusing to be judge. God is your judge." Such a removal of "rightness to punish" is a cost of forgiveness. Before you engage this process, it would be wise to count all the costs and name the potential gifts of forgiving a perpetrator. I'll start a pro/con list with you, and you can finish it in the Question for Reflection at the end of this chapter:

Pro: Freedom. Life lived without physical ramifications of bitterness.

Con: Giving up the right to spit at the perpetrator with friends, alone, or with the perpetrator.

Pro: Ability to move on with life.

Con: You have to move on with life. You have to surrender your victim card.

Pro: Joy. Fullness. Forgiveness from Jesus.

Con: The inability to point to the perpetrator as the reason for any lack in my life.

Initially, it was difficult to give up my right to pay Matt back. Days after going through this forgiveness process, I didn't know how to interact with him without holding a knife behind my back. I missed the weight of it in my hand. I liked the option of stabbing him with his sin so I could watch him bleed. My sinful nature smiled at his pain. I had to remind my soul, "No. There is One who was stabbed already for this sin. Let it go, Laurie." Jesus taught me how to hold Matt's hand instead of holding a weapon to destroy him.

The difference between the temptation to un-forgive and signs of never truly forgiving from your heart is a difference in scale. Before I did the Forgiveness Process, a tiny pinprick would tap the wound and I would explode or implode. After doing it, a bigger poke would hit the healing wound, and I would feel the desire to fight—but not immediately explode. I could reach velociraptor level if I wanted, but I *didn't* want to. The cross sobered my rage. Jesus paid the price. Matt didn't have to anymore.

What Now?

I did the forgiveness process alongside Carolyn when I forgave the molester in the store, and I have done this same terrible/worthwhile process to forgive many people. I engage different parts of it depending on the level of pain and significance in my life. For some "little" pokes like people online who hurt me, I may simply breathe out the pain and the sin onto Jesus. I confess how I responded and see Him die and rise again for us all. Some people for whom I've done this whole forgiveness process hurt me again (surprise surprise, marriage is hard). I may leave out the big lament part, but I make sure I get the sin *and* the feelings out when people with whom I have an ongoing relationship injure me again. I write it out. *Every single time*, I am annoyed at myself for having to do it. But I know of no other way to live. I want to live in freedom. I want to live and not just "pretend to love others, [but] really love them" (Rom. 12:9). I can't do that if I have dead bodies all over my pasture with Febreezed sheets covering them. The stink will affect my ability to freely love. I must get to know Jesus' face and heart, lament with Him, and forgive through His power. You can't. He can through you.

Okay. Who is ready to be done being sad?! Let's talk thankfulness, celebration, and worship alone and in community, and then let's get practical about how to live well if you wrestle with sexuality and want to follow Jesus wholeheartedly.

Reflection Questions:

1. Have you ever experienced something where you thought you forgave someone, but your response to triggers about them indicates you haven't? (Or, could it simply have been that you forgave some pieces of the glass shards, but not all? Were there more to pick up?)

_____

_____

_____

_____

2. Take a couple minutes to rest with Jesus. Ask Him, "Who do I need to forgive? What do I need to forgive?"

_____

_____

_____

_____

3. Make a pro/con list of forgiving that person. The purpose of it is to ask your heart, "Is it worth it?"

_____

_____

_____

_____

Pros of Forgiveness	**Cons of Forgiveness**

4. When will you go through this process to forgive that person? And with whom?

_____

_____

_____

_____

5. Who is someone you feel you really have forgiven? How did that feel? How did you do it?

_____

_____

_____

_____

6. Why do you think all of this heart work is important before we talk about the specifics of living well with sexual brokenness?

_____

_____

_____

_____

CHAPTER 8: A HEAD-ON COLLISION WITH JOY

"Joy is not the absence of suffering but the presence of God."
—*Elisabeth Elliot*[157]

"You have turned my mourning into joyful dancing. You have taken away
my clothes of mourning and clothed me with joy."
—*King David*[158]

Right before Matt and I were married, I left my job as a full-time newspaper reporter to work retail. I loved life as a journalist, but honestly, I felt called to write this book. I could not write articles all day and have energy to write a book all evening. The monotony of my retail job was just enough of a brain reset to give me energy to write. Ideally, I would have written the first draft and been published quickly.

That was over ten years ago. Ahem. Humility is good for a person. God had to do some more refining of my pride, my language, and my understanding of this conversation before letting me speak publicly about it.

What shocked me about my job as an early morning stocker in a large retailer is that I enjoyed it immensely. There was more to the work than simply restocking; there is an art and science to the way retailers design sales space. I loved engaging new parts of my brain, and it did not go unnoticed. I was promoted four times within the first two years, and by the time I left, I was being looked at as a district manager.

Until a shelving unit fell on my head.

You can laugh. It's funny now.

A co-worker and I were in a back stockroom, getting signs and necessary equipment to set the floor. She reached for a table, trying to separate it from others that were all precariously leaning against the base of a fifteen-foot shelving unit. The shelves were heavy with arms, bars, and brackets to build equipment to hold stock on the floor. "Help!" she called as the leaning tables began to lean out of control against the buckling legs of the shelving unit. I ran toward her just as the legs broke, and the shelving unit began to bury us. I don't remember much except feeling box after box filled with metal pieces slam against my head.

"Are you okay?" my co-worker asked as the dust settled. I was dazed and in pain. My head was bleeding. I went to the hospital, but they sent me home after a few hours with a stack of papers and a recommendation to call them if I felt anything weird.

I felt weird, alright. Beyond the dizziness and puking from the dizziness, it was as if the world went from playing a melody I could sing to playing a minor song to which I did not know the lyrics. Every time Matt spoke to me I thought he was yelling—not in pitch but in tone. "Why are you so mad at me?" I asked. He wasn't.

I began to see four specialists a week. I couldn't drive, I could hardly walk without puking, and my head— oh, my head—hurt. After months of recovery, I went back to work with limitations, and then a picture frame fell on my head within the first six months. That's when the debilitating migraines began. I left work completely and went into the dark.

Literally. In our apartment the lights were always dimmed, the shades drawn, and if I wasn't sleeping, I wore sunglasses—even indoors if any light was on. I would have looked cool if I didn't look so sick. I am a fairly in-shape person, but I lost thirty pounds, bringing me to a near-appearance of emaciation. I could hardly eat anything without throwing it up or it triggering a migraine. If you have never had a migraine, they feel like someone takes an ice pick and grinds it through your eyeball to the back of your head for hours or days.

I lived that way for nearly a year.

It was in that year of suffering that I learned about joy.

I could not read books, I could not look at screens, and I could only have visitors for ten to twenty minutes at a time before I grew too over-stimulated and needed to sleep for hours. In the time I was not asleep, I lay on the couch with my eyes closed . . . thinking and praying.

In the early weeks, my thinking often shifted to anger. *This is not fair. I did not do anything to deserve this.* But even anger exhausted me. I knew it would not help me heal. I felt two choices before me once again: the hard, narrow road or the wide, easy road (Matt. 7:13–14). The wide road was one where I complained, whined, and grew bitter about my circumstances.

The second one was uncertain. I did not know if it would work. It was one of gratitude in the midst of pain. I'd never done it on my own.

My parents modeled it well. They took literally Paul's call to "rejoice . . . when we run into problems and trials" and "be thankful in all circumstances" (Rom. 5:3; 1 Thess. 5:18). When there was pain, we had pizza. "What can you be thankful for?" my dad would ask, looking at the twelve faces hungrily devouring the paradox pizza. We were trained to look for the good in the midst of bad.

But the trauma I endured as a kid taught me to expect and look for tragedy in the midst of joy. Without jumping back into too much brain science, when we go through series of traumatic events as kids, our amygdala—the area primarily in charge of regulating emotion and responding well to stress—grows in volume.[159] The more ongoing stress we have as kids, the less we are able to regulate stress as adults. Children with highly stressful and traumatic childhoods often endure increasing depression and anxiety as adults. According to pediatrician Nadine Burke Harris, "High doses of adversity not only affect brain structure and function, they affect the developing immune system, developing hormonal system, and even the way our DNA is read and transcribed."[160] Studies show children who endure high levels of adversity are more likely to develop heart disease and even cancer.[161]

Although heart disease (beyond the metaphorical hole in my heart) is not a part of my story, I have unquestionably walked the dark and stressful paths of diagnosed depression and anxiety throughout adulthood. It is possible the trauma I endured in childhood contributed to it. Although I have not had a brain scan, it is possible my brain has been "wired" to expect trauma and process it poorly. "It isn't fair!" I told Matt after learning this. "I have to live with anxiety and depression because of what random people did to me as a kid?"

No, I don't.

I didn't know it then, but the Alpha and Omega knew gratitude could change my brain. As I laid on the couch, wrestling with choosing either the narrow road of praising God in the midst of pain or the wide road of bitterness, the Holy Spirit reminded me of an interview with Joni Eareckson Tada I heard as a kid. Joni was a healthy teenager when she jumped into a too-shallow Chesapeake Bay, severed her spinal cord, and instantly became a quadriplegic. She couldn't do much, like me, but her spirit was completely different from mine. *She had overflowing joy.* I remember hearing how she thanked God in the mist of pain and was even grateful for what it brought her. "I like to think of my pain as a sheepdog that keeps snapping at my heels to drive me down the road to Calvary, where, otherwise, I would not be naturally inclined to go," she said.[162]

So, I went with my usual, "What have I got to lose?" decision-making skills and tried it. *If what I'm doing isn't working for me, why not try the Jesus way?* You would think by this point in my life, I'd try Jesus's way first, but I am a stubborn sheep with the three-second memory of a goldfish.

"Okeydokey . . ." I thought quietly to myself in the dark of the apartment and in the darkness of my heart. "Thankfulness . . . thankfulness. Gratitude. I am thankful for these sunglasses. I am thankful I am not dead." *Be joyful always; pray continually; give thanks in all circumstances.*[163] "I'm thankful for quiet. I'm thankful I'm not alone." Like forgiveness or lament or anything of these disciplines, I did not want to do it. I chose to do it. As the minutes wore into hours and days and months, gratitude became my default.

I began to see Carolyn again to help me process this trauma, and I remember telling her how glad I was when I was able to walk downstairs and walk even a couple hundred yards in the woods behind our apartment. "I heard a bullfrog, and it was so beautiful." She welled up with happiness, tears coming to her eyes. "A bullfrog!" she said exuberantly. *What did I say? It was just a frog.* She mirrored secret joy I felt deeply and was afraid to show on my face. She was teaching me how to wear it.

With gratitude as my foundation, my prayers shifted from thankfulness to petitions for those I loved. I began cycling through praying for each of my siblings and their families each day. That took about seventeen hours. (I'm kidding . . . but come on. My family is huge.) My heart grew to love them more and more, and when they called to check in on me, I often forgot I was the one in pain. I cared more about their lives than mine—*and I'm not just saying that.*

My brain was changing physically. If trauma stole my ability to process stressful situations, gratitude was giving it back. Recent brain imaging scans show there are long-lasting effects of simply writing down three things for which we are grateful for twenty-one days.[164] I was finding many more ways to be grateful and twenty-one days turned into months. I was still laid up in bed, but I felt closer to God, more joyful, and more in love with my family and friends.

And then I got better. After a solid year of physical darkness around me and growing light within me, my walks in the sunshine grew longer, my legs became stronger, the headaches lessened, and my appetite increased. But as my life grew circumstantially less painful, I forgot about gratitude. My prayers returned to, "Me, me, me, me, me, my family, my friends, me, me, me."

So . . . What? You Failed.

So, why write a whole chapter on gratitude? You can't even do it. Big fail, Laurie.

Yeah. You're right. I have to *work very hard* to remember to thank God. My default (and perhaps my brain's literal default) is to expect the worst. Matt jokes that my Disney spirit animal is Sadness from *Inside Out*. If you haven't seen the movie, see it. It's basically like going to therapy. Sadness is an anthropomorphized personality trait who lives in the brain of a pre-teen girl named Riley. Sadness's most hilarious moment is when she is dragged around by another character, Joy, because she is so distressed by her life circumstances. "I'm too sad to walk. Just give me a few . . . hours," she says. My favorite quote of hers is, "Crying helps me slow down and obsess over the weight of life's problems."[165] Although I am not a crier, my default is to think of life's issues rather than God's faithfulness in them.

So, what does this have to do with caring for the wounds in our hearts? Perhaps your brain—like mine—has been trained to expect the worst. Perhaps you experienced complex trauma as a kid, felt continual rejection as an adult, and now you are left to work through the mess with a brain trained by trauma.

We must rest in God's love for us. We must grieve the pain to us. We must forgive. But we must also rejoice in the midst of it.

What? That sounds insane. No one else has to do that! If anyone has a right to be rage-filled at the Church, I do.

True that. But beyond not being biblical (Rom. 3:5), it isn't going to help. It isn't going to help our brains, our spirits, or our desire for community. We may gather together and throw all our pain in the middle, creating a cesspool of pain to swim in, but will we leave any happier? Will we have any more joy? Will we ever leave that place feeling empowered to live out the calling God has on our lives and perhaps even to do something about the cesspool of pain in front of our eyes? No. We will be stuck. Forever swimming in agony produces more agony, rage to cover up the pain, or dysfunctional behaviors to escape.

Over the last few years, I have read a lot and listened to a lot of conversations about the Church and LGBT+ people. Do you know the predominate *tone* of it? *Pain. Sorrow. Grief. Your life is going to be terrible. It was terrible, and it is terrible—unless you be who you are. If you choose to surrender your sexuality to Jesus, your life will be one of inner and external turmoil.*

I hear that and I'm like, "I don't want that life. Oh, wait. That *is* my life." But it isn't. Even though my story *is their story*, my story is not currently one of pain and inner torture.

When I look at the Bible and compare it to my life of submission to God and seeking to be grateful in the midst of ongoing rejection, I think, this is *normal*. Paul, the apostles, the prophets, and Jesus all experienced what I experience and way more—but they were full of joy.[166] When I look at the world and what it celebrates (a life of ease, success, money, power, comfort, and little to no self-denial) and then look at my life, I think, *why am I doing this again?*

It is in the midst of rejoicing in the pain, with the Word as my lens, that my clarity of calling comes.

How Rejoicing in the Midst of Suffering Looks

Let me give you an example.

This morning I rolled out of bed early and popped "start" on the coffee maker. (I'm a mom of three tiny children; I don't have energy for a French press anymore.) I sat down to listen to the One Year Bible on an app while munching on a muffin. I am learning to start my day with the Bible on my eardrums instead of the world in my eyes through my smartphone. Then, I simply sat with Jesus. Coffee in hand, I closed my eyes and went to my Safe Place with Him. I didn't say anything. I breathed and rested with Him, meditating on his love for me. Sometimes I take time to study, but I knew I was writing this morning. I believe writing this book is warfare, and I wanted to get good and full of His love before engaging in the battle. "May you experience the love of Christ, though it is too great to understand fully," Paul writes in Ephesians 3:19. "Then you will be made complete with all the fullness of life and power that comes from God." Fullness, life, and power come from knowing I am loved.

I drove to work, checked Facebook before writing, and there it was. Someone ripped into me, Matt, our ministry, and what we are doing. The vitriol dripped off the screen. As much as I want to say, "Oh, pfft. Whatever. I'm fine," I wasn't fine. I was hurt. It was not a to-the-core level of hurt, but it bumped up against old wounds of rejection that are at my core. They are healed, but I can find the scars. Lies danced around my head like, "You can't talk. Live in fear. What you say is worthless." I resisted the temptation to close the computer and give up, and instead, I closed my eyes again. I know if I do not address it immediately, I will either write my un-grieved, dysfunctional pain into this book or I will take it out on my husband and kids later. *I'd rather address it now, thank you very much.*

So I sat with Jesus, and I breathed out the pain of what this person said. *Jesus, it hurts.* I did a little lament. I saw what this person said as sin. I saw it on the cross. *Jesus, I give you the sin and the pain. Jesus, what do you say about me?* I saw Jesus wipe it away as if it is nothing. He did not negate the hurt; instead, I sensed Him encouraging me, as a beloved person, by saying it is not as big of a deal as the person intended. *Laurie, trust My love for you, and let this arrow deflect off your shield of faith. They don't hate you; they hate Me* (John 15:18). *Trust My love for you that is as vast as the heavens* (Ps. 36:5).

The arrow intended to destroy me and my job today was removed with the Healer's tender surgery through lament.

But I still felt where it was removed. I needed to fill up the place where this person stabbed me. It's not enough to grieve and get the pain out; we need to fill up with something else. The quickest, most effective way to do this is to get my focus off of the pain and onto the King. I turn on my favorite, God-focused worship music.

As I let my pain linger with the words and worshipped God in the midst of the hurt, I began to feel a balm on the wound. I sensed a reorientation of my thoughts toward God who is Elohim—Creator God, Alpha and Omega—Beginning and End, El Roi—The God Who Sees Me, and Rapha—the Healer. I was rejuvenated. What threatened to tear me down and rip me apart from the inside was made nothing in the presence and praise of God.

Gratitude and praise are not always the starting point for me, but when I engage it while acknowledging my pain, it rapidly increases the speed of inward healing. It may not change my circumstances, but it changes me. "Joy is not the absence of suffering but the presence of God," Elisabeth Elliot, a woman familiar with much suffering, said.[167]

Gratefulness, worship, and praise of God are the final pieces necessary to learning how to walk in lightness and freedom with Christ. Resting in God's love (Safe Place) is foundational. Grief is necessary (lament). Naming sin and pain and giving it to Jesus is critical (forgiveness). But that is not the end. The world cannot know we are Christians by our pain, they must know it by our love. "Your love for one another will prove to the world that you are my disciples" (John 13:35). But the only way to love anyone is to receive true love. "We love each other because he loved us first."[168] We make room for love by getting the pain and bitterness out and letting in the One whose name is Love. "God is love" (1 John 4:8). Thanking Him for His undeserved love multiplies it and tells the world we are His.

The Bumbling Disciple

I will leave this chapter with one more story. Peter is my favorite disciple because in the early days, he was a bit of a bumbling goof. He reminds me of me. He blurted things out when he should have been quiet, he fought over positioning in heaven, and he tried, oh, he tried hard: he tried walking on water, he tried slicing off someone's ear for Jesus, and he jumped out of the boat into icy-cold water after Jesus rose from the dead. I think there were many times Jesus did a holy face-palm when it came to Peter. "Really?! You want to build a tabernacle as I am showing you a glimpse of My holy deity with Abraham and Moses?"[169] Face. Palm.

After Peter denied Jesus three times in Jesus' moment of absolute turmoil, the Lord asks Peter if he loves Him three times. Each time Peter restates his love for Jesus, and Jesus gives him an exhortation: Feed My sheep; feed My lambs. What was Jesus doing? Here are my best thoughts (which were shaped with the help of Beth Moore):[170] 1) Jesus was reestablishing Peter as a beloved disciple. "Peter. I love you. Do you love Me? Let Me offer you the opportunity to make it right, in the amount of times you made it wrong." 2) He was telling Peter what would empower him to be the rock on which Jesus would build the Church[171] and to feed the lambs: love. 3) He was telling Peter what would empower him to die.

"I tell you the truth, when you were young, you were able to do as you liked; you dressed yourself and went wherever you wanted to go. But when you are old, you will stretch out your hands, and others will dress you and take you where you don't want to go." Jesus said this to let him know by what kind of death *he would glorify God* (John 21:18–19, italics mine).

Love is the motivator for death. "No other motivation will last!" Beth Moore writes about this connection. "Opposition is huge. Circumstances will happen in all our lives that will defy discipline, determination, and conviction. Love keeps burning when everything else disintegrates in an ashen heap."[172] Love is the motivator for submission to Jesus's will for us, and it is this love for and this submission to Jesus to the point of death—literal or internal—that will glorify God. The apostle Paul agrees: "If it seems we are crazy, it is to bring glory to God. And if we are in our right minds, it is for your benefit. Either way, Christ's love controls us" (2 Cor. 5:13–14). If we choose to give thanks to God in the midst of pain, we will receive more joy and more love of the Father than we can possibly imagine.

I see it clearly in my favorite chapter of Ephesians. In the third chapter, Paul alludes to his suffering in ministry but says, "Please don't lose heart because of my trials here" (v. 13). Why? God. Paul immediately jumps into worship of God. "When I think of [the wisdom and the scope of God's plan], I fall to my knees and pray to the Father, the Creator of everything in heaven and on earth" (vv. 14–15). Paul knows his ministry is hard. He's been beaten to the point of death many times. (I think some mean words people wrote online are hard?!) But his comfort comes when he acknowledges his pain and brings it to the Creator. He lifts his eyes above his pain in glory, gratitude, and worship of the King.

What comes next? An awareness not only of God's glory but of His marvelous love (v. 17). I wish I could tattoo the next verses on my heart: "And may you have the power to understand, as all God's people should, how wide, how long, how high, and how deep his love is. May you experience the love of Christ, though it is too great to understand fully" (3:18–19). Paul began with his pain, looked to Christ in worship, and received love in exchange. His next words are bursting with joy. "Now all glory to God, who is able, through his mighty power at work within us, to accomplish infinitely more than we might ask or think. Glory to him in the church and in Christ Jesus through all generations forever and ever! Amen" (3:20–21).

Tears sting my eyes as I write this. I've heard such a tone before from Joni Eareckson Tada. I felt it when I smiled at the sound of a bullfrog. I saw it in Carolyn's face as I described the bullfrog. I experienced it today when I worshipped through the pain of the person being mean to me online. This is a feeling of hope, love, and joy *in the midst of suffering—and I can't help but worship because of it.* Glory be to God.

Do you see the pattern? I may use different words, but what we have been discussing is the gospel on repeat in every day and in every way. We begin with remembering our identity as beings created by God for love (Safe Place), we move to dealing with sin before God (lament/confession/forgiveness), and then we end with giving glory to God as we receive love from God (celebration/gratitude). We begin with love and end with love.

It's all because of God, it is all for God, and we get to simply dive into the rhythm of love and receive joy in the midst of it. "Oh, how great are God's riches and wisdom and knowledge! How impossible it is for us to understand his decisions and his ways! . . . For everything comes from him and exists by his power and is intended for his glory" (Rom. 11:33, 36).

Yes, many of us who wrestle with sexuality have endured some incredible pain, but we also have opportunity for incredible joy in the midst of pain because we are His.

Reflection Questions:

1. When have you experienced a time of joy (or at least closeness to God) in the midst of suffering? What happened?

_____

_____

_____

_____

2. How could you begin to receive more of God's love for you? Which of these practices could you put into place today?

_____

_____

_____

_____

3. When you read in this chapter how trauma affects kids' (and therefore adults') brains, did any of that resonate with you? What specifically?

_____

_____

_____

_____

4. What is a worship song that helps to refocus you from your pain to your Creator?

_____

_____

_____

_____

EXERCISE 12: PRAISE IN PAIN

When was a recent time you felt rejected? What did you do with that pain? Take some time right now to center your heart in the presence of Jesus, offer Him the pain, name the sin involved, and then fill that place of wounding praise. As you do, let His love be a balm for your pain.

_____

_____

_____

_____

CHAPTER 9: I HAVE A CONFESSION

"Why would anyone be shocked to hear of my struggles with past and present sin when the Cross already told them I am a desperately sinful person?"
—Milton Vincent[173]

"Son of man, these leaders have set up idols in their hearts. They have embraced things that will make them fall into sin. Why should I listen to their requests?"
—God[174]

Before I knew this love, before I was taught how to do all of this inner work, God gave me glimpses of His love *while I was yet sinning.*[175] It was a foundation of love that gave me freedom to confess to God without shame or self-hatred.

One gorgeous afternoon in May, Heather and I were doing things we should not be doing. Heather left for a minute, and I fell to the floor, staring at the carpet. I wanted to die. I dragged my head upward to glimpse outside. It was a beautiful day. I had not noticed when the weather shifted from frozen to warm. It happens so quickly in Michigan.

I dug my nails into the palms of my hands to punish myself and release some of the pain. I did not deserve to look at this beauty. The sun cut through the perfectly blue sky, and I could see evidence of a slight wind rustling the new growth of leaves on the trees.

I felt dirty. *I am dirty. I deserve death.* From March through May of my junior year of college, I often had earbuds jammed in my ears to distract me from these death-thoughts. I looked down at the white shag carpet of my room and wept. *I hate myself, I hate myself, I hate myself.* I imagined stabbing knives into my chest. *How can I keep doing what I am doing? How can I stop?*

"God, why don't You just kill me?" I raged at the window, toward the smiling sunshine. I did not expect Him to answer. He did.

In a flash, all the foggy, delirious, death-ridden haze disappeared, and I saw myself as Jesus truly saw me. He did not want to kill me. He did not want to yell at me or even backhand my face like I begged Him to do often. *I deserve it*, I thought. He did not want to squash me and start over with a new model—an upgrade from this version of broken human. Instead, I felt a surge of joy and a flood of His love. *Jesus loves me.* I gasped. *He so loves me.*

I blinked a few times, looking out the window again and hearing birds for the first time in months. *He loves me.* It was as if His heart connected to mine and restarted it. They beat as one again for the first time in years. Yes, He was sad about what I was doing, but for a few seconds, I knew He also hoped for me. God is full of hope. "Oh, return to me, for I have paid the price to set you free."[176] His whispers of love felt like a refreshing rain shower.

"Oh, Laurie," I sensed. "Oh, Heather. My dear girls. Come here, and let Me hold you." He's a good Father. Abba. Papa. He wanted to hold us in a safe, non-sexual, *good Father-ly* way like He did with the children while He was on earth.[177] He was not scary. He was inviting—so inviting, kids wanted to be with Him. "Did you know I am the answer your hearts crave? I am the only answer." As I let myself feel the love, I did not sense any hidden agenda. I knew His truth; I equally knew His love.

Heather opened the door quietly, looking at me with guilty eyes I saw many times in my own reflection. *What now? Is she going to end our relationship again?* she might have wondered. We had broken up and gotten back together so many times. We wanted our friendship to work. We couldn't make it work without ending up where we were.

I looked her in the eye and spoke from a place inside of me that had not held words in a long while. It was the space in my heart where hope lived.

"Heather," I said, confidently. "He still loves us."

"Who does?"

"Jesus." She looked away. "He still loves us, Heather. I know it. I don't know how I know, I just do."

And then the feeling disappeared. Self-hatred descended, and the storm returned.

Idols of the Heart

God loved me. I knew it for seconds every few weeks when He pulled back the curtain of heaven just enough so I could peek inside His heart. It left me breathless. As much as I knew it to be true, I didn't know how to experience it for more than those few seconds of sobriety. *How do I stop? I keep confessing and falling. Is there any freedom? Where do I begin?*

Let's look at some solutions today.

When I was with Heather (another God-fearing Christian), I dealt with sexual temptation by hanging out with it. When I felt the sexual attraction toward her, instead of running the other direction like Paul, Solomon, and Jesus advise,[178] I sauntered around it, waiting for . . . whatever may happen. Why would I do that? I was a Christian. I loved Jesus. Didn't I know it would make it harder for me? Yes. I did. But like I said earlier, sin is fun, and sin works . . . for a time.

Let's back the train up to understand again some deeper reasons I might not have wanted to run from her. I was born with a hole in my heart and also possibly with a sexual attraction toward women. This hole in my heart is filled with Core Needs for many things, and many were met well when I encountered parents and siblings who loved me like Jesus does. They showed me how He loves well. But a few which were not met as much as I needed were a desire to be seen, noticed, and treasured uniquely. (Again, no parent—myself included—can ever meet all Core Needs in a way that points our kids perfectly to the love of God.) I also wanted to be safe and nurtured. How we define nurture is "Being taken care of physically and emotionally; being held." I was hungry for someone to safely notice and nurture me. When I was assaulted by men and a woman at different times growing up, they essentially looked at those Core Needs and punched them. "Sure, we see you. Sure, we will take care of you physically—but not because we treasure you, but because we want to take from you. You were made for us. Your worth comes in what you can give us," they said. People say that to us in many ways outside of direct sexual assault.

By the time I met Heather, all the attractions I felt toward women, all the attempts I had made to feel seen, safe, and nurtured through flirting with everyone, getting perfect grades, and being a perfect spiritual leader culminated in this one person. At last my soul has found the one I have been searching for!

At first, I simply enjoyed her company. We were quickly close. We enjoyed similar activities, laughed about the same things, and had a great group of God-fearing friends. But as our friendship grew, my attraction to her personality increased, and the hole in my heart screamed, "This is the one who will help your heart," the more possessive and addicted to her I became. I began to filter my every thought through, "What would she think?" I felt a snarl of jealousy anytime she hung out with someone without me, especially girl friends. I was alone, but she was having fun with someone else. I tried to be cool about it, but inside I was worried she would replace me. "The best way to tell if you are addicted to something is not . . . when things are going well, but when you are in trouble," Tim Keller said. "We are all in bed with something, but you can tell when it's taken away."[179] This is known as idolatry.

Idolatry is prioritizing anything before God. The first two commandments God gave us are, "You must not have any other god but me. You must not make for yourself an idol of any kind or an image of anything in the heavens or on the earth or in the sea" (Ex. 20:3–4). Worshipping—literally bowing down and serving tangible, made-of-gold idols was a big deal when God gave those commandments to the Israelites. To worship man-made idols was in style. Today, we worship other things: money, fame, ourselves, or people. That hole in our hearts was made to be filled with something.

> We are *"tellic"* creatures—purposed people; we have to live for something. There has to be something that captures our imagination and our allegiance, which is the resting place of our deepest hopes and which we look to calm our deepest fears. Whatever that thing [or person] is, we worship it, and so we serve it. It becomes our bottom line, the thing we cannot live without, defining and validating everything we do.[180]

So, how was Heather an idol? I coveted her. I wanted her first in my life. Paul says, "Put to death the sinful, earthly things lurking within you. Have nothing to do with sexual immorality, impurity, lust, and evil desires. Don't be greedy, for a greedy person is an idolater, worshiping the things of this world" (Col. 3:5). I was greedy for Heather's time, her attention, and her eyes on me. There was never enough time, attention, and eyes on me. When I felt this greed, it occurred *before* anything physical happened between us. "[Covetousness] is not a deed of the body," John Piper said. "That follows—a fruit on a branch. It starts in the heart, craving, wanting, enjoying, being satisfied by anything that you treasure more than God. That is an idol."[181]

My persistent attractions toward women simply put the icing on the idol cake. It only made sense to move from her meeting the needs in my heart to letting her meet physical and sexual desires. She saw me relationally, so why not move it up a level? I consciously did not intend for something sexual to occur, but I didn't stop it. I sauntered near it, hoping it might. When it began, I was shocked at first that I, a "good Christian girl," could do something like this, but then I stopped feeling shocked. It was fun. It met a need until it didn't. She was never enough.

Little did I realize I was exactly following the script of Romans 1. In it, Paul describes "ungodliness and unrighteousness of men, who by their unrighteousness suppress the truth" (v. 18, ESV). Was I an ungodly and unrighteous person when I first met Heather? I was a Jesus-loving Christian who had just completed a stressful semester studying abroad in England, and I was wrestling with self-hatred while I was there—not because I was attracted to women, but because I was not perfect. Although I was a Christian, my identity was based on achievements, and anything other than straight-As was failure. Therefore, I was a failure.

You can already see idolatry in my heart. I wanted God and an identity of perfection. Pre-England, my identity was based on God and people seeing me as a spiritual leader at my Christian school. Pre-Christian university, my identity was based on God's love and how many people liked me. Pre-people liking me . . . I can't remember. That one has been instilled for a long time.

But my ungodly and unrighteous behavior began before my same-sex behavior and relationship. It began when I said, "I need God *and* . . ." I journaled about it frequently. "God, I know you're there, but why don't you send me a friend? Someone to eat lunch with. Someone with problems. God, I just need someone to put an arm around me. And say they love me for who I am, and not expect me to share all my heart, and will just sit with me. God, can you send someone like that? Is there someone even out there? So I don't have to cry anymore?" Post-England I decided two things: Yes, I need God, but I also need a friend. Isn't this simply an expression of a healthy person? Wasn't I asking for the Body of Christ? Jesus "with skin on"? Sort of. I did need people in my life, but not on the same level as I needed God. If I was truly honest with myself, I wanted a person—*my person*—more than I wanted God. If our priorities are a pyramid, God is at the top. People are the supporting structures. I *said* God was number one, but I hungrily searched for a person more than I searched for Him.

God says through the prophet Jeremiah, "My people have exchanged their glorious God for worthless idols! . . . For my people have done two evil things: They have abandoned me—the foundation of living water. And they have dug for themselves cracked cisterns that hold no water at all!" (Jer. 2:11, 13). Two sinful things are referenced here: rejecting God, and finding a God-replacement. When I made the decision I needed God *and* something else, I sinned in the first way: I forsook God. "No one can serve two masters. For you will hate the one and love the other; you will be devoted to one and despise the other. You cannot serve God *and* . . . " Jesus says (Matt. 6:24, italics mine). Anytime I filled the hole in my heart with people's approval, my achievements, or even the idea of someone *seeing me* as much as I needed, I sinned the second way. I replaced God with a cracked, fallible cistern. I replaced my emptiness with more emptiness. "Son of man, these leaders have set up idols in their hearts. They have embraced things that will make them fall into sin. Why should I listen to their requests?" (Ez. 14:3). I made an idol in my heart.

EXERCISE 13: PRIORITY PYRAMID

Remember this Tim Keller quote from earlier in the chapter? "The best way to tell if you are addicted to something is not . . . when things are going well, but when you are in trouble." Let's think about that. If you lost your job, if someone close to you died, or if you were in a car accident, who would be the first you would call (spouse, BFF, sister, God)? Or, what would you do first (work really hard to fix it, get angry, etc.)? Then what next? Put the first response or person on the top line, and the next below.

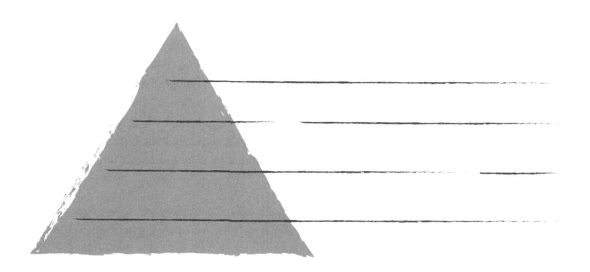

What do you think about your order? What does this say about idols of your heart?

Orientation Toward Anything but God

I am oriented not only toward attraction for women but an attraction toward anything *but God*. (Or at least *God and* _____. That seems more holy.) But God cannot share the top spot with anyone or anything else. I thought He could. So did the people Paul described in Romans 1. "They knew God, but they wouldn't worship him as God" (v. 21). I didn't worship Him alone—I hadn't in years. He wasn't cutting it for me. "Instead of worshipping the glorious, ever-living God, they worshiped idols," Paul goes on to say in Romans 1:23. So did I, and I have my entire life . . . as a Christian.

This is why I love Romans 6, 7, and 8 so much. I relate to Paul's angst with himself. "I know that nothing good lives in me, that is in my sinful nature," he says (Rom. 7:18). "I love God's law with all my heart. But there is another power within me that is at war with my mind. This power makes me a slave to the sin that is *still within me*" (Rom. 7:22–23, italics mine). There is stuff inside of me—even after I "prayed the prayer" of salvation at six years old—that needs to get out. Not gay stuff, but *selfish stuff.* God and [insert anything here] stuff. *Idols.* Anytime I make the Romans 1 exchange of worshipping "the glorious, ever-living God" for *anything else,* it displays my orientation toward fulfilling my needs with something other than Jesus Christ.

My sinful orientation didn't begin with my same-sex attractions or with Heather, it began at birth when I reached for anything other than God.

God doesn't share the top spot. "I, the LORD your God, am a jealous God" (Ex. 20:5). God's jealousy dawned on me while I was reading a theology book alone as a freshman in college. I stormed into our dorm's lounge and said to the group of women there, "Why do we *have* to worship God? He seems so selfish!" One of the wiser ones in the room said, "It's because He's deserving." The answer didn't satisfy—nor should it have. Yes, God is deserving, but He is also way wiser than I am. I am dust, and He invented the dust of the cosmos. He knows what I need. He knows the black hole of our hearts will only find rest in Him. "There is a righteous and holy jealousy and an unrighteous and weak and insecure jealousy," John Piper describes. "And God's jealousy is not only righteous—in that he deserves our deepest and strongest affections and admiration—but he is loving. It is a loving jealousy because we were made to find our greatest joy when he is our greatest treasure."[182] His apparent selfishness is actually selfless—it is *for our benefit we worship Him alone.*

Worshiping God and *anything* else is impossible. God immediately steps back when we ask Him to hang out with our replacers of Him. We cannot hug both God and our idols. He isn't crossing his arms, waiting in rage, but He will wait. He may use consequences to get our attention, but He may also do like He did with the people in Romans (and like He did with me): they rejected Him for idols, "So God abandoned them to do whatever shameful things their hearts desired" (Rom. 1:24). They began worshipping idols with their bodies—which included same-sex behavior. That was exactly me.

So What Can We Do?

You may be reading this squirming a bit. "Gah, Laurie, I get it. I already believe as you do. But what can I do about it?! How do I confess, and live in practical freedom?" You may relate to Paul's exclamation, "Oh, what a miserable person I am! Who will free me from this life that is dominated by sin and death?" (Rom. 7:24) The answer for us is the answer he immediately gives himself, "Thank God! The answer is in Christ Jesus our Lord" (v. 25), and he launches into the starting place of the gospel, "So now there is no condemnation for those who belong to Christ Jesus" (8:1).

Dee Brestin, author of *Idol Lies*, writes, "Idols are how we replace God. Peering into the gospel is how we replace idols."[183] I am so grateful we spent time going through the practical "how" to peer into the gospel via listening prayer. Had we not done that, what I am about to describe would sound like formulaic legalism.

Practical Confession via the Gospel

I am going to walk you through confession. Confession falls under the "Fall" category of the Creation, Fall, Redemption, Re-Creation pattern of the gospel. What are we confessing? That's a critical question. We are not confessing our desires for sin; we are confessing when we sin. Attractions are not sin.[184] Jesus himself "faced all of the same testings [temptations] we do, yet he did not sin" (Heb. 4:15). Do you think He wrestled with lust? What about same-sex lust? I cannot begin to answer either in the affirmative or negative, but knowing He wrestled with temptation and lived a sin-free life is a comfort to this sinner.

I used to ask God to change my attractions. I felt full of shame every time I watched a movie and had to turn my eyes away when overtly sexualized women came on the screen. Why do I have to do this? Straight women don't have to. The men didn't faze me, but the women . . . I felt so much shame. "God, why am I still like this?" I asked. "Take it away!" I had been married to Matt for over six years at this point, but my wrestling with same-sex lust was still present.

Stop asking Me to take it away, I heard the next morning during my quiet time with Him. *My grace is sufficient for you. My power works best in your weakness.* My eyes flipped back to a page in my Bible that's so worn with underlining, stars, and tears, it may fall out one day. "Three different times I begged the Lord to take it away," Paul says of a metaphorical thorn in his flesh. "Each time he said, 'My grace is all you need. My power works best in your weakness'" (2 Cor. 12:8–9). Why did Paul only ask three times for the thorn removal surgery? Why not three million like I had? *You need Me, Laurie. This thorn is keeping you tethered to Me.*

And so I have not asked God to take it away again.

Instead, I notice the attraction, I am kind to myself when I feel the draw toward idolatry of women or a desire to connect in a way that is not God's will, and I only confess when I cross those lines into sin.

I cannot believe God is prompting me to be this vulnerable, but humility needs to be the posture I speak from constantly. Why not make it permanent in a book? I am going to walk you through a confession of mine that happened yesterday.

1: CREATION

"Then God looked over all he had made, and he saw that it was very good!"—Genesis 1:31

A. Notice the sin and redirect

I went for a run outside in a common running area. While jogging, I was trying to catch the eye of many women who were passing by me. *I wonder if she is gay,* I thought about several attractive women. I wanted them to see me, and me them. Around mile two, I caught myself doing it. *Oh my word, Laurie.*

Now, in moments like these, I have three options: 1) Berate and shame myself. *Laurie! You are the worst! You are literally writing a book on how to live well with sexual brokenness, and you can't live a day without falling.* 2) Give into it. *No one knows what I am doing. I mean, I'm married. I can look at other women. Straight women do this. I look straight. It's just called comparing. Who cares where my mind is going, really? No one knows.* 3) Notice. Stop. And rest in love. Okay. *Yup. That's me. That's how I struggle. It's really hard right now.*

After wrestling with each option, I finally chose the third option, directed my eyes toward the road, changed the song on my music to something distracting, and ran.

I did not berate myself, I did not give in, I simply noticed and redirected.

B. Know you're loved

If I had not been in an ongoing practice of reading about God's love and resting in Safe Place in Jesus' love, I would have flipped to my old default of shaming, self-hatred, and begging God to kill me like I did at the beginning of this chapter. Or . . . I would have given in. Starting my day with the gospel of "all fall short and all are loved" gets my brain in shape for moments like yesterday.

> When I begin my train of thought with the gospel, I realize that if God loved me enough
> to sacrifice His Son's life for me, then He must be guided by that same love when He speaks
> His commandments to me. Viewing God's commands and prohibitions in this light, I can
> see them for what they really are: friendly signposts from a heavenly Father who is seeking
> to love me through each directive, so that I might experience His very fullness forever.[185]

When I view the guidelines of God through the starting point of His love for me, I don't hate myself when I sin, I simply observe it. *Yup. That's me: a beloved sinner,* I say and then move onward toward confession.

When I returned home, I went to that common resting place with Jesus in my mind, and let Him love me—as a sinner. As I write this, I still have not confessed to God, but I am working toward it.

2: FALL

"For everyone has sinned; we all fall short of God's glorious standard."—Romans 3:23

2A. Reject shame

One of my options yesterday was to shame myself. Oh, shame. You are gifted to us straight from Satan's hands. Shame says, "I am worthless." Conviction of sin leading to true confession says, "What I did is not worth it." When working with clients on confession, I often ask, "What is your shame-ometer" level?" before we go to the Father to confess. I describe what I mean: "If 10 is 'I am the worst human in my sin-prone state,' and 1 is 'I know I am crazy loved even in my sin-prone state,' where are you at on a scale of 1 to 10?"

EXERCISE 14: WHAT IS YOUR SHAME LEVEL RIGHT NOW?

Using the scale of 1 to 10 that I just described, what is your own shame-ometer? How do you think God feels about you right now? What do you believe about who God is in this moment? Do shame and your thoughts about God relate?

Sometimes, clients know their shame level immediately; others take a bit longer to process. One came back with a written reflection:

> Last time I spoke with Laurie, she kept asking me what number of shame I was . . .
> I didn't feel shame, and I didn't know how to respond to her question. I felt anger,
> hurt, and a number of other feelings, but not shame. She said that was a mask emotion.
> So this week I kept my eyes out for shame to see if it existed and if I could identify it.
> It took a while, but it came. I felt shame at a 10 out of 10 one night and again a couple
> days later. [She went on to describe a dream where someone called her derogatory
> names directly referencing her sexuality.]
>
> I think I've gotten confused with confession of sin or that feeling of guilt. Shame has
> nothing to do with guilt. Shame can and typically happens when you have done nothing
> wrong. Shame happens when someone judges you, labels you, rejects you, condemns
> you, or when you do this to yourself. Shame isn't deserved. That's where I was
> confused, too—covered up by all the other emotions. I thought I deserved shame . . .

The God of all Creation speaks truth. He labels us "new creation," "beloved," "searched," "understood," "known," "protected." We are not condemned. If he is for us, who can stand against us?[186]

Of the forty-five good things she said in here, one stands out for me: the need for someone to be present for shame to hurt us. Psychologist Dan Allender agrees. "Shame is an interpersonal affect; it requires the presence of another, in fact or in imagination, for its blow to be felt."[187] This is why believing truth about God is so critical to removing shame. If we believe He is a Divine Shamer (One who says, "You are worthless") we will throw out conviction with shame and land where many of my peers land: "This is who I am. If God loves me, then I throw away all of these negative feelings. A free life = a deletion of shame + a deletion of conviction." Instead, I believe: "This is not who I am, but it is how I acted sinfully. God's love defines me, makes me whole, and convicts me. I throw out shame but let conviction drive me to the One who has paid the price for my sin. A free life = a deletion of shame + a confession of sin + a receiving of the grace of God."

2B. Confess

While finishing my run, I felt the finger of God point to where I had crossed the line in my mind. *Right here, Laurie. Confess this, this, and this. Not because I hate you, but because I want to free you. You are most free when you are closest to Me. I can't be close to sin. So let it go. I want to take it and hold you. Return to Me. I have paid the price to set you free* (Isa. 44:22). This was not shame of Laurie; this was conviction of Laurie. So I did like I do when I am forgiving someone: I went to Safe Place, I hung out with Jesus's love, and then I pictured the cross—all while finishing my run and then driving home. Where Jesus pinpricked to confess, I saw it as sin nailing Him to the cross. I confessed trying to catch the eye of women (putting what they thought of me above God's thinking of me, i.e. idolatry), lusting after them, and trying to flaunt myself in front of them (pride). I didn't want them to see God in me. I wanted them to see me.

After putting our daughters to bed, I apologized to Matt. If you are married, this is a great way to cultivate intimacy. If you are unmarried, you may have an accountability partner who can walk with you through this process and can hear your sin. This is a great way to cultivate friendship authenticity. "Confess your sins to each other and pray for each other so that you may be healed. The earnest prayer of a righteous person has great power and produces wonderful results" (James 5:16).

It is very important to have another person hear how you have fallen. Just like shame needs a real or imagined person for its sting to be felt, confession needs a real or imagined person for freedom to be felt. (The Holy Spirit can be imagined, but He is really here—so no imagination necessary.)

"When we are in the middle of a shame storm, it feels virtually impossible to turn again to see the face of someone, even someone we might otherwise feel safe with. It is as if our only refuge is in our isolation; the prospect of exposing what we feel activates our anticipation of further shame," Curt Thompson wrote in his incredible book, *The Soul of Shame.* "[I]t is in the movement toward another, toward connection with someone who is safe, that we come to know life and freedom from this prison."[188] People seeing us in our mess and loving us removes shame.

Plus, good grief, how much do we long to have authentic community? If we each had an authentic community where people were equally looking to the cross, equally sharing their fallenness, and equally exhorting one another to love—how incredible would that be? *That is the Church.* "The more open I am in confessing my sins to fellow Christians the more I enjoy the healing of the Lord in response to their grace-filled counsel and prayers," Milton Vincent wrote in his brilliant book, *A Gospel Primer.* "Experiencing richer levels of Christ's love in companionship with such saints, I give thanks for the gospel's role in forcing my hand toward self-disclosure and the freedom that follows."[189] Amen and amen. I have experienced it as truth. Have you?

One last reason to confess to someone is if they know this whole Hole in My Heart model, they can help to get at the heart of the matter. After forgiving me for my mentally cheating on him, Matt didn't shame me. He asked, "Laurie, what do you really need?" By this he means, "what Core Need is missing? Why is the struggle especially loud—not why do you struggle, but why *so hard right now?*" With more questions, thinking through my usual missing Core Needs, and "listening" to them, I concluded, "I'm feeling really alone (unseen). I want to be known." I go to the Father and receive more of His "seeing" of me. And then we begin to put helps and routines in place so I can feel it in human ways—though these are always secondary to getting that need filled by the Father Himself.

3: REDEMPTION

"Since you have been raised to new life with Christ, set your sights on the realities of heaven, where Christ sits in the place of honor at God's right hand." —Colossians 3:1

In my Safe Place, I envision Jesus rising again. Even if I feel like I am "the least deserving of all God's people" (Eph. 3:8), I choose to believe I am "washed . . . sanctified . . . [and] justified in the name of the Lord Jesus Christ and by the Spirit of our God" (1 Cor. 6:11 NIV). I may not feel like it's true. *That doesn't matter.* Feelings are important indicators to tell me how I feel about God, the world, and me, but they are not tellers of what is *true* about God, the world, or me. I *choose* to believe I am washed, sanctified, and justified. I *choose* to believe my sins are made "white as snow" (Isa. 1:18). I choose it, even if I don't feel it. I choose it until I feel it.

After confessing, watching His death for what I confessed, and envisioning Him rise, I often ask, "Jesus, is there something You want to say to me?" Carolyn often asks, "Jesus, is there a gift You want to give Laurie?" Sometimes, I remember a verse. Sometimes, the gift is peace. And sometimes, He gives me a picture of what He is doing inside of me. This can help to realign my feelings about my clean state to what is actually true about my clean state.

The gift yesterday was a removal of shame and an infusion of freedom. What used to lay me out for weeks now takes hours—and sometimes minutes—to deal with, resetting me on a path of freedom.

Do I still wrestle? Yes. Is the attraction of women gone? No. Is my attraction toward any idol gone? "The sinful nature wants to do evil," Paul said in Galatians 5:17, "which is just the opposite of what the Spirit wants. And the Spirit gives us desires that are the opposite of what the sinful nature desires. These two forces are constantly fighting each other . . ." Constantly. Fighting. That sounds like a life of "long obedience in the same direction" as Eugene Peterson said—no matter my sexual, emotional, or physical struggles.

When I say I am given "freedom" after confessing, I mean that I receive a sense of lightness, joy, and hope because of what Christ has done while I was yet a sinner. Paul understood this. After admitting he could not rid himself of the struggle with sin, he said, "because you belong to him, the power of the life-giving Spirit has freed you from the power of sin that leads to death" (Rom. 8:2). Freedom is not a lack of struggling with sin; it is a lack of being owned by the power of sin.

4: NEW CREATION

"And the one sitting on the throne said, 'Look, I am making everything new!'" — Revelation 21:5

Now my only job is to believe I am free. This is difficult when the temptation to shift to shame or self-hatred settles around your brain, whispering for you to go back. The enemy of our souls wants us dead or in bondage. One of the primary ways he tries to do this is through self-hatred.

I mentioned before how I had a hard time with emotional stability after my second daughter was born. Self-hatred was one of the sentiments I wrestled with deeply. I felt worthless. One night while rocking my daughter, I was meditating on my worthlessness. "God, help me!" I begged between thoughts of death. *Laurie, I want to, but you are inviting the enemy into your home with your thoughts of hatred toward My beloved: you.* I looked around my tiny daughter's room, considering what I might not be seeing around me. I know the spiritual battle. *Is it me that is causing not only my own emotional upheaval, but potentially putting my kids in danger?* For me to hate an image-bearer of God—me—opens the door for the enemy to walk through and rip me apart from the inside. For some reason, hating me didn't seem as unholy as hating someone else. *Am I an equally beloved sinner as the next person or no?* I immediately confessed and went to a place of begging God to help me not to hate myself.

It was, and can be hard. But here is something to note: I use the same spiritual muscles to fight the temptation to hate myself as I do to fight lust. I also use the same spiritual muscles to fight pride as I do to fight self-hatred as I do to fight lust. I use the same process. I seek the same God. I have to depend on the same righteousness of Jesus Christ.

I have to believe and rest in the same grace that I am a new creation. "Anyone who belongs to Christ has become a new person. The old life is gone; a new life has begun!" I am washed, I am sanctified, I am justified, and I am made new . . . again.

This gospel is good news for everybody, every day.

Reflection Questions:

1. Have you ever had a moment of "spiritual sobriety" where God cut through a mess and showed you His true heart for you? If so, describe it below.

_____

_____

_____

2. Have you ever had someone look at your Core Needs and "punch them"? Who? What was that like? What lies were planted into your heart in that moment about God, you, or your relationship to the world?

_____

_____

_____

_____

3. What heart idols do you wrestle with most frequently?

_____

_____

4. What did you think about this confession process? How does it differ from your own? How is it similar?

_____

_____

5. Do you have someone you confess to in addition to the Father? If no, what might be the benefits of doing so? If you do, what are the benefits? What might it cost you (and what does it cost you) to confess to someone? In other words, what are the "cons" of confessing to someone?

_____

_____

_____

6. How do you experience the gospel's good news in your everyday?

_____

_____

_____

_____

CHAPTER 10: FRIENDSHIP AND TEMPTATION

"In each of my friends there is something that only some other friend can fully bring out.
By myself I am not large enough to call the whole man into activity; I want other lights
han my own to show all his facets . . . hence, true Friendship is the least jealous of loves.
Two friends delight to be joined by a third, and a three by a fourth."
—C.S. Lewis[190]

"He holds the whole body together with its joints and ligaments,
and it grows as God nourishes it."
—Paul[191]

I sat in a coffee shop, angrily writing to God about what had occurred. I had recently broken up with Heather for the last time, and Matt and I had started "dating." By dating, I mean we were becoming better friends, and he often simply held me as I wept over the end of the relationship with Heather. He is currently a licensed counselor, and we joke I was his first client.

As I grew in friendship, trust, and heart-connected interest in Matt, there was another woman showing interest in me. She had been pursuing me in small ways through personal notes, asking me deep questions, and a silent conversation we were having with one another, which was, "I see you. I know we have a similar interest: each other." She had recently given me another hand-written note, quite obviously reaching out.

According to the Christian world, people like me and this other Christian girl toward whom I was attracted didn't exist. We were either a past tense "that's who you were, now you are good and straight like us," or we were openly gay and should pursue a relationship. The in-between space of "this is *how* I am but not *who* I am" was thought to be non-existent. And yet, here we were. We knew it. As invisible people to the worldly world and Christian world, we were left to create our own reality where we saw each other and could flirt all we want. We looked like two girls simply being kind—or two girls being who they are.

We were neither. And that neither-ness made it all the more enticing and fun. It was hidden. It felt safe. It felt exciting.

I wrote angrily to God because I did not understand why He either wouldn't take away these attractions or simply let me have her. It would be so much easier. As lament turned to whining and complaining, I sensed God's strong, tender hands on either side of my face. *Laurie, look at Me.* I paused. *You are not the boss. You do not know what is best for you. This is hard, I am with you, I will always love you, but hard is not an excuse to quit. This is worth it. You just don't know it yet.* My eyes fell on Hebrews 10:26: "Dear friends, if we deliberately continue sinning after we have received knowledge of the truth, there is no longer any sacrifice that will cover these sins." The author of Hebrews doesn't mess around. I was not sure of all the implications of this passage other than the very clear message: "Laurie, you know what is true. I am serious about sin. Stop whining and trust Me."

I began journaling again with a different tone. "Jesus, you have given me more than enough chances," I wrote. "God, help me to see that You're enough for my heart so that I don't want to go back to that, Jesus! . . . Please show me your tender love to Me, Jesus. Please show Me what a lover You are."

Making Friends Is Hard to Do

I don't know if I ever see more pain written across the faces of people than when I ask about their friendships. No matter how someone identifies or wrestles, there is a loneliness epidemic sweeping our globe. I have felt it most tangibly in my friendships as someone who experiences same-sex attractions, but I am not alone here. Whenever I share my struggles with finding genuine friendships, single, married, straight, gay, cisgender, and queer people all nod in agreement.

After coming out in this middle-of-the-road way, I have been told I'm either too gay or not gay enough. In Christian circles, I have mostly heard the former. "I cannot be your friend *because of that.*" I have had people tell me they don't want me around their kids. "Jesus! It is harder for me to stay in the Church than to leave!" I have screamed at God, begging Him to set me free from church. But He knows it wouldn't offer true freedom. I need Jesus-seeking community—as imperfect as it is.[192]

Before coming out, there were times I was unintentionally marginalized. Because my dad was a pastor and I went to a great church, I would often get an elbow to the ribs when people were talking about "them." "You know what I mean?" they said about the LGBT+ community. I felt like I was physically accepted, but my insides were not. Such marginalization bumped up against a lot of my past abuse wounds. "Oh sure, we see you. Sure, you have value—your good, straight, Christian personhood has value. Your outsides. None of that internal gay stuff." They didn't mean to (and they don't mean to). It was sin. I grieved and forgave it as sin, but I have since learned to also say *Father, forgive them, for they know not what they do.*

Additionally, I felt incredibly isolated in women's small groups. I journaled frequently about how women were able to talk about their "holy, boy-crazy problems" but I did not feel safe discussing the latest breakup with Heather. Would they even know what to say? *Would they kick me out? Would they hug me the same?* The tears I wept in secret were an ocean compared to the few I cried in the presence of my straight friends. "Heather and I . . . just aren't friends anymore," I told them during prayer request time. They were empathetic but didn't understand the reason behind my depth of my emotion.

Granted, I didn't trust them with it. I didn't give them a chance. But I had been shoved aside so many times—first and foremost by self-rejection and then by actual people—that I was terrified to trust again.

This is where I am tempted to dive down the rabbit hole of feeling like my problems are the worst. *It's harder for me to make friends than you. LGBT+ people have it harder.* I have said this to Matt after we have gone places where I thought I surely would have made forty-five friends (or at least one) by the end of the event. "People don't like me! They must know my story and hate me." He often looks at me with half-sympathy and half-an-eye-roll.

"Laurie, you know I love you, and you know I get that there are unique challenges you face," he says. "But as a counselor and as a straight man who would rather talk deeply about emotions than shoot an animal, I can feel out of place." I grimace at his response. I don't want to feel like he gets it. I want him to feel sorry for me. I want an excuse not to try.

I have found that there are unique difficulties to making friendships if you wrestle like I do, but it is not—or rather does not have to be—more difficult than others. If the Church continues on the more inclusive (but still biblically orthodox) road it is going on, my ability to make genuine friendships will be more my responsibility than the Church's. But it will take me pursuing an oft-hated four-letter word: Risk. Risk in sharing the real me. Risk of being rejected. Risk of getting hurt. Risk in making a friend (or three) who become "lifers." It is terrifying—for anyone—but risk can be worth it.

Coming Out

The first time I told a straight female peer that I was attracted to women, I was trembling. Amber was a friend with whom I had reconnected with in college after moving away from our mutual city and church in first grade. She seemed like someone I could trust: she knew grace for herself, spoke with grace about sexual sinners, and was a committed friend. I did not know she would receive me well, but those indicators were enough for me to trust her.

I might have been trembling due to the nerves or simply because it was another cold Michigan day. She and I were hanging out alone in my house. I was not sexually attracted to her, but our spirits aligned in many ways about many things. A like-hearted friend gave me a plaque recently that says, "Your heart and my heart are very old friends." That's how I felt about Amber. "Amber, I need to tell you something, and it may not be easy for you to hear." A counselor taught me to use that opening line as I shared my story with limited people.

"What is it, Laurie?"

I breathed in a prayer of help and courage, and I tried to envision God's care for my heart—even if Amber slapped me across the face and called me "the worst of the worst." An image resurfaced before I went on. It was a picture of myself as the woman caught in adultery from John 8. I first saw it a few weeks earlier in counseling. Accusers stood around me with giant rocks, ready to kill. Like in that passage, Jesus came into the center of the circle. He was willing to die for me. He was willing to take the punishment I deserved. Not only did He stand before the Pharisees who were ready to kill me, but He turned and pointed toward me—not with accusation but with pride. "You're getting it wrong. She's not the worst; she is exactly right." I didn't know whether this was biblical until I found support later in Ephesians 2:4–7. I am going to put it all down here so you can see it build:

> God is so rich in mercy, and he loved us so much, that even though *we were dead because of our sins*, he gave us life when he raised Christ from the dead. (It is only by God's grace that you have been saved!) For he raised us from the dead along with Christ, and *seated us* with him in the heavenly realms because we are united with Christ Jesus. So God *can point to us in all future ages as examples* of the incredible wealth of his grace and kindness toward us, as shown in all he has done for us who are united with Christ Jesus (italics mine).

What. Is. That. Section of verses?! While we were dead we were made alive *because of Christ.* And even though we are dead/alive, He points to us as examples of his incredible wealth of favor. We are nothing, but He still treasures us. I am dead, but I am alive. I am broken, but I am beloved. I am a sinner, and I am loved. The gospel is here too.

God gave me a vision of gospel in that moment, and it gave me the courage to share my story with Amber.

I did. It was messy and laden with fights with fear, but I pressed on. "So, I'm attracted to women," I concluded. "But, don't worry! I'm not, like, attracted to you or anything!" I quickly added. I wasn't, but I was terrified she would think I was going to jump her. Because I wrestle with sexual sin, some people's assumptions are that I am sex-crazy. The opposite is true. I wrestle with idolatry for one person's romantic, same-gendered love of me.

"Laurie," Amber halted my awkward backpedaling. "Laurie, it is okay. Even if you are attracted to me one day, I'm okay. I'm not going to reject you."

I was floored. Not only did Amber call out my fear of rejection, she gave me freedom to be messy. I relaxed, finally smiling. "Thank you," I said. "Thank you for hearing me so well."

The Gift of Mess and of Choice

What so many friends we walk alongside long for is this gift of messiness without rejection: *You don't have to be perfect with us. You don't have to say the right words. You don't have to believe as we do. You are free to be in process. We are not going to quit on you.* We encourage siblings, spouses, and parents to offer this same gift to their sexually broken loved ones.

In the same season as "the phone call" in the introduction of this book, I approached a sibling with whom I did not have the closest relationship. However, I knew he had been though hard things. Maybe he would understand, I thought. *Maybe he wouldn't judge me. It's not that other siblings were judging me* (a couple were people with whom I spoke bluntly and turned to for daily encouragement), but I wanted another voice. It was probably the Holy Spirit prompting me.

I laid out my mess to this brother, and instead of him panicking and trying to control me, he gave me a gift I did not know I needed: freedom. "You could do that, Laurie," he said as I described my desire to call an ex-girlfriend and get back together with her. I described how good it would be. How much better she would make my life. "You could. No one is stopping you." Shock. The chains loosened. For some reason, having all the Church subconsciously keep me from *being who I am* was making me want to come out and *be who I am* more. John's words removed it. "You could do it. Who is stopping you?" *Who? Yeah, who?* I had my own job, my own car, and no debt. *How about I do it?* Then he paused. "All I will say is what you are describing sounds like the twitterpated, starting parts of a relationship. Not the real, gritty portions. What you're describing—this perfect ideal—it's not reality." I wanted to fight him, but I knew he was right.

His words freed me to consider what I really wanted, while simultaneously speaking what was true—not even about sexuality, but about relationships. He alluded to the hole in my heart before I could even feel its need. *She won't meet that need. What you want isn't real.*

His few sentences were critical in getting me to a point of facing God—not the stereotyped religious Church universal in my mind, but God himself. It freed me to face Him and decide, "Do I want You or not?" I was no longer rebelling against a conservative Church; I was facing a holy God.

Why are we not okay with mess? Why are we so terrified of letting people get to this point and choose? When a teenager declares, "This is who I am" (with perhaps a hidden question mark at the end of their statement), why do we flip to fight or flight? Are we afraid that perhaps God isn't in control anymore and we must jump in to save this person? "The LORD's arm is not too weak to save you, nor is his ear too deaf to hear you call" (Isa. 59:1). He's not panicking, so why are we? These teens primarily need space to be in process while in the safety of wise counsel. Parents can set boundaries without micromanaging thoughts.

Amber became a relational safe place for me to share my mess. Part of me was tempted to take my whole suitcase of "Life in Process" and dump it on her, but God instinctively showed me that the relationship I had with Heather, where she was my *one and only* and I voraciously fought for her to be my *one and only* was not healthy. "In each of my friends there is something that only some other friend can fully bring out. By myself I am not large enough to call the whole man into activity; I want other lights than my own to show all his facets," C.S. Lewis said. "Hence, true Friendship is the least jealous of loves. Two friends delight to be joined by a third, and a three by a fourth."[193] Amber was one friend who brought out in me (and me her) parts of me only she could bring forward. I learned to trust other friends with my story who could bring out other facets of my personality.

But remember the Priority Pyramid? As I began to seek genuine friendships, I always did so with God as the top-of-the-pyramid Need Meeter of my heart. *When* my friends failed me, *when* they didn't represent God in a tangible way I wanted by speaking into those Core Needs, *when* they weren't available, I learned to thank God in that moment. "Thank you, God for the pain of rejection—intentional or unintentional. Thank you, God, Amber didn't care for me the way I wanted. Thank you, God, for showing me I cannot depend on one person. Thank You for showing me, again, You are the Need Meeter of my heart." When people failed me and I switched to anger or sullenness, my reaction displayed my heart idols like a billboard. It resembled my relationship with Heather. I tried to surrender to God when I was with her, but I couldn't do it. God wouldn't let me have Heather and Him equally. He is first or nothing.

As I grew in relationship with Amber and began letting other people into different pieces of my life, Matt, my new friend-turned-someone I was interested in at a heart level (and maybe toward marriage?), told me honestly, "You are not very good at making friends." I wasn't. Out of fear of going too deep and becoming too connected with one person, I spread myself out too much with too many people. Matt knew me the best, Amber knew me quite well, but I was terrified to go deep with more people. Risk was not yet a part of my vocabulary. Some of my hesitation was correct. "It's wise to have a healthy skepticism of yourself," a former pastor of mine once said. However, I needed to give myself permission to go deep with some people, move some to a different section of relationship, and break up with others. Matt helped me and many other clients do this, and I offer it to you as an exercise.

EXERCISE 16: RELATIONSHIP HOME

We are not meant to be best friends with everyone, nor are we meant to live life alone. "Two people are better off than one, for they can help each other succeed. If one person falls, the other can reach out and help. But someone who falls alone is in real trouble" (Eccl. 4:9–10). The following exercise is a self-diagnosis to see where you can place your current friends and where you may need God to pour into you.

None of the numbers or specific examples are absolute truth. Certain people in your life may fit into different roles than are given in the examples. This is offered as a general guideline to self-diagnose ways to reshuffle relational needs. Consider the people in your life as belonging in different places in your "relational house":

Crowd: 100–1000 people

<u>House position</u>: Front door; people can know where you live, but they don't come in.

<u>Reality</u>: These people know your name, general age, family demographic, but they don't know much more. The relationship develops because of: proximity, they are near you or are in your friend circles

<u>Examples</u>: Facebook "friends", large church crowd, neighborhood relationships

Social: 20–40 people

<u>House position</u>: Living room; people see a curated, cleaned up version of your life.

<u>Reality</u>: These people know some facts about your life and some of your values, but not much more. The relationship develops because of: convenience, closer proximity

<u>Examples</u>: People in a class, work friends, neighbors you know, parents on your kids' soccer team

Close: 6–10 people

<u>House position</u>: Kitchen; people see where life really happens—the celebrations and the mess.

<u>Reality</u>: These people are invited into the mess of your life and you into theirs. You go out of your way to support one another and celebrate one another. You inconvenience yourself to be in each other's worlds. The relationship develops because of: common interests, beliefs, and ideals.

<u>Examples</u>: Small groups, intentional friendships, roommates, accountability groups

Intimate: 2–3 people

House position: Master bathroom; not many people make it in here.

Reality: These are people who see you with your makeup off, hold your hair back when you're throwing up, and are willing to come alongside you as you clean up your most personal messes. These are people who see your true sorrow, your true pain, and your true victory. The relationship develops because of: covenant, i.e. I am with you no matter what.

Examples: Spouse, best friends

Social Media and Friendships

We placed Facebook relationships up at the top with "crowd." I must admit I have developed some deep, sometimes close, possibly even bordering on intimate, friends online. Some of these people I have never even met in person. God can use social media and the Internet as a tool to help us worship him. Matt and I use things like Skype to mentor people. We believe it is about 90% as effective as in-person interactions. (Which is a high percent!) Additionally, I share authentically at the "crowd" level on social media but never things that are in process or are focused on me-worship. If I can't answer the question, "Is this about me or about honoring God?" with the latter before I decide to post, I don't post. I don't need likes, but God deserves glory.

No big shock here: social media and Internet relationships can hurt us. "Social" media fosters friendships that are a mile wide and an inch deep.[194] Some of us share some of our deepest struggles online without having to risk sharing such personal pieces in our real-life kitchen—let alone in the master bathroom, letting a friend see us puking up a mascara-running lament. We post our prettiest photos, our happiest times, or even perhaps some of our most ugly moments—but when people do not respond like we want (and need), we can react in large ways.

I believe the primary reason for exaggerated reactions is because social media can be fueled by fear, and the neural reward system fuels more fear. "Will anyone like what I said or that picture I posted? Was that caption misspelled?" Or, "Oh no! I didn't wish a happy birthday to that one college friend I knew that one semester ten years ago! Maybe she hates me now!" Or, "I posted that one thing that was maybe too controversial, and now some random stranger is saying all sorts of terrible things about me and my character! My life is ruined!" The dopamine hit we get from getting "likes" (or not getting likes) compels us to addictively share.[195] The fear associated with getting likes only increases the addictive nature of it. "It's a little bit like taking a drug," Adam Alter, a professor at New York University and author of *Irresistible: The Rise of Addictive Technology and the Business of Keeping Us Hooked*, said. "It's the unpredictability

126

of that process that makes it so addictive. If you knew that every time you posted something you'd get a 100 likes, it would become boring really fast."[196] Fear of man is in control on social media.[197] As a result, we are a becoming a bunch of socially thin, emotionally emaciated, full-of-fear people.

Such a result is not as frequently seen in real-life relationships. If I were to forget one of my closest friend's birthdays, she would unquestionably forgive me. This is because we have been developing a connection that can weather the storms of life. Social media-only relationships cannot develop such a weatherproofing. One misspelled word can get you unfriended. One missed birthday greeting. One political post. One too many cat videos.

I understand the draw to withdraw and only hang out online. I am an extreme introvert. If left to myself, I would be by myself. I get the pain of risking and getting rejected in real relationships. I know, however, if I do not intentionally seek to fill and maneuver *real life in-person* people into the relational room where they belong (front door, living room, kitchen, or master bathroom), I will be someone who is spiritually, emotionally, physically, and socially thin. We are made to belong, and social media doesn't cut it. Without real-life connection, our hole-riddled hearts will begin to wander.

What Do You Do When You Are Tempted?

Okay, so if Amber was someone who was not difficult for me to grow close to, what do I do with the people that stop me in my tracks because they are so attractive to me? What do I do when I am attracted to someone with whom I am in an ongoing relationship?

1. I set myself up for success.

I cannot simply wake up and start my day. Every time the sun rises, I begin with zero. In addition to a vat of coffee, I need my day to start in the Word and with Jesus. This is not because I am gay; this is because I am a Christian. "Eyes do not rove, nor do fleshly lusts rule when the heart is fat with the love of Jesus."[198] I have to begin my day with a fat heart.

In addition to starting the day with the gospel of love, grace, and truth, through the rest of the day I am not going to thoughtlessly saunter around areas of the Internet, places in the mall, or people who I know are difficult for me. Instead, I set myself up for success. I make small decisions that help guide me toward wholeness and holiness. "Good and evil both increase at compound interest," C.S. Lewis said. "That is why the little decisions you and I make every day are of such infinite importance."[199] Some little decisions I make are not parking near lingerie stores at the mall, telling a few intimate friends when I am going to meet with someone who is difficult for me, and shutting down any screens when I am in a time of intense temptation.

There were two years where Matt fasted from a smartphone. It drove me crazy at times because he was so disconnected, but the gift of him learning how to be present and not escape into pornography or other forms of smartphone escapism saved our marriage.

If I am in a season of wrestling hard, I tell people. I have an accountability partner, a prayer partner, friends, and an entire prayer team who I can reach out to when I am struggling. Again, this is not because I struggle with sexual sin, it is because I am a sinner. Every Christian should have such teams in their corner—it's called the Church being the Church.

2. I notice.

Like in the first step of confession, I notice the attraction. I neither call it good or bad. I neither dive into a sexual relationship with a person nor do I shame myself for the attractions. I simply notice.

3. I scale.

Matt and I (and my accountability partner and I) ask each other, "On a scale of 1 to 10, 10 being, 'I am about to have an affair,' and 1 being, 'Meh. Hardly wrestling,' what are you feeling on your sexual-lust-ometer?" If I am at a 7–8, I am on "lockdown." This is when screens disappear, and I distract myself with healthy distractions until the wave of temptation (and this level of intensity is a wave—not permanent) recedes. If I am at a 5–6, I am able to do some of the following reflection (in step 4) until it I get my lust-ometer down to about a 4, where I am aware of the attraction but I am able to live well.

4. I assess.

What I am assessing is, "Is this about the person or about me?" Often it is a combination of both. Let's begin with looking at the person.

4A. Temptation + People Assessment:

I am not attracted to all women. Neither are all straight men or women attracted to everyone of the opposite gender. There are some who catch our eye more than others. The following categories are not perfect but are a general guide.

If you are not attracted to the same gender, the following assessment may not apply directly. Shift it to someone of the opposite gender, if that is more your struggle, or consider your relationships to other temptations. What sort of boundaries do you need to put around them, not legalistically but just practically? "If your eye causes you to sin, gouge it out. It's better to enter the Kingdom of God with only one eye than to have two eyes and be thrown into hell" (Mark 9:47). What do you need to remove or what fence do you need to put up so you can better focus on the soil of the pasture where you live?

Unsafe People for Close Relationship:

There are certain women toward whom I am attracted 80–100% of the time. There is no getting around the fact that they are attractive to me. They are safe in the "crowd" level of friendship and perhaps the "social." This is where I have had to move ex-girlfriends and people I meet who are immediately attractive. It may be their physical appearance, their personality, or the way they carry themselves. If I have had a dating or intense relationship with them, I distance myself because it is because it is too easy to fall back into it. The neural pathways have been built.

There is often something I perceive inside of these women I think I am missing in me: confidence, attractive appearance, athleticism, or grace. I subconsciously think that being close to them in many ways will fix the lack in me.

Sometimes-Unsafe People for Close Relationship:

There are some people who are difficult for me more often than not. I can be friends with them, but letting them into my inner circle either socially or intimately would not be wise. Side note: if you directly wrestle with same-sex attractions like me you may be thinking, "This stinks! Other people don't have to do this!" You're right. It does stink. But there are other areas of their life where they have to step aside from temptation: food, other-gendered people, their cell phones, alcohol, etc. Grieve it, celebrate that one day we will be on the new earth with only holy relationships, but today . . . this is your and my post-Fall reality.

Mostly Safe People for Close Relationship:

Then there are the many women toward whom I may have a glimmer of attraction, but more often than not, I can be close with them. I would consider them safe for the "social" or "close" circles.

Almost Always Safe for Close Relationship:

These are the Ambers, the other women with whom my personality connects, but the attraction isn't there. It reminds me of Anne of Green Gables describing her dearest friends as "kindred spirits." You are drawn to them, but it's not primarily a sexual draw. There is a kindred spirit, heart connection. These women are safe in the "intimate" or "close" circles. Since I intentionally began to pray for and seek healthy same-gendered friendships, God has brought women into my life with whom I connect in heart but there is hardly any struggle for me with my mind wandering. If I feel the attraction—even with the "almost always safe" group, I never shame myself. I simply think, "Yup. That's how I am," and move forward. I don't tell the person (it would make things too awkward and hard for me); I simply recognize it.

There are those who believe as I believe theologically but would not agree with the delineation I make friendship-wise. They encourage close friendships with people toward whom they are almost always attracted. They find God in that tension. Maybe I am simply a weaker person with a weaker ability to resist, but when I lean into the attraction, I have a more difficult time resisting it. I don't find God in that tension, I find a wandering mind about to fall. It is wiser for me to be kind, to put the person mentally in the right circle and then "run from sexual sin!" like Paul says (1 Cor. 6:18). "Put to death the sinful, earthly things lurking within you. Have nothing to do with sexual immorality, impurity, lust, and evil desires. Don't be greedy, for a greedy person is an idolater, worshiping the things of this world" (Col. 3:5). I'm not going to put the person to death, but I am going to work to put to death what my sinful nature desires. My favorite writer, Tim Keller, again: "A Christian doesn't play games with sin—they put it to death." But do we simply run from sin? No. We must turn from sin and stare at the gospel. "Sin can only be cut off at the root if we expose ourselves constantly to the unimaginable love of Christ for us," Keller continues. "Sin grows when we think we deserve something from God, or life. Godliness grows when we remember we are debtors to God, throughout life."[200] When I am wrestling quite a bit with temptation toward someone or with temptation in general, I run from it and then look into my heart through the lens of the gospel. This is how

4B. Temptation + My Heart Assessment:

After assessing the person toward whom I have an attraction, it is time to look in my heart. We will turn this part of the look at temptation into an exercise using the book of James.

EXERCISE 17: THE JAMES PROGRESSION

In James 1, the author talks about how blessed we are when we patiently endure temptation. He also reminds us that God is never the one to tempt us. Rather, "Temptation comes from our own desires, which entice us and drag us away. These desires give birth to sinful actions. And when sin is allowed to grow, it gives birth to death" (James 1:14–15). In therapy, Matt uses a tool he calls "The James Progression" taken from these verses to help clients self-diagnose what their heart needs in temptation. I like it and use it in my own life.

It's difficult to go from, "I'm feeling tempted," to answer the question, "What Core Need is lacking right now?" This verse helps to map it out a bit further. Let's make it visual:

CORE NEEDS → DESIRES → ⋮ SIN → DEATH

We believers can overly focus on the line between temptation and sin. *Just don't sin don't sin don't sin.* But we often fall into sin eventually. Instead of staring at sin and focusing on "Just say no," it's more helpful to turn our perspective around toward the desires that get us into the temptation.

That word "desires" can be good or bad. The Greek for "evil desires" is *epithymía*, from *epí*, "focused on" and *thymós*, "passionate desire." These can be positive or negative, depending on whether the desire is *inspired by faith* (God's inbirthed *persuasion*) or not.[201] This is interesting when we put those desires—good or bad—in relationship to Core Needs. Core Needs are good. Core Needs that drive us toward desires (epithymía) that make us focus on God more are great. Core Needs that shift into evil desires (epithymía) that lead us into temptation and then sin and death are not great.

So, let's lean into that good/bad desires place. In fact, let's drive there. See the car? Let's call it a Life Situation car. It drives you from your need to your good/bad desires. There are different brands of the car depending on what is lacking in your life at the moment. Instead of asking the question, "What Core Need is empty?" right now, it's easier to ask, "What life situation of mine is lacking?" and look into your garage.

Your car brands may be similar or different from mine.

Brand of Life Situation Car:

"What feels lacking in my life?"

i.   Work

ii. Friends

iii. God

iv. Self-perception

v.   Marriage

Then, ask yourself, what is fueling this car? How am I not filling this car up, or with what am I filling it that is not actually satisfying?

False Fuel for the Car:

"What about it feels off or lacking?"

i.   **Bored:** "I feel aimless."

ii. **Stressed:** "I am tired."

iii. **Lonely**: "I feel like no one cares about me."

iv. **Rejected**: "I feel brushed aside."

v. **Responsible**: "I feel like I will only be safe when this situation is figured out. The weight of the world/this person/this situation is on my shoulders. I feel I must control it, but I can't. So I will escape or hyper-focus on it."

vi. **Hormonal**: "I am feeling crazy and know this will level me out for a while. I want to feel 'normal,' or at least feel something."

Then ask, what need or needs does this Life Situation Car need to fuel it instead of what I am doing?

Core Need Fuel for the Car:

"How can I practically get this need met in a way that will alleviate the need and glorify God?"

For bored:
- *I need purpose. I need to do something productive. (Purpose, belonging, seen, desired, unique . . .)*

For stressed:
- *I need to rest (or nurture myself), or I really need to buckle down and work. (Purpose)*

For lonely:
- *I need connection with people. (Belonging, nurture) I need to reach out to a fun or serious friend.*

For rejected:
- *I need to be nurtured and cared for. I do not feel seen. I need to be seen by God first and supported by people. (Nurtured, seen, belonging, desired)*

For responsible:
- *I need to rest in God's safety, surrender what I can't control, and move into what I can. (Rest, safety)*

For hormonal:
- *I need to channel this energy somewhere that will truly rest my soul, honor God, and bless my life and others. (Rest)*

The key is to fuel the car with the right things so it will drive us to right desires and we avoid the temptation/sin/death altogether.

I need to say that practically getting these needs met through hanging out with friends, getting work done, or channeling our hormone craziness toward the right place won't completely satiate the need forever. We won't experience that type of fullness until we are made whole in the New Heaven and New Earth. The goal pre-Heaven is to fuel the Life Situation car in a way that drives us more *toward* the One who gave us the practical fuel in the first place. For example, if I keep wrestling with being tempted with pornography, I can recognize the aching *Life Situation Car* is my *job*, the fuel I've been sadly filling it with is *boredom*, and the Core Need fuel I actually need is *purpose*. When I recognize this, I may go and get a new job. This great, new job helps me feel purposeful for a while. I feel full. However, the Life Situation Car will only stay fueled if I stare at the Giver of gifts—not the gift itself. "God, thank you for this job. Thank you for this renewed purpose." Gratitude multiplies the gift and fills the emptiness within. But we cannot stare at the gift. If we do, it simply turns that good desire into a bad one, and we are tempted to worship the gift. Worship of anything but God is a sin, and sin, according to James, leads to death. This could then be called the James Regression.

Additionally, let's talk about shame here because it is an unwieldy beast that likes to show up anytime we confront sin and temptation. A great way in this space to remove shame from your wrestling with temptation is to ask Jesus if He gets it. "Jesus, when did You ever experience rejection from a friend?" (Judas betrayed Him; He felt forsaken by his own Father as He hung on the cross.) "Jesus, when did You ever feel like no one cared about You?" (The disciples ran away in the garden; His own family thought He was crazy.) "Jesus, when did You ever feel like too much was before You?" (In Gethsemane.) "Jesus, when did You ever feel tempted to escape Your pain and suffering through Your own ways?" (When He experienced temptation from Satan in the wilderness.) When I know the Savior relates to what is driving me toward sin, shame is removed.

5. I confess.

The last step of my temptation journey is to confess where I have fallen. To see how I do that, go back to the last chapter on confession.

Phew. We did it. I hope it is both spiritually and practically helpful. Now, let's reflect.

Reflection Questions:

1. This is a lot. What is one piece from this chapter that you want to implement today?

_____

_____

_____

2. When have you experienced similar frustration to mine about weakness? ("I wrote angrily to God because I did not understand why He either wouldn't take away these attractions or simply let me have her. *It would be so much easier.*") When have you experienced God's strong rebuke to your whining (not lament)? What was it like?

_____

_____

_____

_____

3. What did you think about the Relationship Home? If you haven't, take some time to fill it out, praying as you go. If you see blank spaces, ask Jesus to help you not shame yourself but rather to help you find quality friends that love Him for those spots.

_____

_____

_____

_____

Crowd/Front Door (100–1000 people)

Social/Living Room (20–40 people)

Close/Kitchen (6–10 people)

Intimate/Master Bathroom (2–3 people)

4. What are three ways you can "set yourself up for success" before you are tempted the next time?

_____
_____
_____
_____

5. Honestly assess your relationship to screens/social media/the Internet: How is it a tool for God-glorifying relationships? How might it not be?

_____
_____
_____
_____

6. What sort of boundaries do you need to put around your greatest temptation (like the boundaries I have around friendships)?

_____
_____
_____
_____

7. Consider The James Progression. Think through a recent time of temptation. What Life Situation Car was running on the wrong fuel? What were you fueling it with? What Core Need fuel did/do you need to fuel it with instead? After discovering this, ask Jesus, "When have You felt _____[insert your feeling word or place of lack]?" and ask the Holy Spirit to help you connect your heart to Emmanuel's.

_____
_____
_____
_____

CHAPTER 11: TO MARRIAGE, ONENESS, AND BEYOND

"We know the sexual life; we do not know, except in glimpses, the other thing which,
in Heaven, will leave no room for it. Hence where fullness awaits us we anticipate fasting."
—C.S. Lewis[202]

"[A one-flesh union] is a great mystery, but it is an illustration of
the way Christ and the church are one."
—Paul[203]

I never wanted to get married. Sure, there were moments where I was like, "Oh, that would be nice," but I never dreamed about it. When my college friends and I proposed a list of the order in which we each would marry, I was always last. I did not feel I needed people—especially a man-person in a permanent marriage. I had me and Jesus, and I was good.

That's what I thought. Then my Core Need to be seen began speaking louder. Heather met that need to be seen until she couldn't meet it enough. God did not allow our relationship to flourish.

Then God wrecked me with his love—again and again. I learned I needed humans, but I needed God first. I did not understand how that worked in marriage. Six years after I exchanged vows with Matt, we were not one in mind, body, spirit, and purpose. We were best friends, but I withheld significant pieces of my heart from him.

I didn't realize how independent I was in our functionally dysfunctional marriage until Matt had his conversion in our sixth year. After he met Jesus in a deeper way, after he rid his life and our home of pornography, I was no longer alone. Matt was attentive. Caring. Leaning into me. Before, he was focused on his screens and nursing his own self-hatred. He didn't have emotional or mental space for me. I felt a slight sting of rejection and annoyance at his apathy, but I didn't mind it completely. In many ways, it worked out better. I could be independent in our marriage, toss him the occasional piece of my body, and then go on with my life. It was me and Jesus. Me and my friends with Matt on the side. I liked that.

But God called us to oneness. Not only oneness of body but also one-fleshness in mind, heart, and spirit. When Jesus asks us to deny ourselves, He isn't just saying, "Give Me your sexuality," or "Give Me your beliefs in the afterlife," or "Give Me your bad habits." He is saying, "Give Me everything—your fears, your future, your money, your life, your desire to isolate." If marriage is an example of Christ's relationship to us, then marriage requires submitting our whole selves to God, letting Him mold two sinners into one flesh while He gets all the glory for the miracle.

I don't like that.

My selfish nature doesn't like that. I want to run and hide. There is a certain type of brokenness required in receiving love. There is a certain tearing down of self-protective walls. The fortress I build around my heart to keep me safe also keeps the love out. Here's an often-quoted thought on the subject by C.S. Lewis:

> To love at all is to be vulnerable. Love anything and your heart will be wrung and possibly broken. If you want to make sure of keeping it intact you must give it to no one, not even an animal. Wrap it carefully round with hobbies and little luxuries; avoid all entanglements. Lock it up safe in the casket or coffin of your selfishness. But in that casket, safe, dark, motionless, airless, it will change. It will not be broken; it will become unbreakable, impenetrable, irredeemable. To love is to be vulnerable.[204]

I don't get to pick one or the other. The willingness to suffer in relationship is required for love. Just look at Jesus. You cannot more blatantly show the necessity of suffering for love than a near-naked, arms-out death on a cross for His beloved.

It's unconditional. It's undeserved. It makes me squirm with discomfort. There are many people who have loved me well. Two of those many people are Matt and our mentor, Dave. After a meeting with the three of us, Dave followed up with an incredibly encouraging email. He concluded his words with, "I am very fond of you both!" I knew he meant all he said, including those odd final words that sounded like a letter from the 1800s. I was overwhelmed by his overt love, as you can see in my response to him:

> I am sitting here letting your gracious, kind, thoughtful, loving words wreck me like a wave over and over. The love you display to us is similar to the love Matt shows me. And when I let it hit my heart, it feels it has the potential to destroy me. I do not know how to be loved . . . as me. Unconditionally. You both are teaching me how to be loved.[205]

There is nothing like love to highlight hidden places of darkness. With as much as I have worked on my heart, with as much as I have moved toward Jesus, there are places in my heart I have left off limits to God, Matt, or anyone. Because Matt is the closest human to me, I can push him the farthest away. This is not because my default is an orientation toward women; this is because my default orientation is *getting my own needs met because I know what's best for me*. i.e. my default orientation is self.

The Cat and the Gate

Let's look at this another way through our original pasture analogy. When we are married, we let another sheep into our pen. Baa. Welcome, sheep spouse. Let's call our marriage covenant the fence, but look, there is a gate. More times than I would like to admit, I leave this gate *slightly* cracked open. Part of me is aware, but most of me doesn't care. I like it ajar. It keeps me safe from having to be too vulnerable. The open gate on our marriage tells me I don't have to stay—at least mentally. The somewhat problematic part of this is that the cracked-open gate always lets in a sleek, Persian cat named, "What If?".

My sinful nature likes her. She comforts me when Matt does something I don't care for or when I am bored, hungry, angry, lonely, or tired. Her purring tells me I'm wanted, valuable. *What ifff?* she purrs. *What if you weren't with Matt? Let's think about that for a while.* I can carry her in my arms as I go through my day. I am in control of this little pet, until she is bored, hungry, and tired herself. Then she angrily requires more of me. Pet idols do that.

She isn't always here. There are times I wake up to the wrongness of her presence, grab her by the scruff of the neck, and drag her out while she claws the ground the whole way. After slamming the gate and latching it, I spin around to assess the mess she (and I) have made of our marriage. There is fur everywhere. Dander. Sheep Matt is sneezing, and he doesn't know why. The cat is invisible to him, but he feels the effects. The longer we are married, and the closer we are to Jesus and each other, the more quickly he senses her presence. The time I wasted feeding, watering, and playing with her could have been used for getting to know Matt and deepening my relationship with God (who lives here too). It is when I assess the time, energy and money I spent on her that I wake up—as if a bucket of cold water dropped on my head. Oh no . . . what have I done?

Have I ever cheated physically? No. But I have definitely disobeyed Jesus' words about looking at someone lustfully (He says it's adultery). And so has Matt.

I am not the only one who opens gates to our marriage. Matt lets in animals, too, and I feel them even if I do not see them.

But this is not just a mixed-orientation marriage issue, nor even a marriage issue. It is a capital-C Church-that-is-full-of-sinful-humans issue. We cannot be one in marriage, with God, or in the Church if we walk around with our ever-needy pet idols. We are an increasingly lonely culture, but we can't seem to get into our heads that it is our pet sins keeping us from true community and oneness. "It's your sins that have cut you off from God. Because of your sins, he has turned away and will not listen anymore" (Isaiah 59:2). God won't listen if we are petting our idols. And if He is the head of the Church—the place we are one—do you think He will allow oneness in relationships (including marriage) if we are cheating on Him with idols? Will He let us have true community while we turn our backs on the Creator of community? We don't get to pick and choose which we get. Our life is made up of idols + no God + no true community or submission of desires + God + true community.[206] It's all or nothing.

The Church and Oneness

I have spoken on quite a few panels, where we offer our advice and stories to a wondering crowd. More times than not, someone asks a question along the lines of, "If God is calling all of us to submit our sexuality to Him, what if I am never supposed to get married to someone of the opposite sex? What do I do? I have to have a sad life with no intimacy? Where do I go for intimate relationship?"

My answer? *"The Church."* John 17 has completely destroyed my old paradigm of what I believed church was supposed to be: a bunch of nice people hearing a nice sermon and singing a few nice songs, then going home to their nice homes where they live their real (not so nice) life. No. Not according to Jesus. "I am praying not only for these disciples but for all who will ever believe in me through their message," Jesus prays to the Father about disciples who walked with Him physically and those of us who walk with Him now (John 17:20). "My prayer for all of them is that they will be one, just as you and I are one, Father." Jesus didn't pray for financial blessings, a nicer group of people, or the end of suffering. He prayed for oneness—*just as the Father and Son are one.* What are the results? "[T]he world will know that you sent me and that you love them as much as you love me" (John 17:23). Oneness in the Church is how the world will know God loves them. I read this and want to believe it, but I definitely don't live like I believe it.

I love how Francis Chan describes his bafflement at this section of verses in a talk he gave titled, "End Time Sins are in the Church." (Sounds like a real upper, doesn't it? It is amazing. I have watched it at least five times now, and it has over 500,000 views as I write this.) He looks into the crowd and asks someone his name. "Greg," is what he hears. Francis replies, "I don't know you, Greg, but I'm assuming because I have the Holy Spirit in me that I could put up with you, and you could put up with me, we could worship together, and maybe be in a small group together—for maybe six months or so." The crowd laughed. "That's what I think when I think of John 17 unity. I don't think, 'I pray that Greg and I are one, *like you and the Father are one*—just as you and the Father are one.'"[207] Have I ever prayed that? Not in a, "I want her to notice me," sort of selfish oneness, but a *"God, make me one with my local church and the Church universal! Make us one, Father, so the world may know You!"* (Do I even pray this for my marriage?) Honestly, I don't get how it works. All I know is the way many of us love one another doesn't exemplify the selfless, intimate oneness Jesus Christ prayed for.

I think one of the reasons I cannot even begin to grasp a vision of oneness in the Church is most of the sermons I have heard on the subject revolve around marriage. Oneness, intimacy, and sex are interchangeable words—and they are often only uttered in the context of a heterosexual marriage sermon.

Marriage is the ultimate relationship, and sex is the ultimate connector in marriage. What is the climax of every romantic comedy? A scene in the bedroom. What has been called "the glue that holds marriage together"? Sex. All of you celibate, single people? You're in trouble. Good luck with enduring a terrible life of extra suffering.

There is no way such an interchange is true if Jesus and Paul call for oneness while they themselves were single. If sex = the ultimate intimacy = the ultimate oneness, then Paul, Jesus, and every single person who ever died celibate and single must have lived a life of lack.

Sex is not the ultimate connector. It is a fruit of one-flesh, male/female covenant marriage—it is not ultimate. It is a glimmer of what is to come. C.S. Lewis describes the difference between sex on earth and oneness in heaven as being like telling a pre-pubescent kid who is just learning about sex that sex is great. The greatest "great" he knows at his age is chocolate. So, he asks, "Is there chocolate with sex?" When he hears, "No," he is disappointed. "The boy knows chocolate: he does not know the positive thing that excludes it," Lewis says. "We are in the same position. We know the sexual life; we do not know, except in glimpses, the other thing which, in Heaven, will leave no room for it. Hence where fullness awaits us we anticipate fasting."[208] As we fast, we seek to promote oneness here on earth as it is in heaven. How do we do that? How do we foster intimacy now, before heaven where there will be no sex?

We work to build up the Body of Christ. Paul says it begins with Christ, the Head of the Body. "[H]e holds the whole body together with its joints and ligaments, and it grows as God nourishes it" (Col. 2:19). I don't hear a sex word in there. I hear heart and spirit language. Jesus Christ is the Head of the Body, and we are held together by his strong sinews. God—whose name is love—holds us together. Love is what "binds us all together in perfect harmony" (Col. 3:14). What is so amazing about love, which is patient, is kind, does not demand its own way, and rejoices when truth wins out, is that this love is invitational (1 Cor. 13:4, 6). God is invitational. One of the reasons He invented humans was to share His communal joy with others. When we love one another, when we are one with one another just as the Father and Son are one, we are invitational. Oneness and love does not exclude someone who is a chaste gay Christian. It is inclusive at our dinner tables, in our homes, in our small groups, and in our churches. Such oneness is true intimacy within the great marriage between Christ and the Church.

Since watching Francis Chan's sermon five times and reading John 17 many more times, I have begun to pray for oneness in my local church and with Matt. I want our marriage to reflect the Church + Christ, and for the Church + Christ to reflect the Trinity's communal oneness. "God, make Matt and I one as You and the Son are one. God, make us one with the Church as You and the Son are one."

But to do this, I need to be brave. I need to throw out the cat (again), slam the gate shut (again), and break down the walls of my lock-boxed heart. The cat is easier. Instagram wandering is a quicker fix. Wandering eyes give me a sense of being desired. I feel safe with the option of "What If," because I don't have to stand completely vulnerable before Matt and God. But I cannot hug both Matt and the option of not-Matt. "Let no one split apart what God has joined together," Jesus said of marriage (Mark 10:9). Let our daydreaming on the idea of "What If" not split apart what God has joined together.

So how do I do this? How does a same-sex attracted woman not only stay married but thrive in her marriage to a heterosexual man? How does she become one with her husband, and therefore promote oneness in the church, and reflect God in all the relationships? After slamming the gate shut on the cat named "What If?" I have a few more ideas.

How Do You Move Toward Oneness in Marriage?

The following is not only true for a mixed-orientation marriage but straight marriages, and much of it (though not all) applies to anyone pursuing oneness in the Church. This would include parents trying to love their kids who are LGBT+ or wrestling with sexual brokenness better.

1. Remember the good.

When things are difficult between Matt and me, we remember the beginning: why did we first fall in love? What were some activities we did in the beginning that cultivated our friendship?

Then we do them. Personally, we lean toward side-by-side activities like walking as a family, running, hiking, playing Frisbee, cooking, and simply laughing. We look for where we agree and meet there. We remember where we used to have fun and lean in. It is shocking how something like a quiet walk around the neighborhood can re-center us as friends and open our mouths to have some deep conversations in the context of friendship. The *eros* love—romantic love—can follow. It doesn't always, but it can. It isn't mandatory; it is fruit.

2. Remember who the enemy is.

The enemy is not a human. My enemy is not Matt. It can be difficult to remember this when the pain of my unmet Core Needs are not alleviated with his help; when he is being unloving, when I am stressed, or when I simply want to blame him for something going wrong. Whenever the Spirit, a friend, or Matt remind me, "I am on your team," it shakes me awake to the reality of the battle we are in for oneness. "For we are not fighting against flesh-and-blood enemies, but against evil rulers and authorities of the unseen world, against mighty powers in this dark world, and against evil spirits in the heavenly places" (Eph. 6:12). We would do well to have this tattooed on the back of our eyelids.

3. Quit isolating.

We have to quit thinking we can do marriage on our own. You can't. I can't. You have to give up and ask God to be your strength. "Jesus, I cannot do this. I cannot love _____. I cannot be close to _____." This marriage is impossible. Not just a mixed-orientation marriage but marriage. One-flesh marriage is impossible without supernatural power of Jesus Christ.

We also need people in our corner. We have friends who specifically ask us marriage questions and a mentor who does the same, and at times we have professional counselors in our lives. Isolation is a petri dish for sin. We need human mirrors to tell us where we are both doing well and failing. These people must not be afraid of stepping into your worst moments, and you need to give them permission to do so.

The hardest part about finding friends for such a role is they don't quite "get it." But no one can quite "get it." Straight couples don't have an exactly matched straight couple mirror. Mixed-orientation-marriage (MOM) couples don't have an exactly matched MOM mirror. "Laurie, you need to ask the Lord to help *you* be married to *Matt*," Carolyn advised before we were married. "Your marriage is unique to you." This is not because we are a mixed-orientation marriage; this is because we are unique humans.

The critical pieces to find in helpers are: 1) Grace-filled people who have *done their own heart work.* 2) People who have your same theology of sexuality. 3) People who know how to journey with you, or are willing to learn from you. 4) People who are brave and willing to tell you what is true with grace. When we have found such people, we boldly ask, "We want you to ask us hard questions. Will you do that?" And they ask us the same thing. We are all leaning into the same goals: oneness in marriage, oneness in our friendship, and oneness in the Church.

4. Lament.

"God, this is hard. I don't know how to do this." If the pain is in your heart, you might as well get the infection out through lament. What is important to remember is lament never begins with our friends. I puke my entire lament on God first, and then I let Him put a few things back in my hands to take to the team of people who are *pro-my-marriage*. These are people who are a part of the solution, and their job is to pray and speak into how Matt and I can become *more* one. If I sense they are trying to separate us, they lose the privilege to speak into my life or marriage.

5. Confess.

I never want to tell Matt when I have sinned against him. Never ever. But when I do, the freedom that follows tells me it is worth it. I never want to confess, but I am always glad I did.[209] This is true not only for sexual sinning, but also for when I am self-seeking, easily angered, and keeping a record of wrongs (i.e. being unloving, according to 1 Corinthians 13).

This is a big deal for me, and it may be for you: Because I wrestle with feelings of less-than-ness because of my same-sex attractions, I have to bathe my mind, heart, and spirit in God's love before I confess *anything* to Matt. Otherwise, when I say, "I was wrong" (the three hardest words in the English language), I will either go to him with a spirit of, "I am the worst human," or take the opposite approach to self-protect and say, "I am just being me!" even when what I did was sin. I need to remove shame and let confession propel me toward holiness. I cannot let Satan's hateful, shame-filled hands slap me across the face as I confess. I search for Jesus' smile of pride meeting my eyes as I step into forgiveness.

6. Pray together.[210]

My mom told me that when I was young, my dad used to encourage handholding prayer when they were mad at each other. I did not think that was wise or important until I realized how much the enemy likes to split people apart in fights. He cannot hear our thoughts, but he can watch our actions. Fight him with hand-holding prayer—especially when you don't feel like it.

7. Ask each other what you really need.[211]

When I am really struggling or we are in a big fight, we often ask each other, "What do you really need?" We look at the Core Needs list, and ask, "How can I help you meet that need in a healthy way?" Sometimes, it's a date night. Sometimes, it's hanging out with friends. Sometimes, it's shoving the car keys in my hands and saying, "Go to a coffee shop and write for an hour. I have the kids."

8. Speak each other's love language.[212]

This is a big one for us. Love languages are tangible ways to give and receive love. The five of them are acts of service, gifts, words of affirmation, quality time, and physical touch.[213] My top two are words of affirmation and receiving gifts. Matt's top two are quality time and physical touch. (You can see we do not speak love the same way.) However, we have learned the act of choosing to speak the other's language, not only as a gift to the other spouse, but to open our own hearts up toward the person. For example, even though I am not a touchy person, I *choose*—because I love and am committed to Matt—to show him love by stopping whatever I am doing to hug him when he wakes up or when he returns from work. I see his face shift from groggy or exhausted to full of life whenever I do this. The same happens to me whenever Matt says a specific, intentional compliment to me or buys me something small like my favorite coffee.

9. Note rejection words as Core Need clues.

"You don't have time for me." (Seen) "You don't care about me." (Loved) "I don't feel like you ever say nice things about me." (Affirmed) "Your friends hate me." (Included) "You don't like to be with me." (Desired) Our sentences hold insight as to what we need from one another and ultimately from God. Train your eyes and ears to translate complaints into words speaking from a hole-riddled heart.

How It All Began

I want to end this chapter and book with the start of my relationship with Matt. I am hesitant to share it, as it may come across that our story must be yours. Please notice where we placed this story: at the end. We didn't want to put it first as a goal or reason any of us should do any of this heart work. The heart work must be done, no matter who you are or how you identify. How God wants to work out the gospel in any of our lives is *up to Him*. We believe in His design of marriage as two opposite-gendered people in a one-flesh union for life, but a one-flesh union is not a requirement for everyone. "I wish everyone were single, just as I am," Paul said. "Yet each person has a special gift from God, of one kind or another" (1 Cor. 7:7). Anything within God's design is great (celibacy with community, opposite-gendered marriage with community). But even if you have or will go outside of that design, we still love you and are committed to you. God loves and is committed to you, too.

The following is how He worked and is working the gospel out in my life and Matt's. When I met Matt, I was living in what I call hopeless tension. I live in tension now—but with hope. I was going to Christian university, leading worship, leading small groups, getting frequently promoted in my news-reporting job, and I was in a same-sex relationship. You would think I would have been happy, but I wasn't. I was despairing. The Spirit of God within me wasn't leading me to this despair but pointing me toward repentance. Instead, it was the enemy of my soul who capitalized on that conviction and ripped me apart with self-hatred and shame.

I had already shared with my favorite professor what was going on behind the scenes, and I had recently started meeting with her counselor-husband, Dave, for help. He was gracious, and kind, and somehow he never got around to giving me the bill for hours and hours of counseling. It was all free. His statement, "Laurie, there are good men out there, they just don't wear signs," allowed me to see men with less distrusting eyes. He—a man—demonstrated it.

EXERCISE 18: CELEBRATION

One powerful bit of homework Dave offered me was to celebrate my sexuality. God made me a sexual being, and that is a good thing—not something to be ashamed of. Yes, what I was doing with my sexuality was not glorifying to God, but I am someone who is holistically made to glorify God. "Do something to celebrate your God-created sexuality," he encouraged. "Something you would enjoy and find rest doing with Jesus." I took myself out to breakfast and felt like I was on a joyful, somewhat-awkward date with my Savior. As I ate pancakes, I sensed Him sitting across from me, smiling at me, not ashamed of me. I drew on His love and tried to let it into my hole-riddled heart. "Remain in my love," He whispered, and I leaned in (John 15:9).

When we have encouraged clients to do this same exercise, they find it to be a powerful experience. They might not go out to breakfast, but all of them seem to go on "Jesus Dates" and let Him guide them to a small thing to buy for themselves or to a nature scene that feels painted by God for them.

How and when can you celebrate your sexuality this week?

Back to our story. I was a columnist for our university newspaper. The column I wrote was called, "Get Out!" It encouraged students to get out and off campus to explore the city. For each piece, I visited and reviewed a couple of local eateries and shared my quirky exploits there. My most memorable write-up was on how to effectively sneak a whole pizza into a movie theater. (Hint: Put the pizza on your arm like a waiter, and then throw a coat over it. Boom. Pizza-d.) I realized one day that I had not asked any guys to come with me. I liked to share my friend's experiences alongside mine, but I disliked most men. They terrified and disgusted me. *Who do I know who isn't creepy?*

My answer: Matt Krieg! Yes, friends, it's true. What first attracted me to my husband was his lack of creepiness. Cue concluding Disney music.

I invited him and another friend to visit a local thrift shop and a pizza place with me. (We chose not to sneak the pizza anywhere . . . this time.) What I discovered was not only did he lack the creep factor but also he was funny. He was kind. He didn't look at me with lust-filled eyes as I assumed many men did. He looked at me like a sister. Over the next few months, we grew in our friendship. The "he's not creepy" bonus points turned into points for leaning into my quirkiness. When I said something I thought was dumb, he took that dumb thing farther. When I pretended I was a knight in the Dark Ages, he took the name "Sir Mattathias" alongside my "Lady Laurienidas." When I said, "Let's go rollerblading through the grocery store," he strapped on his blades. When I said, "Let's pretend we are a married couple and mess with furniture sales people," he pretended for as long as I would. (Sorry to all of you furniture sales people. We were bored.) When I got a black eye during Ultimate Frisbee, he said that was the moment he secretly knew he wanted to marry me. I began to relax in his presence and wonder, *is he different?*

Another month went by, and it became clear he wanted to date me. *Hold the phone, bro,* I thought. *You have no idea what's going on behind the scenes.* While we were becoming better friends, I was still with Heather. Granted, our relationship was in a state of turmoil because of my wrestling with the Word, the Spirit inside of me, and what I wanted, but it was all hidden. Matt didn't know. "Let's pray about it," I said to Matt. "Let's take a month."

While he prayed about dating me, I prayed about telling him my story and dating him. I didn't want to date every man; I wanted to get to know Matt better. I didn't know if we were supposed to be together forever, I knew just enough to "do the next thing," as Elisabeth Elliot advised.[214]

But . . . Heather. But . . . women. That same month, Heather and I took a break from our relationship.

This is the part of the story I cannot say is at all worth duplicating. The day before I was going to share my story with Matt, I met with Heather after our month long break. I thought the time apart might break the ties of connection toward one another. I thought we could just be friends. I was wrong. If anything, the separation made the desire for her stronger. What started as a fun day ended in the darkness of her car just the two of us. *Get out, Laurie*, I thought I heard the Holy Spirit whisper. *Get out. There is still time.* It seemed impossible. *Put your hand on the car handle. Stand up. Walk out. Now.*

I did, mechanically, obediently, and with every step away, I felt like a bucket of cold water dumped on my head. *What did I do?*

The next morning, I begrudgingly opened my Bible. I hoped to hear from God, but I felt guilty for lingering around temptation for as long as I did. Although the draw toward Heather and women in general had not fled during the month apart, my ability to hear God's voice was improved with the fast from her. I heard the Spirit more loudly than I had a month before.

EXERCISE 19: FASTING

To fast means to take a break from something important to you (such as a meal or three, social media, coffee, or chocolate) in order to better reveal our idols and discern the voice of God. "More than any other Discipline, fasting reveals the things that control us," Richard Foster wrote. "Anger, bitterness, jealousy, strife, fear—if they are within us, they will surface during fasting."[215] Fasting allows us to feel our neediness so we can know how and where we need the Need-Meeter.

Do you need to fast from something? Not do you *want* to fast from something, but do you *need* to fast from something that has become an idol in your life so you can better feel what that idol is trying to fill? So you can feel the hole in your heart?

"God, I am so sorry," I journaled after feeling that gentle rebuke from Jesus. "Please, Jesus, forgive me. I stepped back into it! With Heather! I kept hearing You. I heard Your voice so clearly. I heard it crystal clear in my ears . . . Please, forgive me." I paused, considering the day's events. I took a big breath. "Matt might totally reject me today," I wrote. "Totally. He might spit in my face. I won't allow that, but Christ, where do You stand with me?"

I closed my eyes, imagining his response. Then I picked up my pen again. "Who dares accuse whom God has chosen for his own?" I quoted Romans 8:33–35. "No one—for Christ Jesus died for us and was raised to life for us, and he is sitting at the place of honor at God's right hand, pleading for us. Can anything ever separate us from Christ's love?"

My answer? No. Nothing. Not my dawdling around sin, not Matt's rejection. Christ loved me, no matter what.

My hands trembled as I walked to the designated meeting spot in a park underneath a gazebo. I arrived about twenty minutes early, shivering. I wished it was sunny and warm, but even in June, winter decided to cough up its last breaths.

Jesus, help. I prayed silently. I held my breath as I saw his rusty white Toyota pull into a parking space. This was the moment I had been praying for all month. All Matt knew was that I was going to tell him something about my past. I surmised this topic was not one that would be in his list of ideas about what I might say. "How's it going?" I smiled, trying to regulate my nervous system.

"It's all right," he said. I could tell he was anxious in the way he quickly smiled back.

I shivered again, and then dove in with my opening line. "I have something to tell you, Matt, and it might not be easy for you to hear." For the next thirty minutes, I shared my story. I did not cite specifics when it came to what we did physically, other than to say it became "very physical." He did not need to know. I finally finished, and looked up from the woody grain of the picnic table to see how he was received my words. I waited for the flash of fear or disgust. It never came.

Matt held my gaze, not looking off to gather some politically correct response. He spoke from his heart. "There is nothing that you said that makes me not want to be with you," he said. "It was not what I was expecting," he continued, "but I don't look at you any differently." And he didn't. I could see it.

This conversation began my dating relationship with Matt—while I maintained a friendship with Heather. For months, we tried to keep it platonic, but I know I cheated on Matt. *Stop it, Laurie. Just be friends. Don't do physical stuff together.* I didn't know the friend levels I highlighted in this book. I didn't recognize Heather was in the "always attracted to" level of friendship. Additionally, we had already engaged in so much physically that the connecting neural pathways had already been developed. We had engaged in the dopamine and oxytocin "biochemical love potion" too many times.[216] Backing up from such a level of relationship to friendship was impossible.

I decided I could no longer date two people. I told my brain I was only dating Matt, but deep down, I knew what I was doing. I finally gained the courage to end my relationship with Heather for the final time through a conversation with Matt. He wanted me to be friends with her but was beginning to see perhaps it wasn't possible. One night, after a big fight between Heather and I, Matt wisely asked, "Laurie, what does Heather need?" The Holy Spirit aligned with my mind, and I knew the only true answer: "Not me. She needs not me." I could not end it for me; it had to be for her good.

Within a few days, Heather and I were done. I thought I would die. It felt like half my heart was ripped away. The holes in my heart felt like a chasm of unending need. That's what idols do: they satisfy until they leave you worse than you began. I wanted to call her. I wanted to stare at her picture. I wanted to do anything but feel this pain. Instead, I fasted from anything to do with her. I celebrated a minute without her, then an hour, then a day. I didn't shame myself for missing her. I simply noticed and tried my best to pour my heart out to God . . . allowing Him to put balm on my ripped apart, hole-riddled heart. *I'm sorry, Jesus. Help me.*

The first months of our dating relationship were filled with his sitting with me while I wept over the breakup with Heather.

When I could smile again, I woke up to the idea that there was someone next to me after going through so much pain . . . and it was a guy. A kind, wise, Jesus-loving, me-loving guy. And I was falling for him—not men, but him. One day in Advanced Grammar class, in my final semester of college, I tore out my journal to write an epiphany. "I don't want to get married," I wrote, "but I want to marry Matt." Matt and I had just had breakfast together, and I couldn't help but see our hearts were intertwining. I knew we couldn't, wouldn't, and didn't want to have a stereotypical marriage I saw depicted on TV—where the wife is outwardly subservient and secretly resents him (and he her). I did want a permanent partnership with Matt. Not with all men—but Matt.

We prayed about it, and within months God broke us up, too. "I'm sorry," I said in a coffee shop. "God is directing me to say, 'no.'" I knew it like I knew my eyes were blue. It wasn't supposed to be.

That was when the start of this book began. Every minute of every day, I thought a woman was right for me. Matt was hardly a thought.

I am so grateful for that season because none of what I wrote here—this entire Hole in my Heart journey—would have happened. I have no doubt if we had married before I engaged in the journey with Carolyn, our story would have ended very differently. At best, we would have had a marriage filled with incredible turmoil, and at worst I would have left him within the first year.

We are now staring down the barrel of our eleventh year of marriage, and it is good. So good. It is also very hard. But I don't know one super-straight marriage, friendship, or church trying to pursue oneness who wouldn't use the same descriptions: deep relationships are good and hard—difficult but worth it. It's how my relationship with Jesus is.

How We Began Again

A few months into my healing journey with Carolyn, I attended a small, local church that was definitely more on the charismatic side of things. I liked it. It threw me enough out of my comfort zone to help me feel safe. They prayed and sang loudly, and I stood there, crying anonymously.

But I wasn't anonymous to God. As I lamented one Sunday morning, I thought I sensed the Lord saying to me, *Laurie, you need to receive from Me.* Receive from Me . . . what? "What does that mean, God?" I instantly got an image of two baby girls in my mind. *Daughters.* No way. "Who would ever marry me? How could I ever have kids?" I know it is possible and wonderful for single parents to adopt children, but I did not sense that as my calling. I felt I would be single forever—super single. Just me. Me and Jesus. I wanted to get my doctorate and teach on one of the coasts. *Daughters? Who would ever love me or take me with my history?*

Within seconds, a total stranger made a beeline to me from the back of the church. She was a very soccer-mom-looking mom. Someone you might chat with at the grocery store while waiting in line. "I'm so sorry," she said, "you don't know me, but God just told me to come up to you and tell you to receive from Him." My jaw dropped. I didn't get this sort of stuff happening to me on the regular. I went to a non-denominational church for most of my life. We didn't have "words" for each other. But she did. God did. My tears turned to sobs. She hugged me and walked away. I never saw her again.

About two months later, one of Matt's friends called me, and I messaged Matt about the funny conversation I had with this friend. Matt and I broke up so amicably that we still talked occasionally in a very friendly, platonic way. I thought we were permanently done, but our friendship wasn't. When I pushed "send" on the message to him this time, however, it was as if a wave washed over me. *Oh no, I still love him.* I felt all the connection return. God paused our relationship when we broke up, but when I pushed "send" He un-paused the love.

I emailed Matt after a week of arguing with God over the matter. *What if he is in love with someone else? Don't mess with me, God! You know how sensitive I am!*

Matt and I met at a burger shop one week later, and I put my heart on the table next to the French fries. "So . . . I still love you." He was shocked. He thought I was meeting to tell him I was seeing someone else. "I am interested, it's just . . . there is another woman," he said. It was the woman he had liked for four years before I came along. He was going to visit her that weekend.

So, we left it as, "We will see."

We did not see the literal lightning strike coming. While Matt watched the Little League World Series,

God let a lightning bolt out of His hands to hit Matt's house. Matt was safe, but everything electrical he owned was fried. He couldn't afford to visit the other woman because he had to replace his stuff. Instead, he visited his family. "Laurie is back in the picture," he said to them. "I don't know what to do."

"Laurie? We love Laurie!" they replied. He prayed, wrestled over our differences, thought through how we connected, and made a decision.

I knew none of this. I may or may not have checked his Facebook status one thousand times over the next two weeks.

I also prayed, surrendered my will, un-surrendered my will, prayed, re-surrendered my will, and tried not to let my heart either detach or hope too much in Matt. I wanted my hope to be primarily in God, with people as the supporting cast. But I was a baby at learning how to live this out. I knew how to live solitarily or obsessed with another person. I was learning balance.

We met for coffee in the same spot we broke up. Matt smiled, "If you're in, I'm in. This is it. There is no more praying about it, no more waiting. If we get back together, we are on the road to marriage." I agreed.

We were engaged the next month and married four months after.

Nearly six years later, our first daughter was born. Two years later, we met our second baby girl. I could be wrong, but their faces look a lot like the images I saw that morning in church when I thought I heard God say, *Receive from Me.*

God was, has, and is restoring me, and I am learning to receive the fruit of it. He was, has, and is restoring Matt, and he is learning to receive it. He has not changed anything about my sexual attractions (I'm still attracted to women . . . so is Matt, come to think of it), but He has taught us how to journey with hope while giving us gifts along the way: Matt, our daughters, Amber, Dave, my professor, our mentor, our friends, and the Body of Christ.

How We Are All One

I must take a minute to look into the eyes of the single person. My kids, Matt, and my friends are a gift in obedience to God, but your gifts may be different. If God is calling you to celibacy as a way to honor God with your sexuality, gifts for you may be a fulfilling job, a great group of friends, a solid mentor, and overflowing joy. God chooses how He will both refine and gift us. He knows our Core Needs. He knows the God-honoring vehicles that will help us meet those needs. It may not look like we want, but it will look like He wants—with Him at the center, with Him as each of our husband.

"Fear not; you will no longer live in shame. You will no longer remember the shame of your youth and the sorrows of widowhood. For your Creator will be your husband. The LORD of Heaven's Armies is his name! He is your Redeemer, the Holy One of Israel, the God of all the earth. For the LORD has called you back from your grief . . . For the mountains may move and the hills disappear, but even my faithful love for you will remain. My covenant of blessing will never be broken," says the LORD, who has mercy on you (Isa. 54:4–6, 10).

As we learn and grow in oneness with the Body of Christ, our marriage to Jesus becomes more fulfilling and holistic, we become more whole, and we find a place to belong in this mysterious thing called the Body of Christ. What we need is not more good, old-fashioned heterosexual marriages, but more humans who are willing to surrender *all of who they are* to Jesus Christ no matter what. Such surrender may lead to a male + female marriage, but it may also lead to a celibate life of surrender. It may lead to committed, platonic friendships in community. But it unquestionably leads to oneness. "I pray that they will all be one, just as you and I are one—as you are in me, Father and I am in you. *And may they be in us*" (John 17:21).

May they be in us. Not "may marriages be in us" or "may people who struggle with holy sins be in us," but may "disciples" and "all who will ever believe in [Jesus] through their message" be in us (John 17:20). If we believe, if we lean into love, and if we begin living into the calling He has for us, we are offered oneness.

Perhaps you have experienced a glimmer of this while serving your church, playing on a sports team, hanging out with your family, or doing your job. Have you ever had a moment where it feels like the team is not a bunch of individuals, but one joyful unit? I am convinced that even if the location is Christian or "secular," those moments of oneness foreshadow the oneness God designed for His image-bearers.

There are times my ministry team and I look at each other and simply smile. Our hearts are full, our callings united, and our mouths can't help but overflow with sentences of love and joy. "I love you guys," our chairman said at the end of an especially uplifting and deep conversation surrounding our calling. It was still early in our relationship, and he might have felt the risk of saying it, but he still let it bubble out of his mouth. We said it back, "Love you, too!" and we meant it. Matt and I looked at each other and smiled as we walked down the stairs and into the sunshine. In that moment, we felt closer to one another in our marriage, we felt closer to our mentor, closer to our team, closer to the Body of Christ, and closer to Jesus. There was no sexual action involved in any of this oneness facilitation. There was love. Love does not always involve sex, but it always involves invitational, submitted-to-God-and-each-other oneness. "Make me truly happy by agreeing wholeheartedly with each other, loving one another, and working together with one mind and purpose . . . Be humble, thinking of others better than yourself" (Phil. 2:2–3). "Above all, clothe yourselves with love, which binds us all together in perfect harmony" (Col. 3:14). "[Christ] holds the whole body together with its joints and ligaments, and it grows as God nourishes it" (Col. 2:19). "Just as our bodies have many parts and each part has a special function, so it is with Christ's body. We are many parts of one body, and we all belong together" (Rom. 12:4–5).

When the world sees our marriages, our teams, our churches, and the growing Body of Christ leaning into this loving oneness, "the world will believe [God] sent me," Jesus said (John 17:21). When we, as broken, beloved, wandering sheep, love one another, lament together, forgive one another, confess to each other, celebrate together, fast together, work to till our fields together, and submit all of us to Jesus together—married, single, gay, straight, porn-addicted, anxiety-addicted, cheating, prideful, prone to alcoholism, or something else—those are the moments the world will know Jesus Christ is Lord.

The gospel is here, too. From death comes life. From surrender comes hope. From losing we win. From giving up we find belonging. It is the upside-down Kingdom, and it is the way to care well for our hole-riddled hearts.

Reflection Questions:

1. If you are married, can you relate to leaving a gate open on your marriage covenant? Do you let any animals in named "What If"? If you are not married, how committed are you to your friendships and church? Do you let the gate open on your own commitment to a cat named, "What If"?

2. Have you seen sex be ultimate (an idol) in the Church and in the world? How so? How have you seen it be ultimate in your life?

3. Think of a close relationship you have, and consider the eight ways to move toward oneness we recommend. Which two do you need to focus on this week? How can you "do the next thing" with a focus on those two?

4. Have you ever had a moment where it feels like the team is not a bunch of individuals but one joyful group of comrades? How did you get there?

5. What stood out to you from our story? Where can you relate? Where do you differ?

_____

_____

_____

6. Have you had a moment when you knew God was speaking to you? What was it?

_____

_____

_____

7. What is the next practical step you can take as you close this book? What is the next thing for you to do? A study? A reflection on a certain chapter? Reaching out to one friend who seems to be safe? Take some time to rest with Jesus in Safe Place and ask Him.

_____

_____

_____

_____

EPILOGUE: THE END OF THE PHONE CALL

"A disciple is someone who moves toward their bankruptcy, their poverty, toward their need for God . . . and that's where [they] find him. That's where God can be unleashed in and through us. All we need is need."
—*Rod VanSolkema*[217]

"I pray that God, the source of hope, will fill you completely with joy and peace because you trust in him. Then you will overflow with confident hope through the power of the Holy Spirit."
—*Paul*[218]

When no one called me on my pink flip phone, I made a commitment in that moment: *If I make it, if somehow I make it through this impossibly hopeless tension, I want to be that hope-calling voice for someone else. I want to look even half-a-step behind me at someone walking my same path and say, "Hey, don't give up, there is hope for you."*

A decade later, I finally offer you my hopeful, hole-riddled heart. It is my greatest desire that what I wrote here is not a one-time read, but an ongoing resource of life-giving information because it is tapping into the bottomless source of hope: Jesus Christ.

This is where we end the phone call, but not forever. You are welcome to reach out anytime. It's what I wanted when I was wrestling the most, what I received through Carolyn, and what I can receive and give now alongside friends and mentors. I hope you can find your own Carolyn and your own group you can trust, but until then, we want to be here for you.

Don't give up. If there is hope for me, Matt, and other sexually broken people, there is hope for you, too. This is not because we are all especially broken—but because we are all especially loved.

APPENDIX A: GLOSSARY OF IMPORTANT TERMS

Affirming

People who are affirming believe the Bible affirms or allows same-sex marriage.

Cisgender

Pronounced "sis-gender." People who do not experience any disconnect with their biological sex. So, a woman with no disconnect to her gender and no attraction to her same sex would say, "I am a cisgender, straight female."

Come out

To tell people about your journey with sexuality and/or gender. This is a very big, often terrifying step in the life of any LGBT+/SSA person because micro- and macro-rejections are frequent and traumatic.

Gay lifestyle

This is a phrase that should not be used. What do we mean when we say "gay lifestyle"? Lots of gay sex and pride marching? Is that true of every gay person? What about celibate gay people who are submitting their sexuality to the lordship of Christ? Is that a gay lifestyle? (What's a straight lifestyle?) To preach the gospel, we would do well to say, "He/she is 'out.'" or "They identify as gay, and she is partnered," or, "They engage in same-sex behavior," etc.

Historical Christian view of marriage

We use this term to mean we believe God's design for marriage is one man, one woman for life. This is also known as *non-affirming*. [See also "marriage."]

LGBT+

Lesbian, gay, bisexual, transgender people. These can be Christians or not and celibate in their experience or not.[219] (You may see written LGBTQ+ with a "Q" toward the end. The "Q" stands for "Queer." This word is being used more as a catchall to describe sexual minorities. "The queer community" can be exchanged equally for the "LGBT+ community.")

+

You say, "plus." Plus is used to include people who identify as another letter in the sexual identity alphabet.

Love the sinner/hate the sin

People who identify as gay and believe same-sex behavior/marriage is allowed by God do not see it as sin. Rather, it is simply who they are. To say, "I hate your sin but I love you" does not make sense. You might as well say, "I hate you." Instead, say, "I love you. No matter what." When it comes up you could say, "I believe God defines marriage as two opposite-gendered people in a one-flesh union for life, but I still love you. No matter what."

Marriage
We define marriage as two opposite-gendered people in a covenant one-flesh union for life. When people of the same gender decide to marry, however, we do not describe their marriage as a "marriage" (with quotes) out of respect to them as image-bearers of a holy God.

Orientation
Your default sexual attraction.

Other letters in the LGBT+ alphabet
There are many. This book's primary purpose is not to explain what they are, but rather to get at the heart behind some of the reasons someone may want to be called a certain letter. All I will say about these letters is to encourage you not to laugh at them, but to honor the person who wants to identify as one of them. Use the words someone wants to be called so the gospel can be preached at the heart level.

Queer
This is an umbrella term for sexual minorities or those who may identify as LGBT+. This was once a rude term, but it has become commonplace and acceptable among LGBT+ people if used kindly.

Pronouns
To use the name/title/pronoun of the individual requesting it is kind, graceful, and hospitable. It also helps us earn the right to speak to hearts—which is what matters most. "You blind Pharisee! First wash the inside of the cup and the dish, and then the outside will become clean, too," Jesus said in Matthew 23:26. Let's not foster Pharisaism by demanding an exterior change first.

Reparative therapy/orientation change therapy
The definition of the very controversial practice of reparative therapy varies. The overarching goal of reparative or orientation-change therapy is to change a person's orientation from gay to straight. This is not nor has it ever been a part of Hole in My Heart Ministries' practice.

Same-sex attracted (SSA)
People who choose not to identify as gay, lesbian, bisexual in referring to their sexual attraction may say, "I experience same-sex attractions," or "I am someone who has same-sex attraction." People choose to do this for a myriad of reasons. This is how Laurie chooses to identify.[220]

Sexual and gender fluidity
This is the idea that sexual preference or gender identity is malleable and even choosable.

Straight

Heterosexual. These are people who do not experience same-sex attraction.

Transgender

An umbrella term for anyone who doesn't identify with their biological sex or feels some sort of disconnect with their biological sex. They most often wrestle with gender dysphoria, the condition of feeling one's emotional and psychological identity as male or female as opposite to their biological gender.

APPENDIX B: SOME PROMISES AND SOME CAUTIONS

Our Promise:

Our only promise to you as you walk through this book is to read a story of hope because of the power of the gospel. We pray you will find hope because of Jesus, community, your own vulnerability, and in the power of the gospel in your life.

We Do Not Promise:

Please do not read this book thinking your orientation will change or something broken will automatically be "fixed." God knows what will glorify Him most and simultaneously fill us with abundant life. That may come in the form of a brokenness with which you may journey your whole life. Thanks be to God for His faithfulness through it all.

Some Cautions:

Caregivers (therapists, pastors who counsel, camp counselors, youth pastors, mentors, small group leaders) and **Care-Abouters** (You care about people and may be a friend, spouse, sibling, neighbor, etc. of someone wrestling with something related to sexuality):

This book can be helpful for you, but please do not offer this book to anyone without first reading it and understanding the main concept: The gospel is equally good for you as it is for me. If by the end you see yourself equally as broken and beloved as the next broken and beloved person, then and only then do you have our blessing to offer it as a gift to someone to read or not read. (They choose. Forced obligation will only change behaviors, not hearts. The behavior change breeds resentment, and from what we have seen, it only causes changes that last between 1–6 months.)

For Parents of LGBT+ Kids:

You get your own category because you potentially care for and/or about an LGBT+/SSA person—depending on their age. This book can help you understand some of the heart behind your own broken sexuality and your child's to be able to care for and about your child better. Our hope is these pages will help you have the eyes of Jesus for them and words to approach their hearts so that relationships stay intact no matter what.

We strongly recommend not going through this book with your child or demanding they read it. The reason for this is not because you are the cause of your child's sexuality, but you have emotionally injured your child in some way at some point. Let me say it again: You are not the cause of your child's sexuality, but you have wounded them. Matt and I know every word written in here, but we have and will hurt our children. Children cannot grieve with us the pain we have caused them. Matt's and my kids will need a counselor and/or spiritual mentor outside of our counsel for their pain. So will yours—no matter how they struggle.

So why even read this? Our hope is that this book may give you better understanding and better vocabulary to improve the relationship with your child.

We *do* recommend that you *offer* your children a godly mentor or counselor. If your child lives in your home, we recommend working through your own heart while reading these pages, and then offering (only *offering not demanding*) it to your child if you think they would benefit. We recommend finding a mentor for them to go through this book with them. This mentor should love God, have the same traditional, biblical perspective of sexuality as you, and grasp what is written here for themselves and their own hearts first.

We also recommend you find a group for yourself with whom you can grieve and pray. The healthiest parents we meet are those who realize their own need for a Savior and have a group of people with whom they can pray, grieve, and live in hope-filled tension together. Your child has caused you pain as well, but as the parent, you do not get the freedom to bleed all over your child. Take that grief to God and your prayer group. If you take it to your young or adult child, they may feel responsible for you and potentially resent you for put a weight on them they were not meant to carry. You have real grief, but your child is not the recipient of your grief. God, your family, and your friends are.

APPENDIX C: WHY DON'T I CALL MYSELF GAY?

I identify as a Christian who experiences same-sex attractions. Actually, my favorite way to describe myself is, "a beloved and broken human who, when she struggles with lust, it's toward women." Yes. I like the long-form description as opposed to anything else. However, I will use "I experience same-sex attractions" to shorten it a bit.

The term "same-sex attraction" sets some people on edge. They feel it is a nod to the days of reparative therapy, implies self-hatred, and is an inaccurate description of someone's personhood. To say "same-sex attracted" (SSA) is to take an integral part of you and put it to the side of a person—an impossible task.

For me, it is a more accurate description of how I see the world. I was never burned at the hands of reparative therapy or some sort of evangelical agenda who forced the phrase down my throat. I found it and chose it. The phrase simply helps me describe how I am, not who I am. I am a Christian. How I see the world is as someone who experiences same-sex attractions.

To be honest? I would like to be able to call myself "gay." It is my default attraction and orientation, but I simply cannot do it. When I mentally put on the glasses of "gay" and look around, I begin to posture myself in ways in relationships to other women that is either in a position of need as a victim or of trying to receive from them via flirting. I, Laurie Krieg, cannot worship God that way. I cannot stay committed to Matt that way.

Identifying as gay would make my external life so much easier, but I do not believe I would honor God or my husband in my mind. I would be more tempted to get my need to belong, to be affirmed, and to be seen as unique (Core Needs) from my gay identity. I would more frequently cheat on both God and Matt with idols in the secret spaces of my hole-riddled heart. You may not see it, but God would.

But that's just me. It is not everyone's story.

Greg Coles, a friend of mine who identifies as a gay Christian and wrote the book *Single Gay Christian*, helped me understand why identifying as gay (while maintaining a chaste life) is the most God-honoring thing for some people to do. "In some ways, I wish I could call myself same-sex attracted," he said. "I could fit into the evangelical church so much more easily if I did. But for me, doing that would be more prideful than calling myself gay. I would be distancing myself from other sexual minorities, pretending that I'm not *really* like them, just to gain more respect from church communities. It is humbler for me to identify as gay."[221] God will use whatever will make us most like Him, and He is humble. "You must have the same attitude that Christ Jesus had. Though he was God, he did not think of equality with God as something to cling to. Instead, he gave up his divine privileges; he took the humble position of a slave"

(Phil. 2:5–7). For Greg the humblest position is to take the descriptor of "gay." For me, it is to say, "I experience same-sex attractions" or my favorite long-form description.

You may choose to follow me, Greg, or someone else in this. But no matter what, all of us need to remember the secret places of our hearts matter most to God. "People judge by outward appearance, but the LORD looks at the heart" (1 Sam. 16:7). The self-descriptor that keeps Him in the top position of worship in our hearts is the identifier we must choose.

APPENDIX D: SIGNS OF SAFE PEOPLE

AKA: How Do You Know If Someone Is Safe to Come Out To?

Before I answer that question, I must say what I mean by "come out." I am advocating for everyone who experiences a same-sex attraction, another type of attraction, or incongruence with their biological gender to *come out* as someone who experiences this. People may choose a sexual minority letter or not. Although I do not often choose to identify with a letter, I refuse to cast a stone on those who do. I will not rest until every type of temptation or struggle is allowed within the Church—no matter how anyone identifies. Our motto at Hole in My Heart Ministries is "All fall short. All are loved." That is either true for all of us, or it is true for none of us. "*All* fall short of God's glorious standard," Paul said in Romans 3:23 (my emphasis added). "God loved the *world*," Jesus said in John 3:16. He didn't love part of the world or only the straight world, but the whole world—from drag queens to transgender people to straight folk.

But just because God says He died for us equally and loves us equally, it doesn't mean everyone in the Church believes it. Some do, some don't. What we really believe comes to the surface when we are tired or stressed—when we don't have our church face on. (Or sometimes exactly when we do.) "I mean, I don't want to judge, but . . ." You better believe that 99% of the time the end of that sentence is judgmental. "We vilify the sins we don't struggle with," my friend Preston Sprinkle says.[222] So, how can we weed out the safe people from the not-safe? Honestly, truly, you can never know for certain. I have thought certain people were safe. I had been in relationship to them for a long time, but the outright rejection they expressed at my sharing my story was excruciating.

So, how can you know if someone is safe? Even if you may not know know? Here are some tests to see if someone is safe before you share your story or ask them to journey with you:[223]

Tests to Know If Someone Is Safe:

I. **Ask about national issues concerning the LGBT+ conversation, and look for how the person responds.** The question might be, "What do you think about the some of the laws our president is putting in place concerning LGBT+ people?" [224]

- **Unsafe Person**: They might be spitting mad, overtly happy, or pulling out his or her prepared monologue on how same-sex behavior and LGBT+ people are one of the primary things destroying our nation. You would hear things that would signify they do not see LGBT+/SSA people as individual people with hearts made by God, but as an issue to be silenced. You may also hear the other side: They say how thrilled they are with certain bills being passed that do not hold to a traditional, biblical perspective of sexuality.

- **Safe Person:** Safe people display thoughtful empathy and compassion for humans, while kindly nodding to the need for honoring God's design for family. They might say things like, "I have wrestled with this," and "I really care about the hearts of LGBT+ people," and "It is difficult to navigate grace and truth well." You do not hear rage. You hear wrestling.

II. **Ask about policies in your local church concerning the LGBT+ conversation.** A question may be, "One of my gay friends wants to come to church with me. What do you think the church policy is on that?"

- **Unsafe Person:** You will hear some of the same reactions as Unsafe People reacting to national issues: Extreme emotions and an unwillingness to see all sin as equal. (If you ask a follow-up question about whether your friend who is sleeping with someone of the opposite gender could come and they say, "Yes," that's sin inequality.) Easy paragraphs will slip off their tongue of unrighteous anger and sweeping generalities. On the other extreme, you may hear phrases like, "I am so glad that more and more churches are coming to their senses by allowing same-sex marriage in the church. I hope our church does the same."

- **Safe Person:** You will hear similarities to Safe People reacting to national issues: Wrestling with how to carry out a biblical theology, concern for LGBT+/SSA people they *know* (not a deal breaker, but it is ideal if they know someone well), and an awareness of their own weak areas. Safe people do not speak in us versus them language. They see everyone as needy.

III. **Directly ask their theology of sexuality.** "What do you think the Bible says about same-sex marriage? What do you believe?"

- **Unsafe Person:** Unsafe people are on either extreme of this conversation. They will say something like, "The gays are the downfall of the church!" Or on the other side: "Paul got it wrong, and Jesus wouldn't want anyone to be sad. Love is love."

- **Safe Person:** I am always listening for five things when I ask about sexuality directly:

  1. Humility. I want to hear statements of equality about our need for Jesus. The gospel raises the bar for all of us and cuts us all off at the knees with its conviction.

  2. Belief. I want to hear a statement of what they believe marriage is. "I believe marriage is for one man, one woman for life." Ideally, they also have well-thought-out reasons behind what they believe. They have studied good books (on either side).

3. Wrestling. The one-woman/one-man phrase should feel weighty when they say it. They cannot easily say, "It's wrong!" I want to hear people who have and are wrestling currently with how to live biblically. "This is tough. It is hard to love our neighbor with grace and truth."

4. Apology. Even if it is not overt, I want to hear some grief over how the church has held a theology of sexuality in the past. "We have done this poorly. We have handled marriage and sexuality in general poorly."

5. Relationship. If someone already knows an LGBT+/SSA person and is *still in a gracious relationship* to them, I can likely assume they will have a good relationship with me.

6. Offering. God is a gentleman. He did not make us robots who are *required* to give up all things for the sake of the cross. He does not demand; He offers. I know people are safe when they simply offer the love that has wrecked them.

IV. **Share your story.** After prayerfully evaluating their responses above during time spent with them, I would encourage you saying something to the effect of, "I want to share with you some of my own journey, and it may not be easy for you to hear." What you share doesn't have to be specific or explicit, but I would advise you not to veil pronouns. If you are a woman and dated a "she," say it. If you are a man and you have wrestled with gay pornography, say it. Yes, you may be rejected. But those people's rejection of you is not everyone's rejection of you and certainly not God's. "I am as likely to reject my people . . . as I am to abolish the laws of nature!" (Jer. 31:36) and "Even if my father and mother abandon me, the LORD will hold me close" (Ps. 27:10).

If I confidently share my story with a crowd—without apologizing even in my tone for my temptation—I am saying to the crowd, "I love me—flaws and all; God loves me—flaws and all. You can love me—flaws and all." This is never easy, even though I have come out in different ways to thousands of different people. It is difficult every time. But three things help:

1. Reaching out to friends for prayer and encouragement beforehand. Those friends reflect God by telling me they love me no matter what.

2. Immersing myself in the love of Christ through worship, meditating on verses, and quiet time alone.

3. Finding a spot in the room where I can envision Jesus. He's always for us. He is slow to anger, quick to love (Ps. 103:8). He is proud of me. Proud of you. Like my older sister Renee says, "He's always winking at you across the room when you feel unseen." I

picture Him in an empty chair every time I speak. Do it. It helps. As long as you are seeking Him even a shred, He will seek you back (James 4:8). He is for you even when people are not.

- **Unsafe Person**: Will reject you. They will see you as gross, wrong, terrible. They will look at you with conditional love. "You better stop that or God will condemn you." Or, they will tell you things that will not encourage you to dwell in a place of safety because it is not biblical love. They will encourage you to experiment or be "who you are" by engaging in same-sex behavior or relationships.

- **Safe Person**: Will encourage you to come out as someone who wrestles with this. They will hear your struggles. They will hear your pain. You can say anything—even, "This is who I am, and I am going to go sleep with someone of the same gender right now!" and they will stick with you for the long haul. They will not react, they will respond. "I hear you. I am not going anywhere." If they do react, they will apologize. They will be humble.

A Few More Thoughts:

For Caregivers/Care-Abouters: You may read some of the above and think, "I am not safe. I literally was not safe today." When we fail each other, let's commit to saying, "I was wrong." And "Would you please forgive me?" A broken spirit and a contrite heart God will not despise, and neither should we (Ps. 51:17). There is something about exemplifying the humility Christ embodied that speaks to God's image-bearers (i.e. people). It quells rage. "A gentle answer deflects anger" (Prov. 15:1).

For LGBT+/SSA People: No one is 100% safe 100% of the time. The church will fail you—no question. People will fail you—undoubtedly. You will fail the church and people—absolutely. But if we can go to God, forgive those who have hurt us, and understand how equally in need of the cross we all are (whether straight or LGBT+), then perhaps when we fail we will look with forgiving love at our brother and grateful love at the Father.

APPENDIX E: HOW CAN I PRACTICALLY LOVE MY LGBT+ NEIGHBOR (LIKE, TODAY)?

Have you heard of micro-aggressions? Try micro-kindnesses.

Micro-Kindnesses:

- Tip your LGBT+ baristas and servers well—especially if you talk about Jesus with them.
- Smile at the person whose gender you do not know. Ask them about their day, with no agenda except "I want to show love to this person" in mind.
- In conversations with LGBT+/SSA people, look for where you agree. "You like dancing? Me too!"
- When in a conversation with an LGBT+ person, if it makes sense, apologize for the church's way they have handled theology. (Not apologizing for theology, but how we have presented it.) We carry all of the Church's history on us the minute we say "I am a Christian." Even if we aren't Westboro Baptist, we carry the blood of their protests on us.
- Be humble in learning how you can live your theology better. (Before, you might never have gone to the Pulse massacre site in Orlando, but now you might—to lay flowers and grieve with those who grieve.)
- If in doubt, switch it out. If all you think is "gay people!" when you look at someone who is gay, mentally switch out their behavior with a sin you can more easily process (like sleeping with some one of the opposite gender before marriage, pornography engagement, etc.).
- Go out of your way to invite LGBT+ people to sit with you at church if they attend.
- Hug LGBT+/SSA people if they are okay with it (ask first).
- Ask questions to hear the answer, not say your thoughts. Then ask more questions.
- Don't use these words:
  - "Gay lifestyle." (What is a gay lifestyle?) Instead, use "she is out" or "engaging in same-sex behavior."
  - "Hate the sin, love the sinner." For affirming gay people, there is not sin involved. It is either "I am this" or "I am not." To say this phrase is ignorant of how it comes across. Instead say, "I love you as a person. No matter what." That's Jesus' heart toward us—no matter what.
  - Any "us versus them" language. Instead, try to see everyone equally in need of a Savior.
  - The word "normal." I hear that sometimes. "You seem so normal to me!" Is "normal" heterosexual? Is your sexuality—even heterosexual—not abnormal because of the fall? Who on earth has a pure, unblemished sexuality? So, "normal" is really a broken sexuality—not heterosexual sexuality.

Macro-Kindnesses:

- Get involved in LGBT+ homelessness and sex-trafficking work.
- Go to the Pulse Orlando massacre site and lay a flower. Grief is grief. There is not gay pain and straight pain. There is human pain.
- Support graceful, biblical initiatives of inclusion of people at your church.
- If laws are passed that make an LGBT+ person feel afraid (even if you agree with the law), go out of your way to tell them they are loved and seen. Because they are.
- When forming policies at your church regarding sexuality, make sure an LGBT+/SSA person is involved. They see things you do not.

APPENDIX F: THEOLOGY 101

The following excerpt was first posted on Dr. Preston Sprinkle's site, *The Center for Faith, Sexuality & Gender*. It is used with permission.

15 Reasons For Affirming Same-Sex Relations—and 15 Responses[225]
by Dr. Preston Sprinkle

If we were having this discussion 30 years ago, or even 20 years ago, very few people would have expected affirming Christians to defend their view with biblical arguments. For the most part, two positions dominated the dialogue: one that used the Bible and another that didn't. Most Christians thought that if you simply read the Bible, you'd clearly see that the Bible condemns all types of same-sex sexual behavior. End of story. No debate.

Regardless of whether you think the Bible is clear on this issue (and I actually think it is), there are a growing number of Christians, even evangelical Christians, who now hold to an affirming view of same-sex sexual relations. The debate is no longer about what the Bible says; it's about what the Bible *means*.

This distinction is crucial, and it means that people who wish to uphold the traditional Christian sexual ethic can no longer be content to ignore opposing views. Even if you are 100% convinced that the Bible condemns same-sex relations, it's still very important for you to know, wrestle with, and even consider the affirming arguments if you want to maintain a traditional view of marriage with any degree of thoughtfulness and credibility.

In this paper, we'll seek to understand why some Christians affirm the sanctity of consensual, monogamous, same-sex relations. We'll start with the biblical arguments used by affirming Christians, most of which have to do with the biblical prohibitions against same-sex sexual behavior found in Leviticus 18:22, 20:13, Romans 1:26–27, 1 Corinthians 6:9–10, and 1 Timothy 1:9–10. Then, in the second half of this paper, we'll address some general arguments against the traditional view of marriage.

Old Testament Prohibitions

The Old Testament doesn't say a whole lot about same-sex behavior. But there are two laws in Leviticus that clearly condemn it: Lev. 18:22 and 20:13.

"You shall not lie with a male as with a woman; it is an abomination." (Lev. 18:22, ESV)

"If a man lies with a male as with a woman, both of them have committed an abomination; they shall surely be put to death; their blood is upon them." (Lev. 20:13, ESV)

Both verses condemn male same-sex sexual behavior.[226] So how do affirming Christians address these two prohibitions?

Reason 1: Old Testament Laws Are No Longer Binding on Christians

Some affirming Christians point out that these commands are in Leviticus—the Old Testament law—and that Christians are no longer under the Old Testament law. Sure, it was wrong for Israel to engage in same-sex sexual behavior. But it was also wrong for Israel to eat pork, trim their beards, and gather sticks on Saturday. Christians, however, don't need to abide by these laws. They were for Israel. And they've been fulfilled and done away with in Christ.

While this affirming argument can still be found on Google, most thoughtful affirming Christians don't use it any more. It's not a very good argument, and here's why: Just because some laws in the Old Testament are no longer binding on Christians doesn't mean that no laws are. There are many Old Testament laws that are still binding on Christians, including several prohibitions right here in Leviticus: incest (18:6–18; 20:11–14, 17, 19–21), adultery (18:20; 20:10), child sacrifice (18:21; 20:1–5), bestiality (18:23; 20:15–16), theft (19:11), lying (19:11), taking the Lord's name in vain (19:20), oppressing your neighbor (19:13), and many others—all written within one chapter of the laws prohibiting same-sex behavior.

Just because *some* Old Testament laws aren't binding on Christians doesn't mean no laws are.

In fact, if you read Leviticus 18, you'll see that this chapter deals almost exclusively with sexual immorality, and all the laws about sexual immorality are carried over into the New Testament—adultery, incest, bestiality, and same-sex sexual behavior.[227] Ancient Jews used the word *porneia* to describe all these sexual sins, and *porneia* is roundly condemned by New Testament writers (e.g. Matt. 5:32; 15:19). Scot McKnight, a New Testament scholar, says it like this: "When you double click on the term *porneia* . . . it takes you to Leviticus 18."[228] It's hard to imagine why Lev. 18:22 and 20:13 would not apply to Christians, while these other laws would. In fact, when Paul prohibits same-sex behavior in 1 Cor. 6:9, he uses a word that formed from the same-sex prohibition in Lev. 18:22 and 20:13.[229] According to Paul, then, the Leviticus prohibitions carry authority for new covenant believers.

Reason 2: The Old Testament Was Patriarchal

Another way affirming Christians deal with the prohibitions in Leviticus is to point out that sexuality at that time was profoundly patriarchal. That is, men were more valued than women, and women were seen as little more than sexual receivers and baby makers.

What does this have to do with the same-sex prohibitions in Leviticus? Some affirming Christians argue that men were forbidden from having sex with other men because such an act would *treat another man as a mere woman.* In male same-sex intercourse, one man must act "like a woman" in the sexual act—receiving rather than giving. In a patriarchal culture, where women were viewed as property and much less valuable than men, such an act would be disgraceful.

So was a low view of women driving the same-sex prohibition? And if so, should we follow a command that's inherently demeaning towards women?

Here are two responses to this challenge. First, while the Old Testament world was deeply misogynistic (that is, it devalued women), the Old Testament itself is not. Certainly, there are some laws and statements that seem to uphold men as more valuable as women, but when considered against the backdrop of the rest of the ancient world, the Old Testament is quite liberating towards women. Several women are held up as heroes of the faith, more courageous than the men around them (Rahab, Ruth, Deborah, and Abigail, to name just a few). Plus, the creation account of Genesis 1 makes the claim—radical for that time—that women and men equally possess the image of God. Many ancients believed only kings possessed God's image. The Old Testament says all people, including every single female on the planet, were created in God's image. So, while the ancient world was misogynistic, it doesn't seem that the Old Testament itself reflects the same degree of patriarchy.[230]

Second, and most importantly, there's nothing in the actual text of Scripture (in Leviticus or elsewhere) suggesting that the reason men shouldn't have sex with each other is that they shouldn't act like "mere" women. Read through Leviticus 18 and 20 for yourself. Or read through the entire book of Leviticus. There's nothing in Scripture which says that men shouldn't have sex with other men because this would treat another man as a lowly, baby-making, kitchen-bound woman. The commands in Leviticus simply state in absolute and unqualified terms: men shouldn't have sex with other men. Affirming Christians who pump these commands full of patriarchal assumptions assume things about the text that are not clearly there.

Reason 3: Same-Sex Prohibitions Were Really About Domination and Exploitation

Another point sometimes raised by affirming Christians is that consensual, monogamous, same-sex relations didn't exist in the ancient world. Sure, it was common for masters to have sex with their male slaves, older men to have sex with younger teenage boys, or victims of war to be raped by their male conquerors. But these are acts of *sexual exploitation*, not consensual love.

So are the prohibitions in Leviticus only talking about *exploitative* same-sex acts (for instance, a master raping his male slave)? Or do they ban consensual same-sex acts as well?

The answer is both. Of course exploitative acts are forbidden. The Bible would never sanction a master raping his slave, or any other act of sexual violence. But *there's nothing in the biblical text that limits the prohibition to such acts of sexual exploitation.* Again, don't just believe me. Go back and carefully read the prohibitions. Do they mention masters or slaves or prostitutes or rape or older men having sex with teenage boys? The language of Leviticus simply says that men (not just masters, or older men, or victors of war) shouldn't have sex with other men (not just slaves, or younger boys, or war victims). There's nothing in the text or around the text that limits the prohibition to acts of exploitation.

Some affirming Christians say that the biblical text doesn't need to specifically mention exploitation since *every same-sex relationship in the ancient world was exploitative.* But this simply isn't true either. For what it's worth, we know very little about same-sex relations in the ancient world. But the evidence we do have is somewhat diverse. Sure, we have evidence of exploitative same-sex relations, but we have evidence of consensual relations as well.[231] So we can't just assume that all relationships back then were abusive. Some were, but some weren't. And Leviticus doesn't limit its same-sex prohibitions to abusive acts. All types of male same-sex behavior are condemned.

In short, if you look at the text and study its historical context, there's no evidence that Leviticus was only prohibiting certain types of same-sex behavior.

Reason 4: The Sin of Sodom Was Not Homosexuality

Before we leave the Old Testament, we need to mention the story of Sodom (Genesis 19). As you may recall, a couple of angels show up to Lot's house in the city of Sodom and the men of the city mistake the angels for men. After trying to have sex with the two angels, the Sodomites are struck with blindness as divine punishment for their evil attempt.

Some Christians point to this passage as clear evidence that God condemns same-sex sexual behavior. However, it's important to notice that what's happening in Genesis 19 is *not* consensual same-sex love; it's *attempted sexual violence*—like an ancient version of modern-day prison rape. If a man in prison rapes another man, it's usually not because the perpetrator was gay. It's an act of domination and power. Likewise, the men of Sodom were trying to gang-rape Lot's guests. If we're going to examine the text fairly, in this case, exploitation is the issue. The men of Sodom were not courting Lot's guests, bringing them flowers and asking them out for a romantic stroll under the moonlight. Consensual same-sex love is not the focus; sexual violence is. And, for what it's worth, whenever the Bible refers back to the sin of Sodom, it never mentions same-sex sexual behavior.[232]

It's true that if the men of Sodom had gone ahead and raped the two men (or angels), they would have violated Lev. 18:22 and 20:13. But it's important to stay focused on the main point of the passage and the main sin depicted there. Consensual same-sex sexual activity is nowhere to be found in Genesis 19, and yet consensual same-sex love is the pressing ethical question facing the church. To use the Sodom story as evidence that God prohibits consensual same-sex love is like using Donald Trump's Twitter account as evidence that cell phones are sinful.

Those of us who do hold a traditional sexual ethic must resist the temptation of racing uncritically to certain passages and overlooking what they actually say in order to find support for our view. We need to step back and think through how we're interpreting the Bible and how we're applying it to this discussion.

For an in-depth investigation of the story of Sodom, see our Pastoral Paper "Was Homosexuality the Sin of Sodom?" (Available at centerforfaith.com.)

New Testament Prohibitions

Three passages in the New Testament prohibit same-sex behavior. The most important is Romans 1:

> For this reason God gave them up to dishonorable passions. For their women exchanged natural relations for those that are contrary to nature; and the men likewise gave up natural relations with women and were consumed with passion for one another, men committing shameless acts with men and receiving in themselves the due penalty for their error (Rom. 1:26–27, ESV).

The other two times same-sex sexual behavior is mentioned are in 1 Corinthians and 1 Timothy:

> Or do you not know that the unrighteous will not inherit the kingdom of God? Do not be deceived: neither the sexually immoral, nor idolaters, nor adulterers, nor men who practice homosexuality, nor thieves, nor the greedy, nor drunkards, nor revilers, nor swindlers will inherit the kingdom of God (1 Cor. 6:9–10, ESV).

> [U]nderstanding this, that the law is not laid down for the just but for the lawless and disobedient, for the ungodly and sinners, for the unholy and profane, for those who strike their fathers and mothers, for murderers, the sexually immoral, men who practice homosexuality, enslavers, liars, perjurers, and whatever else is contrary to sound doctrine (1 Tim. 1:9–10, ESV)

In English, at least, these passages seem rather clear. So how do affirming Christians interpret them? Again, it's important to make sure we actually listen to and try to understand these arguments. Listening doesn't necessarily mean *agreeing*. But you can't disagree until you actually understand what it is you're disagreeing with. Real dialogue in search of the truth only happens when people on *both* sides of a conversation are willing to hear all the evidence, even evidence that threatens to change their minds. You can't be proven right unless you take the risk of being proven wrong.

Reason 5: It's Exploitation—Again

One of the most popular affirming interpretations for these New Testament passages is the same "exploitation argument" we saw in the Old Testament. Again, some say that the only type of same-sex relations that existed in the ancient world, including the Greco-Roman world of the New Testament, was exploitative—rape, prostitution, and pederasty, which refers to older men having sexual relations with teenage boys.

Our two-fold response to this argument is same one we gave above. In short, *look at the text* and *study its context.*

As with the Leviticus passages, there's nothing in these New Testament passages that mentions masters or slaves or prostitutes or rape or older men having sex with boys. In fact, there are several different Greek words for "pederasty," and none of them are used in these passages.[233] (None of them actually occurs in the New Testament.) Of course, the biblical writers would have condemned pederasty, but they didn't *only* condemn pederasty. All types of male-male sexual relations were considered to be outside of God's will and design.

What's fascinating is that several affirming scholars actually agree with this point. For instance, the late Louis Crompton, a self-identified gay man, was a brilliant scholar who wrote a 500-page book called *Homosexuality and Civilization.*[234] In it, he says:

> According to [one] interpretation, Paul's words were not directed at "bona fide" homosexuals in committed relationships. But such a reading, however well-intentioned, seems strained and un historical. Nowhere does Paul or any other Jewish writer of this period imply the least acceptance of same-sex relations under any circumstance. The idea that homosexuals might be redeemed by mutual devotion would have been wholly foreign to Paul or any other Jew or early Christian.[235]

Bill Loader is the world's foremost scholar on sexuality in ancient Christianity and Judaism, and he's an affirming Christian. He's published thousands of pages in eight books on the topic. Still, *he rejects the argument that the only same-sex relationships in the ancient world were exploitative.* Loader says that Rom. 1:26–27 included, but was by no means limited to "exploitative pederasty," "sexual abuse of male slaves," or "same-sex acts … performed within idolatrous ritual contexts."[236] And again: "It is inconceivable that [Paul] would approve of any same-sex acts if, as we must assume, he affirmed the prohibitions of Leviticus 18:22 and 20:13 as fellow Jews of his time understood them."[237]

The idea that New Testament writers were only prohibiting exploitative same-sex relations is neither biblically nor historically accurate.

Reason 6: Paul Condemns Having Sex Against One's Own Nature

This argument is based on Rom. 1:26–27, where Paul says, "For their women exchanged natural relations for those that are *contrary to nature*." Some affirming Christians argue that God is only condemning heterosexuals who have abandoned their natural desire for the opposite gender and pursue sexual relations with the same gender. In other words, the "nature" Paul's referring to is their natural sexual orientation. Straight people shouldn't have gay sex.

This interpretation, however, doesn't follow what Paul is actually saying. He does not say "contrary to *their* nature," but "contrary to nature" (*para physin* in Greek). The Greek phrase *para physin* was often used by other ancient writers to describe same-sex sexual relations.[238] The phrase wasn't used to describe sexual orientation. The Stoics, for instance, believed that same-sex relations were *para physin* since they went against the order of nature—a sort of moral code build into creation. Christians and Jews believed something similar, though they spoke in terms of a personal Creator who could be known through creation (a point made clear in Rom. 1:19–23).

The point is, Paul is not saying some people left behind their innate heterosexual urges to pursue same-sex partners for whom they felt no innate desire. He's saying that some people have gone against the Creator's will and design for sexual expression (that is, male-female marital relations) to pursue sexual relations with members of their same sex.

Given the context of Romans 1 and how para physin is used by other writers in Paul's day, it's unlikely that Paul is talking about people simply deviating from their own sexual orientation.

Reason 7: The Real Problem Was Excessive Lust

A similar affirming argument says that same-sex relations were condemned because Paul considered them the result of excessive lust. That is, straight men got bored having sex with women, and out of their lust, they explored new and kinky territory with other men.

Whereas the previous argument focuses on the *types* of same-sex relations, this argument focuses on the reasons why men were having sex with other males. Both arguments are trying to distinguish between same-sex relations back then and same-sex relations today.

It's easy to see how someone reading Romans 1 might come to this conclusion. Paul says that men "were consumed with passion for one another" (Rom. 1:27), which sure sounds like lust. But pay close attention to what Paul is writing. Is lust the only reason why these relations were wrong?

Paul doesn't actually say this. If you look at the broader context, Paul's point is that men departed from their Creator's intention by having sex with other males. Of course there's passion and desire involved. That kind of goes hand in hand with any sex act—gay or straight! (Could any couple have sex and *not* be "consumed with passion for one another?") But the passion or lust is not the reason why Paul says same-sex sexual behavior is wrong.

Other Theological and Relational Arguments

The arguments we'll cover in the second half of this paper deal with broader themes and questions that go beyond interpreting the five prohibitions against same-sex sexual behavior.

Reason 8: Understanding Same-Sex Laws Along a Trajectory Ethic

This one has arguably become the leading argument by thoughtful affirming Christians. In many ways, it's an attempt to get around the counterarguments I've given to the previous affirming arguments.

A trajectory ethic assumes that the Bible doesn't always give us a complete or fully developed position on all ethical matters. Take slavery, for example. The Bible never comes out and condemns slavery as an institution. However, we can see some rumblings of the institution being challenged, especially in the New Testament. That is, we can identify a *trajectory in the Bible that doesn't quite condemn slavery but is moving towards this goal.*

Some argue the same thing with women in the Bible. (The trajectory argument isn't the only argument for women's ordination, by the way.) The Old Testament appears to be patriarchal, but the New Testament is moving towards full equality and liberation. Some argue, therefore, that the biblical trajectory is headed towards the full inclusion of women into all areas of ministry and leadership. Since the Bible gives us an incomplete ethic (so the argument goes), we still see a residue of patriarchy in passages where Paul tells women to keep silent in church (1 Corinthians 14) and forbids them from holding leadership and teaching positions (1 Timothy 2). Follow the trajectory towards its logical conclusion, and these patriarchal commands fade away.

Let's just assume a trajectory ethic for slavery and women. The question is: Can we also identify the same trajectory for same-sex relations? Does the Bible begin to move away from prohibiting same-sex sexual behavior? Is there anything in the Bible to suggest that gay marriage might be included as part of God's intention?

Many affirming Christians say, "Yes!" But there's really no evidence for this. From Genesis to Revelation, there are almost no changes to God's parameters for sexuality and marriage. I say "almost" because there are some. Polygamy, for instance, is allowed in the Old Testament, but we see the New Testament moving away from it. Divorce too was allowed in the Old Testament, but Jesus himself tightened up on those laws in the New. Think about it. *When the Bible augments its vision for marriage and sexuality, it moves towards a stricter ethic, not a more expanded one.* We see movement towards the Genesis 1–2 ideal of one man and one woman bound together in an inseparable one-flesh union.

Reason 9: Christians Have Often Been on the Wrong Side of History Before

I often hear people point out that for hundreds of years, the church believed slavery was okay. We only recently realized, they say, that slavery is a horrible evil. Is not the current debate about same-sex relations the same thing? Non-affirming Christians are like our slave-owning forefathers. One day, we'll realize that we were on the wrong side of history.

In some ways, Christians have been on the wrong side of history when it comes to the LGBT+ conversation. Some Christians have mistreated, shunned, dehumanized, and failed to love LGBT+ people. We've not taken the time to listen or to learn from LGBT+ people, and some Christians wish that gay people simply didn't exist. History will look back and say, "What was wrong with you Christians?" just as we look back on our slave-owning forefathers and say, "What was wrong with you people?"

But this is a posture problem, not a theological problem. Believing that marriage is a one-flesh union between two sexually different persons and that God intends sexual expression to take place within this covenant of marriage doesn't mean we should mistreat or shame LGBT+ people.

Plus, the church's historic view of slavery is not the same as its historic view of same-sex relations. For the last 2,000 years, the church has always and unanimously viewed same-sex sexual relations as immoral. But the same unanimity has not existed in its view of slavery. Throughout church history, various religious and political leaders have opposed slavery. William the Conqueror (1027–1087), Saint Wulfstan (1009–1095), Anselm (1033–1109), Pope Paul III (1468–1549), and even the great theologian Thomas Aquinas (1225–1274) all said slavery was sin. Sociologist Rodney Stark writes, "The problem wasn't that the leadership was silent. It was that almost nobody listened."[239] In fact, not only did historic Christians dissent against slavery, but Christians also led the way in ending slavery in the 18th and 19th centuries.

Christians are far from perfect; it's why we need a perfect Savior. But it's not as if the entire body of Christ for 2,000 years was pro-slavery. The church has, however, held to a uniform belief about same-sex relations until the late 20th century (in the West). Yes, we should consider the possibility that we might have been wrong side of history. But we also need to consider the possibility that we might have been right—that perhaps 2,000 years of unanimity are not mere coincidence.

Reason 10: I Was "Born this Way," How Could It Be Wrong

This argument is often invoked on blogs and in popular media, even though scholars realize that it's not scientifically accurate. Some affirming Christians argue that gay people are "born gay" and should therefore be allowed to express their love within the context of a consensual, monogamous relationship. Put differently, since God made some people gay, he shouldn't punish them for engaging in same-sex relations.

There are several things wrong with this line of reasoning. First, it misunderstands God's involvement in human birth. While God is Creator and He gives life to the womb, every human since Adam is born into a fallen world where things "aren't the way they're supposed to be."[240] People are born with all sorts of biological, mental, and emotional traits that aren't naturally aligned with God's will. Simply because a person experiences a desire that appears to be inborn doesn't mean they should act on that desire—no matter how strong or seemingly fixed that desire is.

So even if some people were born with a fixed same-sex orientation, this wouldn't in itself mean they should engage in same-sex behavior. Even Justin Lee, founder of the Gay Christian Network, doesn't buy into this argument. He says:

> Just because an attraction or drive is biological doesn't mean it's okay to act on . . . We all have inborn tendencies to sin in any number of ways. If gay people's same-sex attractions were inborn, that wouldn't necessarily mean it's okay to act on them, and if we all agreed that gay sex is sinful, that wouldn't necessarily mean that same-sex attractions aren't inborn. "Is it a sin?" and "Does it have biological roots?" are two completely separate questions.[241]

And Justin is an affirming gay Christian. Still, he believes that the "born this way" argument isn't a good way to construct a Christian sexual ethic.

But are people "born gay?" Without getting caught in the weeds of research, the best scientists who have studied the question of orientation say that it's not that simple. There's most likely a complex blend of nature (biology) and nurture (environmental influences) that shapes same-sex desires. According to the American Psychological Association,

> [N]o findings have emerged that permit scientists to conclude that sexual orientation is determined by any particular factor or factors. Many think that nature and nurture both play complex roles.[242]

A recent major study on sexual orientation by Johns Hopkins University comes to similar conclusions.[243] Keep in mind, these aren't fundamentalist Christians trying hard to prove the "born this way" argument wrong. These are just scientists doing good scientific research.

So whether the cause of same-sex attraction is nature or nurture (or both), the Bible still prohibits same-sex sexual behavior.

Reason 11: Shouldn't Christians Just Love Everyone?

Many people say that the non-affirming view is inherently unloving. It's unloving, they say, to "deny a person's right" to pursue the romantic relationship they desire. After all, a same-sex relationship isn't harming anyone. Why do Christians care about what two people do in the bedroom? And didn't Jesus teach his followers to love people—all people—especially those have been marginalized?

Before wrestling with this argument, we must all check our hearts and ask: Have we been unloving towards gay people? Have you told a gay joke, laughed at a gay joke, looked down upon a gay person, or ignored someone who's wrestling with same-sex attraction? There are many ways in which straight Christians have not been loving towards gay people. When we hear the "What about Love?" argument, we need to first repent from any unloving thing we've said or done.

We also need to make a clear distinction between a societal ethic and an ethic for the church. I don't think it's the church's job to project a Christian ethic on the rest of society. When we talk about same-sex sexual relations or same-sex marriage, we are embodying and articulating a distinctive *Christian* ethic for the church—one that's based on Scripture and confirmed by tradition. Christians should be able to love people without forcing them to adhere to a Christian ethic.

As for the argument itself—that we should just love everyone—it rightly prioritizes love but wrongly defines it. Jesus tells us to "love one another as I have loved you" (John 15:12), and that last part is important. When Jesus loved his disciples, he didn't always (or usually) affirm their behavior or desires. It's worldly love, not Christian love, that says: if you love me, you'll affirm everything I desire to do and everything I believe to be true about myself. When Jesus loved people, He loved them towards holiness, not away from it. And this includes sexual holiness—as defined by Scripture.

Christian ethics can't be reduced to the secular code of "do whatever you want as long as it doesn't hurt anyone." It's true, most sins end up hurting other people. But some don't. If I bow down to an idol in the secrecy of my basement, I'm not hurting anyone. If my wife and I didn't have kids, and we happened to "fall out of love with each other," we wouldn't hurt anyone by getting a divorce. But the Bible never uses the "do whatever you want as long as it doesn't hurt anyone" logic for determining what is right and wrong.

As we love people, we must love them as Jesus loved them—towards holiness, not away from it.

Some people describe this posture with the phrase "love the sinner, hate the sin." I actually don't like this phrase. It sounds too self-righteous—as if we are standing over here shrouded in all our holiness, while loving all those other dirty sinners over there. At least, that's how the phrase sounds when gay people hear it.

Instead of "love the sinner, hate the sin," how about "love the sinner, hate your own sin, and let's pursue Christ together!" That's the texture of Christian love.

Reason 12: The Bible Hardly Talks About Homosexuality

It's true that Scripture mentions same-sex relations less than a dozen times. And for "verse counters," this must mean that it's not all that important. After all, the Bible mentions greed and the misuse of money in more than 2,000 passages! Why aren't we more concerned about the abuse of wealth than we are same-sex sexual behavior?

Let's linger on that last line for a second. Are we more concerned about same-sex sexual behavior than we are about the misuse of wealth? Why? Do we have a strong biblical case for our concern? Do we misuse wealth? Do we give generously to the poor? Will we inherent the kingdom of heaven if we haven't clothed the naked, feed the poor, and visited those in prison? Are you regularly practicing these things—things that Jesus said are essential for salvation (Matt. 25:31–46)?

God addresses the misuse of wealth and calls it a crime 400 times more often than He addresses same-sex sexual behavior.

Now, to be clear, just because some sins are address more often than others doesn't mean they're worse sins; or, if some sins are only addressed a few times, that doesn't mean they are merely misdemeanors in God's court. Followers of Jesus should pay close attention to both frequently and infrequently addressed sins. And just because something is mentioned only a few times in the Bible doesn't mean it doesn't matter to God. I may rarely tell my kids that they aren't allowed to drive my truck, but that doesn't mean it's not an important prohibition. And I may delve into lengthy sermons twice a day about why they need to brush their teeth, but this doesn't mean dental hygiene is more important than underage driving.

The point is, if we truly love Jesus, we will pay close attention to all of God's commands and not try to weigh them on the scale of significance based on frequency. God may have reasons unknown to us (and there are cultural and historical reasons as well) that explain why he mentioned some things only a few times while other commands seem to inhabit every other divine breath.

Reason 13: Jesus Never Mentioned Homosexuality

This is true. Jesus never explicitly mentions homosexuality. And some people have understood this silence to mean he either doesn't care about it or he probably would have affirmed same-sex relations. But this is reading way too much into Jesus' silence. Here's why:

First, Jesus was a Jew, and first-century Judaism was the context of his life and teaching. The topics debated with other Jews were always ones that were disputed within Judaism (like divorce or how to keep the Sabbath). But same-sex relations were never disputed within Judaism. Every Jew in and around Jesus' day believed that same-sex relations were against God's will. And this is probably why Jesus never mentions it. It wasn't relevant for his specific, Jewish context.

Second, although he doesn't mention same-sex relations, Jesus does mention "sexual immorality" more broadly. In Matt. 15:19, for example, he says, "For out of the heart come evil thoughts—murder, adultery, sexual immorality, theft, false testimony, slander." Again, every Jew in Jesus' day considered same-sex relations to be immoral based on the sexual laws in Leviticus 18. Even though Jesus doesn't directly mention same-sex sexual behavior, he does so indirectly.

Third, when Jesus *does* depart from a traditional Jewish sexual ethic, he doesn't expand that ethic but tightens it. For instance, divorce was debated within Judaism. Some Jews were strict about appropriate grounds for divorce, while others were more lenient. Jesus holds to a stricter view. The same is true with adultery. Many Jews believed that you hadn't committed adultery unless you actually slept with another person's spouse. But Jesus tightens the Jewish ethic: "But I say to you that everyone who looks at a woman with lustful intent has already committed adultery with her in his heart" (Matt. 5:28). Again, when Jesus does depart from a Jewish sexual ethic, he moves towards a stricter ethic, not a more lenient one. Based on what Jesus does say about sexual ethics, there's no evidence that he would have affirmed same-sex relations if the question came up.

In sum, Jesus' silence on same-sex relations cannot be taken as indifference or affirmation. We must interpret Jesus within his first-century Jewish context (and not our 21st-century Western one). For an in-depth paper on Jesus and homosexuality, see our Pastoral Paper "Why Didn't Jesus Mention Homosexuality?" (Available at centerforfaith.com.)

Reason 14: Isn't This Just an Agree-to-Disagree Issue?

This isn't precisely an argument for the affirming view, but it's often raised by people who question whether non-affirming Christians should even care about this issue at all. Is it really a big enough issue for Christians to fight about and divide over? Can't we all just agree to disagree—like some people do about, say, the timing of the rapture—and not let this divide us?

While I'm not a fan of creating disunity, Scripture always considers sexual immorality to be a very serious issue. Nowhere in Scripture does Jesus shrug his shoulders at sexual sin and say, "Well, there are different viewpoints on this issue, so let's not make a big deal about it." Whenever same-sex relations are mentioned, they are treated as serious deviations from God's will (Lev. 20:13; Rom. 1:26; 1 Cor. 6:9–10)

The Bible does talk about some ethical questions as "agree-to-disagree" issues. Romans 14 and 1 Corinthians 8–9 mention some so-called "grey areas" that Christians can disagree on, but sexual sins aren't among them. Whenever sexual sins are mentioned, they are profoundly serious and nonnegotiable. I'm not saying that Christians should just assume that the traditional view is correct. I believe every Christian should consider the reasons for each view and weigh them against Scripture. But I also think that Christians should consider the grave danger of calling something "righteousness" when God calls it "sin." We can't afford to throw up our arms and plead the fifth.

I don't think the question of what marriage is, or whether same-sex sexual relations are morally permissible, are agree-to-disagree issues. Our God, who created us as sexual beings and institute marriage in the Garden of Eden, has revealed to us his guidance on how to honor him with our sexuality.

Reason 15: Christians Don't Care About Gluttony and Divorce but Still Condemn Same-Sex Relations

This argument doesn't give any evidence for affirming same-sex relations; it simply points out that non-affirming Christians brush over other sins—like gluttony and divorce—so why should they care about same-sex relations?

Yes, it's true, some Christians (certainly not all) have been lax in their view of gluttony and have ignored the wide-spread problem of unbiblical divorces and remarriages. There's no excuse for this. We shouldn't respond in turn with another, "Yeah, but . . ." We should acknowledge it. Own it. And repent from it. In fact, I would go so far as to say that one of the blessings of the LGBT+ conversation is that it has forced the church to reflect on its own sins and ask the question, "How can we be more holy in our marital and sexual lives?"

That said, there's no logical or ethical or biblical reason why laxity in one area (gluttony or divorce) should encourage laxity in another (same-sex behavior). I can't imagine Jesus looking at the church's gluttony and divorce rate and saying, "Well, since you all have really dropped the ball by overeating and divorcing your spouses, I think it's only fair that you lighten up a bit more on my Father's sexual ethic."

With the divorce question in particular, we should acknowledge that not every divorce is against God's will. Jesus allows for divorce if there has been sexual infidelity (Matt. 5), and Paul says that if an unbelieving spouse leaves, the believing spouse is no longer bound to that marriage (1 Cor. 7). While divorce is never encouraged, the Bible does make some allowances. But the same cannot be said of same-sex sexual behavior. There's nothing in the Bible that views some types of same-sex behavior as permissible.

In short, we should respond to the "What about Gluttony and Divorce?" response by taking the gluttonous log out of our own eyes, so that we can help others who are struggling with sexual (including same-sex) temptations.

Conclusion

Here's the thing about these arguments—they're not the real issue. Logically and biblically, the traditional view of marriage makes the most sense of the Bible and Christian tradition. It's not primarily because of these arguments that so many Christians are changing their view about the historic Christian sexual ethic. Most often, Christians are changing their view because they want to show compassion toward LGBT+ people. Most affirming Christians think that the traditional view of marriage is incompatible with compassion, and they think that the only way to love LGBT+ people is to redefine the Christian view of marriage. The arguments discussed in this paper are important, but refuting these arguments won't usually change people's hearts. Love, not logic, contains more power in demonstrating the credibility of your view.

Until Christians can show compassion and empathy toward people LGBT+ people, our views will not carry much weight. Our ethics will feel cold and depersonalized—detached from the lives of real people. Compassion without truth is empty sentimentality; truth without compassion is lifeless and powerless in an age of justice. What we need is both. The gospel demands both: faithful allegiance to God's intention for human sexuality, and radical love extended to the marginalized.

FURTHER READING:

For a more thorough response to some of the affirming arguments mentioned above, please see the following books:

- Sam Allberry, *Is God Anti-Gay? And Other Questions about Homosexuality, the Bible, and Same-Sex Attraction* (The Good Book Company, 2013)
- Preston Sprinkle, *People to Be Loved: Why Homosexuality is Not Just an Issue* (Grand Rapids: Zondervan, 2015)

For a book that contains scholarly arguments for both affirming and non-affirming views, see:

- Preston Sprinkle (ed.), *Two Views on Homosexuality, the Bible, and the Church* (Grand Rapids: Zondervan, 2016)

ENDNOTES

1   Isa. 40:2. [All Bible passages are in the New Living Translation except where indicated.]

2   Henri Nouwen, *Turn My Mourning into Dancing* (Nashville: Thomas Nelson, Inc., 2001), 7.

3   See Christian psychologist Mark A. Yarhouse's book, *Homosexuality and the Christian: A Guide for Parents, Pastors, and Friends* (Bloomington, MN: Bethany House, 2010), for a more thorough explanation of his three categories of Gay, gay, and same-sex attraction—specifically chapter 6.

4   This book's purpose is not to argue for a traditional biblical sexual ethic, but instead to answer the question, "If we hold to a Christian sexual ethic, how do we live well?" For a further dissection of the theology, see Dr. Preston Sprinkle's thoughts in Appendix F.

5   Luke 15:11–32

6   For guidelines on how to lead or start a group, please visit https://www.himhministries.com/journey-well.html

7   See Appendix D: "Signs of Safe People" for more on this.

8   You are going to hear me talk about how I "experience same-sex attractions." For reasons why I describe myself this way instead of calling myself "gay," please see Appendix C: "Why Don't I Call Myself Gay?"

9   For a list of defined terms such as "reparative therapy," please see Appendix A: "Glossary of Important Terms."

10   Isa 49:9

11   Timothy Keller, *Center Church* (Grand Rapids: Zondervan, 2012), 3.

12   Rom. 3:23 (NIV)

13   Isa. 1:18

14   Rom. 6:6; Eph. 4:22

15   Rom. 7:18

16   Milton Vincent, *A Gospel Primer for Christians* (Bemidji, MN: Focus, 2008), 46.

17   Rom. 1:16 KJV, "I am not ashamed of the gospel of Christ: for it is the power of God . . ."

18   Isa. 49:9

19   Ps. 23:2

20   Kenneth E. Bailey, *The Good Shepherd: A Thousand-Year Journey from Psalm 23 to the New Testament* (Downers Grove, IL; IVP Academic, 2014), 37–52.

21   Prov. 15:14

22   Luke 19:10

23   American Psychological Association, "Answers to your questions: For a better understanding of sexual orientation and homosexuality," 2008, http://www.apa.org/topics/lgbt/orientation.pdf.

24   Lawrence S. Mayer and Paul R. McHugh, "Sexuality and Gender," *A Journal of Technology & Society*, no. 50 (2016), http://www.thenewatlantis.com/publications/number-50-fall-2016.

25 Gen. 6:5–6

26 Rev. 20:10

27 *For adultery:* Katrina Woznicki, "US Scientists Discovered Adultery Gene," News Amen (2010), http://www.newsamen.com/101138/us-scientists-discovered-adultery-gene.
For alcohol: "Genetics of Alcohol Use Disorder," National Institute on Alcohol Abuse and Alcoholism, https://www.niaaa.nih.gov/alcohol-health/overview-alcohol-consumption/alcohol-use-disorders/genetics-alcohol-use-disorders. For murder: Barbara Bradley Hagerty, "Can Your Genes Make You Murder?", NPR, July 01, 2010, http://www.npr.org/templates/story/story.php?story Id=128043329.

28 Rom. 8:22–23

29 Gal. 5:17, italics mine.

30 Keller, *Center Church*, 3.

31 Timothy Keller, The Word Made Flesh (podcast), December 13, 2009, http://www.gospelinlife.com/the-word-made-flesh-9207.

32 Rom. 1:16

33 Matt. 15:18

34 St. Augustine, translated by Maria Boulding, *The Confessions* (New York: New City Press, 1997), 35.

35 Ann Voskamp, *The Broken Way: A Daring Path into the Abundant Life* (Grand Rapids: Zondervan, 2016), 105.

36 Nouwen, *Turn My Mourning into Dancing*, 31.

37 Ps. 16:2 (NIV)

38 "Why Watching Porn Is An Escalating Behavior," Fight the New Drug (July 2017), accessed August 05, 2017, http://fightthenewdrug.org/why-watching-porn-is-an-escalating-behavior/.

39 Rom. 6:19

40 "A quote by Jalaluddin Rumi," Goodreads, https://www.goodreads.com/quotes/411483-the-cure-for-pain-is-in-the-pain.

41 Isa. 53:3

42 Nouwen, *Turn My Mourning into Dancing*, 7.

43 Michael Rosen, *We're Going on a Bear Hunt* (New York: Margaret K. McElderry, 2009).

44 *The Institutes of the Christian Religion*, 1.2.2., 43.

45 Acts 17:27

46 Voskamp, *The Broken Way*, 196.

47 The original idea was derived from Terry Wardle's Healing Care curriculum, 2002.

48 Sexual Assault Center, "What is a Trigger?" Psych Central, July 17, 2016, https://psychcentral.com/lib what-is-a-trigger/.

49 "Emotions," Merriam-Webster, https://www.merriam-webster.com/dictionary/emotions.

50 This version of the feeling wheel was created by Geoffrey Roberts, used with permission, https://imgur com/gallery/tCWChf6.

51 Susan David, "The Gift and Power of Emotional Courage," TED, 2007, https://www.ted.com/talks/ susan_david_the_gift_and_power_of_emotional_courage/transcript

52 Ibid.

53 "#58 Journey Toward Healing with Brandi Lea," Interview, *Mom Struggling Well* (audio blog), http:/ www.momstrugglingwell.com/podcast/58-brandi-lea.

54 See 1 Cor. 13:4–7.

55 See Gal. 5:17.

56 Chris Irvine, "Anger Is in the Genes," The Telegraph, May 2009, http://www.telegraph.co.uk/news/ science/science-news/5270316/Anger-is-in-the-genes.html.

57 There may be more, but we have listed the most common ones we see in our practice here.

58 Eph. 1:23

59 "Pleroma - New Testament Greek Lexicon - New American Standard," Bible Study Tools, http://www biblestudytools.com/lexicons/greek/nas/pleroma.html.

60 The following verses are not in their original context. However, they are chosen because even though there are some listed that are directly speaking to Daniel or the Israelites, for instance, the emotion behind God's heart for his creation in these verses is still true.

61 Ps. 27:10.

62 A.W. Tozer, *The Knowledge of the Holy* (New York: HarperCollins, 1978), 1.

63 Ibid.

64 The research data behind Andrew Marin's groundbreaking book, *Us Versus Us: The Untold Story of Religion and the LGBT Community* (Colorado Springs: NavPress, 2016), found that 54% of the LGBT community leave their faith as adults versus 27% of the general American population. 86% come from a church background as opposed to 75% of the general population. Shockingly, 92% of LGBT+ people would not require a change in theology in order to return to their faith. (In fact, the reasons they left are not directly related to theology, but instead because of negative personal experiences.) What we can learn from this is that an adjustment in the way we hold theology is required to care well for LGBT+ people. A change in theology is not. Check out his infographic here: https://books.thedisciplemaker. org/wp-content/uploads/UsVersusUs_Infographic.jpg (accessed September 3, 2017).

65 "Facts About Suicide," The Trevor Project, http://www.thetrevorproject.org/pages/facts-about-suicide.

66 The Institutes, 3.2; 3.6, 585–84.

67 Whenever we use capital-C Church, we are talking about the Church universal.

68 2 Thess, 2:16–17

69 1 Thess. 5:14

70 1 Thess. 5:21

71 For more on this, see "Signs of Safe People" in Appendix D.

72 Christa Black Gifford, *Heart Made Whole: Turning Your Unhealed Pain into Your Greatest Strength* (Grand Rapids, MI: Zondervan, 2016), 44.

73 *Healing the Wounded Heart: The Heartache of Sexual Abuse and the Hope of Transformation* (Grand Rapids, MI: Baker Publishing Group, 2016), 45.

74 Carolyn Schroeder, Healing Care Group discussion, January 7, 2015.

75 I first learned this from Carolyn, but she was taught by Terry Wardle, PhD, author of *Draw Close to the Fire.*

76 Dan B. Allender, *Healing the Wounded Heart*, 45.

77 2 Cor. 12:9

78 2 Cor. 1:4-5

79 John 14:16

80 Jason Moser and Andy Henion, "Talking To Yourself in the Third Person Can Help You Control Stressful Emotions," MSUToday, July 26, 2017, http://msutoday.msu.edu/news/2017/talking-to-your self-in-the-third-person-can-help-you-control-stressful-emotions/.

81 John 8:10-11

82 Henri Nouwen, *Turn My Mourning Into Dancing* (Nashville: Word, 2001), xv.

83 "Sexual Assault and the LGBTQ Community," Human Rights Campaign, accessed September 05, 2017, http://www.hrc.org/resources/sexual-assault-and-the-lgbt-community.

84 "Sexual Assault: The Numbers | Responding to Transgender Victims of Sexual Assault," Office for Victims of Crime, June 2014, https://www.ovc.gov/pubs/forge/sexual_numbers.html.

85 https://www.ncbi.nlm.nih.gov/pmc/articles/PMC3320670/; and https://www.ncbi.nlm.nih.gov/pmc/ articles/PMC3912575/; and http://www.nsvrc.org/sites/default/files/Publications_NS VRC_Research-Brief_Sexual-Violence-LGBTQ.pdf and http://www.hrc.org/resources/sexual-as sault-and-the-lgbt-community and http://www.thetaskforce.org/static_html/downloads/reports/ reports/ntds_full.pdf and https://www.bjs.gov/content/pub/pdf/ccsvsftr.pdf

86 "Bullying Statistics," Bullying Statistics - National Bullying Prevention Center, December 8, 2016, http://www.pacer.org/bullying/resources/stats.asp.

87 Human Rights Campaign, *Growing Up LGBT in America: HRC Youth Survey Report Key Findings*, (Washington, D.C: 2013).

88 Brian S. Mustanski, Robert Garofalo, and Erin M. Emerson, "Mental Health Disorders, Psychological Distress, and Suicidality in a Diverse Sample of Lesbian, Gay, Bisexual, and Transgender Youths," *American Journal of Public Health* 100, no. 12 (December 2010), DOI: http://ajph.aphapublications org/doi/abs/10.2105/AJPH.2009.178319.

89 http://www.thetrevorproject.org/pages/facts-about-suicide

90 Laura Kann, Emily O'Malley Olsen, Tim McManus, et al. "Sexual Identity, Sex of Sexual Contacts,

and Health-Related Behaviors Among Students in Grades 9–12 — United States and Selected Sites, 2015," MMWR Surveill Summ 2016; 65 (No. SS-9): 1–202. DOI: http://dx.doi.org/10.15585/mmwr.ss6509a1.

91 Grant, Mottet, Tanis, et. al. *Injustice at Every Turn*, 3.

92 Ibid, 2.

93 Rachel Banning-Lover, "Where are the most difficult places in the world to be gay or transgender?" The Guardian, March 01, 2017, https://www.theguardian.com/global-development-professionals-network/2017/mar/01/where-are-the-most-difficult-places-in-the-world-to-be-gay-or-transgender-lgbt.

94 Laura E. Durso and Gary J. Gates, "Serving Our Youth: Findings from a National Survey of Service Providers Working with Lesbian, Gay, Bisexual, and Transgender Youth who are Homeless or At Risk of Becoming Homeless," (Los Angeles: The Williams Institute with True Colors Fund and The Palette Fund, 2012).

95 Shahera Hyatt, "Struggling to Survive: Lesbian, Gay, Bisexual, Transgender, and Queer/Questioning Homeless Youth on the Streets of California," California Homeless Youth Project, http://cahomelessyouth.library.ca.gov/.

96 Durso and Gates, "Serving Our Youth," http://williamsinstitute.law.ucla.edu/wp-content/uploads/Durso-Gates-LGBT-Homeless-Youth-Survey-July-2012.pdf.

97 David Finkelhor, G. Hotaling, I. A. Lewis, and C. Smith, "Sexual abuse in a national survey of adult men and women: Prevalence, characteristics and risk factors," Child Abuse & Neglect 14, 19-28, (1990), DOI:10.1016/0145-2134(90)90077-7.

98 "Homelessness in America," Covenant House, https://www.covenanthouse.org/homeless-teen-issues-statistics.

99 Caroline Beaton, "8 Habits That Make Millennials Stressed, Anxious And Unproductive," HuffPost, May 24, 2017, http://www.huffingtonpost.com/entry/8-habits-that-make-millennials-stressed-anxious-and_us_5924f46be4b0dfb1ca3a0f8a

100 Jeremiah rightly talks about healthy shame regarding the promiscuous Israelites who cheated on God with gods. God says through Jeremiah, "That's why even the spring rains have failed. For you are a brazen prostitute and completely shameless" (Jer. 3:3), and "Are they ashamed of their disgusting actions? Not at all—they don't even know how to blush!" (Jer. 6:15). I would put this type of healthy shame under the title of godly conviction. See the chapter on confession where we talk more in depth about conviction and confession.

101 Terry Wardle, "Formational Prayer Seminar," seminar, Ashland Theological Seminary, Ashland, OH, January 13–16, 2016.

102 These two paragraphs are adapted from: John Regier, "The Soul in Pain" (Colorado Springs, CO: Caring for the Heart Ministries, 2009).

103 Alice Park, "Why Deep Breathing Is the Fastest Way to Calm You Down," TIME Health, March 30,

2017, http://time.com/4718723/deep-breathing-meditation-calm-anxiety/.

104 "Meditation Definition and Meaning - Bible Dictionary," Bible Study Tools, http://www.biblestudy tools.com/dictionary/meditation/.

105 John W. Kleinig, "The Kindled Heart: Luther on Meditation," *Lutheran Theological Journal* 20, no. 2 (1986), http://www.johnkleinig.com/files/2513/2695/2230/The_Kindled_Heart_-_Luther_on_ Meditation.pdf.

106 David G. Benner, *The Gift of Being Yourself: The Sacred Call to Self-Discovery* (Downers Grove, IL: InterVarsity, 2005), 40.

107 Ps. 62:5

108 The following process is what I journeyed through and learned one-on-one with Carolyn for about a year. Several years later, Matt and I were trained at Ashland Seminary at a Formational Prayer Seminar with Terry Wardle and the Healing Care team there. Although what we will guide you through here began with Carolyn and was adjusted with Terry, all of what I am writing is coming from our own mentoring and counseling experience. If you would like to learn more about the specifics of Formational Prayer, go to healingcare.org

109 Søren Kierkegaard and Walter Lowrie, *Christian Discourses: And the Lilies of the Field and the Birds of the Air; and Three Discourses at the Communion on Fridays*, (New Jersey: Princeton University Press, 1974), 324.

110 Timothy Keller, *Prayer: Experiencing Awe and Intimacy with God* (New York: Dutton, 2014), 62.

111 Ps. 62:5

112 R.A. *Torrey, Rewards of Prayer* (New Kensington, PA: Whitaker House, 2002), https://books.google. com/books?id=fQr2BgAAQBAJ

113 Matt. 19:26; Luke 5:27

114 Richard Foster, *Celebration of Discipline: The Path to Spiritual Growth* (San Francisco: Harper, 1988), 26.

115 Luke 5:16 (NIV). See also Luke 6:12; Matt. 14:13; 14:23, and Mark 1:35.

116 See Matt. 6:6.

117 Beth Moore, *Beloved Disciple: The Life and Ministry of John* (Nashville, TN: Lifeway Press, 2002), 32.

118 See *Mindsight* for a more thorough explanation of this. Also see: Ruth Buczynski, "Two Chemical Reactions That Happen in the Brain during Trauma," National Institute for the Clinical Application of Behavioral Medicine, August 4, 2015, https://www.nicabm.com/trauma-two-chemical-reactions-that-happen-in-the-brain-during-trauma/; Theresa Burke, "How Trauma Impacts the Brain," Rachel's Vineyard Ministries, http://www.rachelsvineyard.org/Downloads/Canada%20Conference%2008/ TextOfBrainPP.pdf; Adam Young, "Why Engaging Your Story Heals Your Brain," Adam Young Counseling, June 15, 2017, http://adamyoungcounseling.com/story-and-your-brain/.

119 For more on the interaction between sub-cortical and right/left parts of our brain, see: Marla Paul,

"How Traumatic Memories Hide in the Brain, and How to Retrieve Them," Northwestern, August 18, 2015, https://news.northwestern.edu/stories/2015/08/traumatic-memories-hide-retrieve-them/.

120 Lindsay Bicknell-Hentges and John J. Lynch, "Everything Counselors and Supervisors Need to Know About Treating Trauma" (2009). Paper based on a presentation at the American Counseling Association Annual Conference and Exposition, Charlotte, NC.

121 John Rigg, "The Effect of Trauma on the Brain and How It Affects Behaviors," YouTube video, 28:01, posted by "TEDx Talks," March 20, 2015, https://www.youtube.com/watch?v=m9Pg4K1ZKws; Dawn McClelland and Chris Gilyard, "Calming Trauma – How Understanding the Brain can Help," Phoenix Society, https://www.phoenix-society.org/resources/entry/calming-trauma-how-understanding-the-brain-can-help.

122 Read Appendix C: Signs of Safe People for more on this.

123 1 John 4:18

124 Gretchen Cuda, "Just Breathe: Body Has A Built-In Stress Reliever," NPR, December 06, 2010, http://www.npr.org/2010/12/06/131734718/just-breathe-body-has-a-built-in-stress-reliever.

125 Ann Voskamp, "How to Just Keep Breathing {on a Monday}," Ann Voskamp, January 10, 2011, http://annvoskamp.com/2011/01/how-to-just-keep-breathing-on-a-monday/.

126 See Rom. 8:11.

127 1 Pet. 5:8; John 10:10; 1 John 4:4

128 Prov. 18:10

129 1 John 4:4

130 Oswald Chambers, AZQuotes.com, Wind and Fly LTD, 2017, http://www.azquotes.com/quote/545436.

131 Ps. 8:4

132 Steve Miller, *C. H. Spurgeon: On Spiritual Leadership*, (Nashville: Thomas Nelson, 2003), 136.

133 Ps. 31:9–10

134 I am using quotes around "arrived," "heard," etc, because none of it is physical or audible. I "hear" and see this in my spirit.

135 John 8:1–11; John 4:1–38

136 John 11:33 (NIV)

137 D.A. Carson, *The Gospel According to John* (The Pillar New Testament Commentary), (Grand Rapids, MI: Eerdmans, 1991), 415-16.

138 Timothy Keller, "Truth, Tears, Anger, and Grace," *Gospel in Life* (podcast), September 16, 2001, http://www.gospelinlife.com/truth-tears-anger-and-grace-5253.

139 "John 11:33 Commentaries," BibleHub, http://biblehub.com/commentaries/john/11-33.htm.

140 Jon Bloom, "Why Jesus Wept," Desiring God (blog), April 29, 2011, http://www.desiringgod.org/articles/why-jesus-wept

141 Luke 23:42–43

142 Heb. 2:14–15

143 "Lament," Merriam-Webster, https://www.merriam-webster.com/dictionary/lament.

144 Michael Card, *A Sacred Sorrow: Reaching Out to God in the Lost Language of Lament* (Colorado Springs: NavPress, 2005), 21.

145 Prov. 14:10

146 Voskamp, *The Broken Way*, 237.

147 See Tremper Longman's article on lament, "Getting Brutally Honest with God," Christianity Today, 59, no. 3 (April 2015), http://www.christianitytoday.com/ct/2015/april/getting-brutally-honest-with-god html?start=1.

148 The Holy Spirit prompted my remembering of Ps. 46:1.

149 King Solomon said the power of life and death is in the tongue (Prov. 18:21). I want to speak life over me, and Carolyn wants me to speak life over me.

150 Caregiver Note: If the client ever goes "back" to the memory and freezes, after praying against any work of the enemy, I would encourage going back to Safe Place to bring their brain back to a state of home stasis. Work on building the safety with you and with Jesus in Safe Place and simply talking/building rapport before going back again.

151 "Corrie Ten Boom Quotes," GoodReads, https://www.goodreads.com/author/quotes/102203. Corrie_ten_Boom.

152 Matt. 6:15

153 Matt. 5:28

154 A really interesting read on why we default to anger: Deborah Khoshaba, "Masks of Anger: The Fears That Your Anger May Be Hiding," Psychology in Every Day Life, May 29, 2012, http://www.psychologineverydaylife.net/2012/05/29/masks-of-anger-the-fears-that-your-anger-may-be-hiding/.

155 Rev. 1:8

156 Carolyn Schroeder, Healing Care Group discussion, January 7, 2015.

157 "The Elisabeth Elliot Newsletter," letter from Elisabeth Elliot Gren, March 2002, in *The Elisabeth Elliot Newsletter* (Ann Arbor, MI: Servant Publications).

158 Ps. 30:11

159 https://www.intechopen.com/books/the-amygdala-a-discrete-multitasking-manager/traumatic-experiences-disrupt-amygdala-prefrontal-connectivity.

160 "Hardwired," *TED Radio Hour*, August 25, 2017, http://www.npr.org/programs/ted-radio-hour/545024014/hardwired.

161 Ibid.

162 Joni Eareckson Tada, "A Purpose in the Pain: An Interview with Joni Eareckson Tada," *Tabletalk Magazine*, October 1, 2011, http://www.tabletalkmagazine.com/article/2011/10/a-purpose-in-the-pain-

an-interview-with-joni-eareckson-tada/.

163 1 Thess. 5:16–18 (NIV)

164 Jessica Stillman, "Gratitude Physically Changes Your Brain, New Study Says," Inc.com, https://www.inc.com/jessica-stillman/the-amazing-way-gratitude-rewires-your-brain-for-happiness.html.

165 "Sadness (Character)," IMDb, http://www.imdb.com/character/ch0463309/quotes.

166 Heb. 12:2; 2 Cor. 12:2; Acts 16:16–40

167 *The Elisabeth Elliot Newsletter* (Ann Arbor, MI: Servant Publications).

168 1 John 4:19

169 Matt. 17:4

170 Beth Moore, *Beloved Disciple*, 59–62.

171 Matt. 16:18

172 Moore, *Beloved Disciple,* 61.

173 Milton Vincent, *A Gospel Primer for Christians* (Bemidji, MN: Focus, 2008), 34.

174 Ez. 14:3

175 Rom. 5:8

176 Isa. 44:22

177 Matt. 19:13–15

178 1 Cor. 6:18; Prov. 5:8; Mark 9:47

179 Timothy Keller, "How Sin Makes Us Addicts" (podcast), February 14, 1999, http://www.gospelinlife.com/how-sin-makes-us-addicts-5087.

180 Timothy Keller, *Romans 1–7 For You* (New York: The Good Book Company, 2014). Kindle Edition: Location 336/2850.

181 John Piper, "What Is Idolatry?", Desiring God, August 19, 2014, http://www.desiringgod.org/interviews what-is-idolatry.

182 Ibid.

183 Dee Brestin, *Idol Lies: Facing the Truth About our Deepest Desires* (Brentwood, TN: Worthy Publishing, 2012), 158.

184 All scripture references to homosexual sin (i.e. Lev. 18:22; Rom. 1:27; 1 Cor. 6:9) refer to the act, not the attraction. However, the act would include envisioning it (lusting), according to Matthew 5:28.

185 Vincent, *A Gospel Primer*, 18.

186 The client gave permission for this to be used anonymously.

187 Allender, *Healing the Wounded Heart*, 46.

188 Curt Thompson, *The Soul of Shame* (Chicago: InterVarsity, 2015), 34–35.

189 Vincent, *A Gospel Primer*, 34–35.

190 C. S. Lewis, *The Inspirational Writings of C.S. Lewis* (New York: Inspirational Press, 1994), 246.

191 Col. 2:19

192 If your church is spiritually abusive, shaming, or hateful towards you, you do not have to stay. There are good churches; it may take time to find them.

193 Lewis, *The Inspirational Writings of C.S. Lewis*, 246.

194 Katherine Hobson, "Feeling Lonely? Too Much Time On Social Media May Be Why," NPR, March 06, 2017, http://www.npr.org/sections/health-shots/2017/03/06/518362255/feeling-lonely-too-much-time-on-social-media-may-be-why.

195 Nicholas Kardaras, "It's 'digital heroin': How screens turn kids into psychotic junkies," *New York Post*, August 29, 2016, http://nypost.com/2016/08/27/its-digital-heroin-how-screens-turn-kids-into-psychotic-junkies/; Eames Yates, "What happens to your brain when you get a like on Instagram," Business Insider, March 25, 2017, http://www.businessinsider.com/what-happens-to-your-brain-like-instagram dopamine-2017-3.

196 Yates, "What happens to your brain."

197 "Fearing people is a dangerous trap, but trusting the LORD means safety," Prov. 29:25.

198 Vincent, *A Gospel Primer*, 46.

199 C. S. Lewis, *Mere Christianity* (New York: HarperCollins, 1980), 117.

200 "Renew: Romans 8 With Timothy Keller," YouVersion, https://www.bible.com/reading-plans/3461-renew-romans-8-with-timothy-keller/day/2.

201 "Epithumia," Bible Hub, https://biblehub.com/greek/1939.htm

202 C. S. Lewis, "C.S. Lewis Daily - Today's Reading," BibleGateway, http://contentz.mkt4731.com mson/2016/11/18/6EBc45iXVSnK/index.html.

203 Eph. 5:32

204 C.S. Lewis, *The Four Loves*, (New York: Harcourt, 1960), Kindle Edition: Location 1541.

205 Email to Dave Beelen, May 25, 2017

206 "If we are living in the light, as God is in the light, then we have fellowship with each other, and the blood of Jesus, his Son, cleanses us from all sin" (1 John 1:7).

207 Francis Chan, "End Time Sins Are In The Church 2017 – Francis Chan," YouTube video, 55:22, posted by "BRMinistries," January 27, 2017, https://www.youtube.com/watch?v=bQz6R_RqHsg.

208 C. S. Lewis, *Miracles: A Preliminary Study*, (London: MacMillan Publishing, 1969).

209 This is not true for all marriages. We have worked with some people for whom total vulnerability is not possible because the situation is abusive. Please read this article for more on it: Gary Thomas, "Enough is Enough," Gary Thomas (blog), November 29, 2016, http://www.garythomas.com/enough-enough/.

210 This is not one parents may be able to do directly with their LGBT+ kids. They could pray for them, however.

211 Again, parents of LGBT+ kids, this will not be one you can do with each other. The child may not be able to articulate it and may not trust you with that place of depth. That's okay. If you have a sense of

what Core Need they need, then try to lean in via their Love Language.

212 Please see Gary Chapman's 5LoveLanguages.com for more.

213 Visit the site to take a test and discover yours love language: Gary Chapman, "Discover Your Love Language," The 5 Love Languages, accessed August 29, 2017, http://www.5lovelanguages.com/.

214 Colleen Chao, "Do the next thing: Wisdom from Elisabeth Elliot," The Ethics & Religious Liberty Commission, June 16, 2015, http://erlc.com/resource-library/articles/do-the-next-thing-wisdom-from elisabeth-elliot.

215 Richard Foster, *Celebration of Discipline: The Path to Spiritual Growth* (San Francisco: Harper, 1988), 55.

216 Andrea Kuszewski, "The Science of Pleasure: Part II-Your Brain on Sexual Imagery," Science 2.0., August 13, 2010, February 18, 2013 (web), http://www.science20.com/rogue_neuron/science_pleasure part_ii_your_brain_sexual_imagery.

217 Rod VanSolkema, "On Being Desperate," *Grand Awakening* (podcast), February 9, 2017.

218 Rom. 15:13

219 To understand better how Christians can be LGBT+, see Preston Sprinkle's book, *Grace/Truth* (Boise, ID: The Center for Faith, Sexuality & Gender, 2017), 27–30. Available from the Center for Faith, Sexuality & Gender, http://centerforfaith.com/.

220 See Appendix B for reasons why.

221 Personal conversation, June 14, 2017.

222 Grace/Truth chapter 3, page 6. By Preston Sprinkle

223 The following descriptions of Unsafe People are ones with whom we would encourage you to be in relationship to at some level—friends, co-workers, church friends, social friends. We would not recommend you putting yourself in a position of submission to them if you have a choice. (Kids, we understand you do not have a choice.) In other words, we wouldn't recommend getting counseling from them or asking them to be your mentor. The national-to-personal inquiring originated with Darren Calhoun on a panel at the Calvin Sexuality Series, March 7, 2017.

224 The national-to-personal inquiring originated with Darren Calhoun on a panel at the Calvin Sexuality Series, March 7, 2017.

225 This paper originally appeared as chapters 4–5 of a discussion guide by Clare De Graaf and Laurie Krieg titled *Leading your Church to be as Gay-Friendly as the Bible Teaches*. This paper has been slightly modified from its original form.

226 Female same-sex relations aren't mentioned in this text or anywhere in the Old Testament. (The only place they are mentioned in the Bible is in Rom 1:26.) Female same-sex relations are rarely (perhaps never) mentioned outside the Old Testament during this time either. The first clear reference we have of lesbian relations comes in the writings of the 7th–6th century B.C.E. poet Sappho. So the Old Testament is not alone in its silence about female homoeroticism. Perhaps romantic love between

women didn't exist in the Old Testament world, or, more likely, it was kept secret. Either way, it would be unnecessary for Leviticus to prohibit something that wasn't being practiced or was simply unknown.

227 The only possible exception is Lev. 18:19, which says that a man shouldn't have sex with his wife while she is menstruating. Some people say that this law is no longer binding, but I've never actually seen a good argument that shows why it's totally okay for a husband to have sex with his wife while she is menstruating. There's nothing in the Bible telling Christians that after Jesus' resurrection, the Old Testament ban on menstrual sex is overturned.

228 http://www.patheos.com/blogs/jesuscreed/2015/04/06/did-jesus-talk-about-homosexuality/

229 Paul uses the Greek word *arsenokoitēs* (1 Cor. 6:9) to describe male same-sex sexual behavior. This word is made up of two Greek words: *arsēn* and *koitē*. *Arsēn* simply means "male," while *koitē* means "bed" but is often used in a sexual sense (i.e. "to sleep with"). The exact word *arsenokoitēs* does not occur in the Greek translation of the Old Testament, but the individual parts (*arsēn* and *koitē*) do ap pear. In fact, we see both arsēn and koitē in close proximity in Lev. 18:22 and 20:13. The Greek reads: *kai meta **arsenos** ou koimēthēsē **koitēn** gynaikeian* ("and you shall not lie with a **male** with the lying of a **woman**," Lev 18:22) and *kai hos an koimēthē meta arsenos koitēn gynaikos . . .* ("and whoever lies with a male with the lying of a woman..." Lev 20:13). Paul almost certainly has these Levitical passages in mind when he mentions (and prohibits) same-sex sexual behavior in 1 Cor. 6:9.

230 See Paul Copan's book *Is God a Moral Monster?* (Grand Rapids: Baker, 2011). He does a great job looking at the seemingly harsh treatment of women in the Old Testament against the background of the ancient world.

231 See Preston Sprinkle, "Same-Sex Relations," in *Dictionary of Daily Life in Biblical and Postbiblical Antiquity*, Vol. IV (ed. Edwin Yamauchi and Marvin Wilson; Peabody, Mass.: Hendrickson, 2017).

232 See Isa. 1:10–17; 3:9; Jer. 23:14; Matt. 10:5–10. Some think that Jude 7, which mentions the men of Sodom going after "strange flesh" (*sarkos heteras*), supports the traditional interpretation. But in the context of Jude's epistle, "strange flesh" refers not to people of the same sex, but to angels—the ones whom the Sodomites were seeking to rape. The phrase "strange flesh" literally means "other flesh" and ironically contains the Greek word heteras, from which we get heterosexual. If homosexual relations were what Jude meant, it would have made much more sense for him to say "same flesh," not "other flesh."

233 The Greek word *paiderastēs* was widely used to refer to "the love of boys," as was *paidophthoros* ("corruptor of boys") or *paidophthoreō* ("seducer of boys"). Another pair of Greek words, *erastēs* and *erōmenos*, was often used to describe the older man (*erastēs*) and his boy-lover (*erōmenos*). Again, none of these words is used when the New Testament prohibits same-sex relations.

234 (Cambridge, Mass.: Harvard University Press, 2003).

235 Ibid., p. 114.

236 *The New Testament on Sexuality* (Attitudes Towards Sexuality in Judaism and Christianity in the Hellenistic Greco-Roman Era; Grand Rapids: Eerdmans, 2012), 325.

237 Ibid., p. 322.

238 See, for instance, Philo, Spec. Leg. 3.37–42; cf. Abr. 133–141; Josephus, Against Apion, 2.199; 2.273 275; Seneca, *Moral Epistles*, 122.7; Rufus, *On Sexual Matters*, 12; Plutarch, *Dialogue on Love*, 5; cf. Dionysius of Halicarnassus, *Ant. rom.* 16.4.3; Aeschines, *Tim.* 185; Athenaeus, *Deipn.* 13.84 (605d); Diodorus Siculus, *Hist.* 32.10.9.3.

239 http://www.christianitytoday.com/ct/2003/julyweb-only/7-14-53.0.html

240 This is the title of Cornelius Plantinga's excellent book on sin: *Not the Way It's Supposed to Be: A Breviary of Sin* (Grand Rapids: Eerdmans, 1996).

241 Justin Lee, Torn: *Rescuing the Gospel from the Gays-vs.-Christians Debate* (Jericho Books, 2013), 62.

242 http://www.apa.org/topics/lgbt/orientation.aspx

243 http://www.thenewatlantis.com/publications/number-50-fall-2016

Printed in the United States
By Bookmasters